AF804742

Palgrave Studies in Islamic Banking, Finance, and Economics

Series Editors
Zamir Iqbal
Islamic Development Bank
Potomac
MD, USA

Jahangir Sultan
Bentley University
Boston
MA, USA

Mehmet Asutay
Durham University
Durham, UK

The aim of this series is to explore the various disciplines and sub-disciplines of Islamic banking, finance and economics through the lens of theoretical, practical, and empirical research. Monographs and edited collections in this series will focus on key developments in the Islamic financial industry as well as relevant contributions made to moral economy, innovations in instruments, regulatory and supervisory issues, risk management, insurance, and asset management. The scope of these books will set this series apart from the competition by offering in-depth critical analyses of conceptual, institutional, operational, and instrumental aspects of this emerging field. This series is expected to attract focused theoretical studies, in-depth surveys of current practices, trends, and standards, and cutting-edge empirical research.

More information about this series at
http://www.palgrave.com/series/14618

Muhamed Zulkhibri · Abdul Ghafar Ismail
Editors

Financial Inclusion and Poverty Alleviation

Perspectives from Islamic Institutions and Instruments

palgrave
macmillan

Editors
Muhamed Zulkhibri
Islamic Research and Training Institution
Islamic Development Bank
Jeddah, Saudi Arabia

Abdul Ghafar Ismail
Islamic Research and Training Institution
Islamic Development Bank
Jeddah, Saudi Arabia

Palgrave Studies in Islamic Banking, Finance, and Economics
ISBN 978-3-319-69798-7 ISBN 978-3-319-69799-4 (eBook)
https://doi.org/10.1007/978-3-319-69799-4

Library of Congress Control Number: 2017956910

© The Editor(s) (if applicable) and The Author(s) 2017
This work is subject to copyright. All rights are solely and exclusively licensed by the Publisher, whether the whole or part of the material is concerned, specifically the rights of translation, reprinting, reuse of illustrations, recitation, broadcasting, reproduction on microfilms or in any other physical way, and transmission or information storage and retrieval, electronic adaptation, computer software, or by similar or dissimilar methodology now known or hereafter developed.
The use of general descriptive names, registered names, trademarks, service marks, etc. in this publication does not imply, even in the absence of a specific statement, that such names are exempt from the relevant protective laws and regulations and therefore free for general use.
The publisher, the authors and the editors are safe to assume that the advice and information in this book are believed to be true and accurate at the date of publication. Neither the publisher nor the authors or the editors give a warranty, express or implied, with respect to the material contained herein or for any errors or omissions that may have been made. The publisher remains neutral with regard to jurisdictional claims in published maps and institutional affiliations.

Printed on acid-free paper

This Palgrave Macmillan imprint is published by Springer Nature
The registered company is Springer International Publishing AG
The registered company address is: Gewerbestrasse 11, 6330 Cham, Switzerland

Foreword

Policy-makers and regulators globally have acknowledged the importance of financial inclusion for inclusive development. Inclusive development has the dual benefit of reducing poverty and improving welfare. Financial inclusion is about human development and empowerment and about giving people the means to improve their own lives. Moreover, the concept of financial inclusion from an Islamic perspective is not new. Islamic finance offers a sound framework that could enhance financial inclusion and cater the needs of people via a two-pronged approach: (i) using risk-sharing financing instruments to develop microfinance for micro-enterprises and SMEs; and, (ii) using Islamic solidarity-based instruments such as *Zakah, Awaqf, and Qard-al-Hasan* to provide basic social safety nets to the marginalized segment of the society.

This book is about understanding financial inclusion and inclusive development in Muslim countries from two dimensions, namely Islamic institutions and instruments. The book is intended to fill the gap in the academic and policy literature on issues related to Islamic institutions and instruments that could be used by policy-makers in enhancing financial inclusion and inclusive development. Some of the prominent contributors have participated in the 10th International Conference on

Islamic Economics and Finance, which was jointly organized by Islamic Research and Training Institute, Islamic Development Bank, the Qatar Faculty of Islamic Studies Qatar Foundation, and the International Association of Islamic Economics.

I believe that the topic of financial inclusion and inclusive development is a subject of great importance for policy-makers, academics, and practitioners and contribute to the debate on financial inclusion and inclusive development in Muslim countries. Moreover, I hope this book will contribute in sharing knowledge and provide new insights for the various stakeholders. I would like to take this opportunity to congratulate the editors for publishing this important book. Finally, I would like to extend my deepest gratitude to those who have contributed and rendered their support for this publication initiative.

June 2017

Prof. Dr. Mohammed Azmi Omar
Islamic Research and Training Institution
Islamic Development Bank

Preface

Financial Inclusion and Inclusive Development: Perspectives from Islamic Institutions and Instruments

Introduction

A growing interest in inclusive growth arises from the realization that such gaps in productive potential and access are not good for development. The persistence of such gaps has raised interest in the concept of inclusive growth. Inclusive growth is defined as growth that is sustainable and sufficiently broad based to incorporate a number of economic sectors and mobilize large shares of the local labour force (Commission on Growth and Development 2008; De Mello and Dutz 2012). Unlike pro-poor growth, inclusive growth focuses on growth in equity and equality of opportunity across a wider range of firms and individuals. In the least-developed countries, sustainable patterns of pro-poor growth and inclusive development are still a major concern. On the other hand, inclusive development can be referred to a process of improving human well-being by involving all the segments of the society at all the stages of production and sharing its benefits. Achieving this requires growth in productive potential and employment together with unfettered access to markets and unbiased regulatory environments. For policymakers, promoting inclusive growth includes balancing growth across sectors, i.e. between private stakeholders and the government and between tradable and non-tradable sectors (De Mello and Dutz 2012).

Promoting inclusive growth does not mean redistributing assets and opportunities from the rich to the poor or from large firms to small firms and from urban to rural areas. While much of the focus of the existing inclusive growth approaches is reaching segments at the Bottom of the Pyramid (BOP) and extending private-sector activity to disadvantaged groups (i.e. rural areas, SMEs, women, and unskilled workers), this is only part of the story. In the process of economic growth, patterns of specialization and concentration of resources and talents across firms and individuals, cities and sectors naturally arise and are important engines of growth and dynamism. World top exporting countries, high-performing clusters and cities as well as top-notch institutions are an equally important part of the inclusive growth story. They are vital sources of dynamism and specialization, which make the diffusion and diversification of economic opportunities across broader groups possible and sustainable.

The book is about understanding financial inclusion and inclusive development in Muslim countries from three dimensions, namely Islamic theoretical perspectives, institutions and instruments. The book is organized into two parts: (i) Trends and Challenges Facing Financial Inclusion and Inclusive Development in an Muslim Countries; and (ii) Institutions and Instruments for Financial Inclusion and Inclusive Development in Muslim Countries. In Part I, Chap. 1 by Muhammad Tariq Majeed examines poverty effects of finance and institutions using a panel data for OIC developing countries. Chapter 2 by Charilaos Mertzanis analyzes the impact of firm-specific and country-specific factors on the extent to which firms in Islamic countries face constraints to finance. Chapter 3 by Umi Yaumidin, Putri Irma Yuniarti, Diah Setiari Suhodo and Achsanah Hidayatina empirically examine the impact of Islamic microfinance on women's empowerment in Indonesia. Chapter 4 by Amin

Mohseni-Cheraghlou provides evidence that Islamic financial instruments can help reduce poverty and increase shared prosperity through enhancing financial inclusion among Muslim communities.

In Part II, Chap. 5 by Ishrat Hossain outlines a model to use Zakah as a tool to improve food security as well as fulfil the goal of taking care of the poor and needy of a rural locality. Chapter 6 by Muhammad Ayub and Abu Umar Faruq investigates how the Takaful system can be translated as shared responsibility and cooperative risk and reward sharing vehicle. Chapter 7 by Mohammad Nurzaman examines the impact of productive-based *Zakat* program conducted by *Zakat* institution within the perspective of human development approach. Finally, Chap. 8 by Mustafa Omar Mohammed and Umar Ahmed examines the relationship between intention and actual support towards the construction of a modern Waqf-based hospital in Uganda.

Trends and Challenges Facing Financial Inclusion and Inclusive Development in Muslim Countries

Financial inclusion has become an important global agenda and emerging priority for policymakers and regulators in financial sector development in ensuring sustainable long-term economic growth. This significant development reflects the importance and global recognition of financial inclusion to socio-economic development and inclusive growth. The Group of Twenty (G20) Summit in 2010 has recognized financial inclusion as one of the core pillars of the global development agenda. Financial inclusion has also become an integral part of many development institutions and multilateral development banks (MDBs) in efforts to promote inclusive growth.

Financial inclusion, within the broader context of inclusive development, is viewed as an important means to tackle poverty and inequality and to address the Sustainable Development Goals (SDGs). Financial inclusion is defined as a process that 'ensures the ease of access, availability and usage of formal financial services'.[1] It is a state in which all members of the society have access to a full set of financial services at an affordable price and in a convenient manner. Despite the debate among specialists around the term of financial inclusion, there is no widely approved definition of financial inclusion, but the challenges associated with measuring financial inclusion are now being overcome.

Study on the evidence of poverty, finance and institutions from OIC member countries shows that financial development helps to increase the well-being of the poor; however, the liquidity effect is stronger than the private credit effect. The role of institution for the poor of Muslim world turns out to be more conducive than economic growth. Moreover, the role of finance is also important but it is not robust as it depends on the proxy of financial development. The monetization effect is stronger than the credit effect. The stronghold of law and order and stable governments are the important dimensions of institutional framework, which help the poor, while corruption turns out to be one of the major causes of poverty in OIC countries. This study also shows that institutions are the basic prerequisite to help the poor in OIC countries.

Issues related to financial intermediation, development and access to finance in an Islamic environment broadly confirm relevant empirical evidence that access to finance to be one of the most binding constraints on firms' growth. However, occasionally and in some important respects, the results also differ from those in other countries. In line with the most relevant empirical findings, firms' age, size and ownership predict its financing constraints in most of the models used. In contrast, sectoral origin, external audit of accounts, government ownership and investment funding through internal funds have less significant predictive power, and their prediction power is conditional upon the model specification.

On Islamic financial inclusion and poverty reduction in OIC and Arab MENA countries, the study suggests that percentage of unbanked adults due to religious reasons is positively correlated, while negatively correlated with the density of Shari'ah complaint financial assets in an

[1]Sarma, Mandira and Jesim Pais. 2008. Index of Financial Inclusion. ICRIER Working Paper No. 215.

economy. Moreover, Qard Hassan, which is more than simply being an interest-free loan (Qard), seems to be the most effective instrument in Islamic finance industry to address the financial needs of the poor and the vulnerable and pave the path for their inclusion in and access to formal financial services. However, as of now, genuine Qard Hassan is not being widely practiced by IFIs (Zulkhibri 2016).

Interesting finding on financial inclusion for women and the impact of Islamic microfinance on women's empowerment in Indonesia show that microcredit programme by Islamic microfinance institutions do have an effect on the bargaining power of women within the household for a broad range of decisions including child related, health and economic and social mobility decisions. On the other hand, the gender-specific approach for microcredit services may be overrated specifically in the context of urban people in Bandung, Indonesia. *Zakat* management organizations tend to be careful to utilize Zakah fund as a source of capital for economic empowerment. Distribution of this fund only for charity programme without any impact on empowering the poor.

Institutions and Instruments for Financial Inclusion and Inclusive Development in Muslim Countries

Many studies in economic development and poverty reduction suggest that financial inclusion matters. For instance, many empirical evidence suggest that improved access to finance not only pro-growth, reduces income inequality and poverty, but it is also pro-poor (Beck et al. 2007, 2008). On the conceptual level, a range of theoretical models has been used to demonstrate that lack of access to finance can lead to poverty traps and inequality (Banerjee and Newman 1993; Galor and Zeira 1993; Aghion and Bolton 1997). More recently, applied general equilibrium models provide new insights into the microeconomic underpinnings of the relationships among financial inclusion, poverty reduction, income inequality and economic development (Buera et al. 2012).

In the literature, there has recently been a boom in new research due to improved availability of data. The recent availability of new datasets to measure inclusion such as the Global Findex database offers a new opportunity to distinguish between the use of financial services and access for individuals, and therefore to probe deeper into the subject of financial inclusion. For instance, using a new micro dataset, Demirgüç-Kunt and Klapper (2012) find that the likelihood of owning an account is higher among richer, older, urban, educated, employed and married individuals, with greater trust in banks. Furthermore, expanding financial inclusion can potentially reduce informality in an economy with related benefits such as an increased tax base.

The application of Zakah to food security in the context of low-income rural areas in Bangladesh points to the fact that faith-based novel approach to inclusive development would allow more flexibility to integrate moral and ethical codes in the process. The focal point of the model will be a local Zakah management committee to ensure community participation and empowerment. The Zakah fund would include collection from the local community and an appropriate share from the national Zakah fund. A food bank could be created, including some basic nutritious food items, which satisfy local customs, dietary needs and local production practices.

Regarding the transformation of Takaful from corporation to Musharakah al- Ta'awuniyyah, the finding argues that the current Takaful models and practices are problematic, limiting benefits to a few groups and hindering its acceptability among the faith-based clientele at broader levels. The study proposes for changing the structure of Takaful entities to make them mutual and cooperative—alternative musharakah al-ta'awuniyyah-based cooperative model which can serve better in achieving the objectives of Takaful and that of the Shari'ah. With the goal of community well-being, the Takaful entities need to be 'Mutuals' or cooperative entities, as the spirit of Takaful really requires. Furthermore, the model could also be feasible for the corporate world in big-ticket developments for infrastructure projects that are being undertaken almost in all Islamic countries' economies.

The empirical evaluation on the impact of *Zakat* from human development dimension based on the Human Development Index (HDI) suggests that the level of human development of household who receives productive-based *Zakat* is significantly higher than the initial period with improvement in education and income. The study suggests that the welfare of the poor or *Zakat* recipients can be improved significantly if more productive-based *Zakat* is properly targeted. As the *Zakat* recipients receive financing from *Zakat* institution, the improvement towards welfare status might occur due to investment in productive capital.

Understanding the relationship between intention and actual support towards the construction of a modern Waqf-based hospital in Uganda provides interesting observations. The study reveals that three motivating factors, namely attitude, moral duties and religious duties significantly and positively influence the Muslim community's intentions to provide actual financial and non-financial support for the construction of a modern Waqf-based hospital in Uganda. Accordingly, Muslim religious authorities and relevant parties should use these three motivating factors to influence the Muslim community's decision to support Waqf-based projects for their socio-economic development. Future research can extend this pioneering work by including other relevant motivating variables.

A study based on Amanah Ikhtiar Malaysia (AIM)—the largest Islamic microfinance institution in Southeast Asia—regarding market orientation and accountability of Islamic microfinance institutions indicates that management sustainability is influenced by customer orientation and inter-functional coordination. However, only customer orientation affects the financial sustainability of AIM. On the other hand, competitor orientation has insignificant effect on both aspects of sustainability of AIM. The study suggests the importance of market orientation on both management sustainability and financial performance sustainability for policymakers, management of microfinance institutions, practitioners and academics to enhance the microfinance system.

Conclusion

This book provides original works and provoking ideas covering the theoretical and empirical issues related to the state of financial inclusion in Muslim countries. It also provides conceptual frameworks and several case studies regarding the role of Islamic instruments and institutions in improving financial inclusion and inclusive development. As the central economic tenet of Islam is to develop a prosperous, just and equal economic and social structure in which all members of the society can maximize their intellectual capacity, preserve and promote their health, and actively contribute to the socio-economic development of the society. Islam emphasizes financial inclusion more explicitly. The emergence of Islamic finance in many Muslim countries could provide a comprehensive framework to advance financial inclusion and inclusive growth by promoting Islamic microfinance, micro-insurance and SME financing structured on the principles of risk sharing and through Islam's redistributive channels, which are grossly under-utilized.

Jeddah, Saudi Arabia

Muhamed Zulkhibri
Abdul Ghafar Ismail

References

Aghion, P., & Patrick, B. (1997). A theory of trickle-down growth and development. *Review of Economics Studies, 64*(2), 151–172.

Banerjee, A. V., & Newman, A. F. (1993). Occupational choice and the process of development. *Journal of Political Economy, 101*(1), 274–98.

Beck, T., Demirgüç-Kunt, A., & Martinez-Peria, M. S. (2007). Reaching out: Access to and use of banking services across countries. *Journal of Financial Economics, 85*(1), 234–266.

Beck, T., Demirgüç-Kunt, A., & Martinez-Peria M. S. (2008). Banking services for everyone? barriers to bank access and use around the world. *World Bank Economic Review, 22*(3), 397–430.

Buera, F., Kaboski, J., & Shin, Y. (2012). *The macroeconomics of microfinance.* (NBER Working Paper 17905). Cambridge, MA: National Bureau of Economic Research, NBER.

Commission on Growth and Development (2008). The growth report: Strategies for sustained growth and inclusive development. Washington, DC: World Bank.

Galor, O., & Zeira, J. (1993). Income distribution and macroeconomics. *Review of Economic Studies, 60*(1), 35–52.

De Mello, L. & Dutz, M. (Eds.). (2012). Promoting inclusive growth: Challenges and policies. Paris: Organization for Economic Cooperation and Development.

Demirgüç-Kunt, A., & Klapper, L. (2012). *Measuring financial inclusion: The Global Findex.* (Policy Research Working Paper No. 6025). Washington, DC: World Bank.

Zulkhibri, M. (2016). Financial Inclusion, Financial Inclusion Policy and Islamic Finance. *Macroeconomics and Finance in Emerging Market Economies, 9*(3), 303–320.

Contents

List of Figures

List of Tables

Part I

Trends and Challenges Facing Financial Inclusion and Inclusive Development in Muslim Countries

1

Quality of Institutions and Inclusive Financial Development in the Muslim World

Muhammad Tariq Majeed

If the misery of the poor be caused not by the laws of nature, but by our institutions great is our sin.
—Charles Darwin

Abstract This chapter explores the linkages between financial development and quality of institutions with poverty using cross-sectional and panel data sets for Islamic countries. The empirical findings show that financial inclusion and development significantly alleviate poverty in the Muslim world. However, poverty-reducing effect of financial development is not robust to the use of different measures of financial development. In contrast, the poverty-reducing effect of institutional quality remains robustly negative and significant in all models. Corruption turns out to be the most significant predictor of poverty in the Muslim world. This study concludes that both inclusive

M. T. Majeed (✉)
Quaid-i-Azam University, Islamabad, Pakistan
e-mail: m.tariq.majeed@gmail.com

© The Author(s) 2017

M. Zulkhibri and A. G. Ismail (eds.), *Financial Inclusion and Poverty Alleviation*,
Palgrave Studies in Islamic Banking, Finance, and Economics,
https://doi.org/10.1007/978-3-319-69799-4_1

financial development and institutions are important to address the issue of widespread poverty. Nevertheless, these are the institutions, which are prerequisite to eradicate the poverty because institutions also play a mediating role to ensure poverty-reducing effect of financial development.

JEL Classification C23 · D33 · G2 · I32 · O16

Keywords Poverty · Financial development · Financial inclusion Quality of institutions · Muslim world

1.1 Introduction

An extensive literature has focused on the relationship of financial development and economic growth of an economy and has widely recognized the importance of finance for economic performance (King and Levine 1993). Another body of the literature has focused on the linkages between institutional infrastructures to explain growth and emphasizes on the development of institutions to attain long-run sustainable growth rates (Scully 1988; Knack and Keefer 1995). Whereas finance and institutions matter for economic growth, they also have the power to explain poverty outcomes in developing countries. However, surprisingly, the empirical literate has paid little attention to analyze the linkages between institutions with poverty.

The empirical studies provide evidence that development of financial sector helps to eradicate poverty (Honohan 2004; Jalilian and Kirkpatrick 2005; Beck et al. 2007; Jeanneney and Kpodar 2008). These studies point out that one of the fundamental causes of poverty is the inability of a poor to save from his minimum earnings and to invest them into productive activities. In this regard, financial markets are not only the means of enhancing poor's access to formal modes of finance provision but also yield efficient ways of savings, mobilizing and allocating resources.

The favorable outcomes of increased financial development for growth and poverty may be inhibited in the presence of low quality of institutions and widespread corruption. In the presence of weak institutional infrastructure, the resource allocation can be diverted from productive purposes to the inefficient utilization of resources. In particular, low-quality institutions are disadvantageous to the poor because they divert the benefits of financial development and growth from the poor to the rich. Therefore, a financial system embedded in strong institutional setup is necessary to eliminate poverty. Tebaldi and Mohan (2010) argue that improving the quality of institutions is the only way that can help to escape from the poverty trap.

The extant empirical literature on finance and poverty suggests that financial development can have diverse effects on poverty. For instance, Honohan (2004) finds out favorable impact of financial development on poverty. However, some empirical studies find out unfavorable impact of financial development on poverty. For example, Jeanneney and Kpodar (2008) show financial development is not poverty reducing when disadvantages of financial crises exceed the advantages of financial development. The available literature on finance and poverty does not incorporate the role of institutions to explain the links of finance with poverty. In particular, the importance of this relationship is not focused on the case of Muslim countries where poverty is a serious issue. Moreover, the mediating role of institutions to explain the poverty–finance nexus is ignored.

This study incorporates the role of institutions in shaping the finance–poverty relationships and attempts to address the following questions. (1) Does improvement in financial development help to ameliorate poverty? (2) Does financial inclusion alleviate poverty? (3) Does the institutional framework matter in explaining poverty outcomes? (4) Do different dimensions of institutions influence the poor differently? (5) Does quality of institutions mediate the relationship of finance with poverty? In this study, we test the following hypothesis for the Muslim world.

H1: The improvement in financial sector helps to eradicate poverty.

H2: Higher inclusive financial development alleviates poverty burden.
H3: The impact of financial development on poverty varies depending upon the measures of financial development.
H4: Higher quality of institutions ensures eradication of poverty.
H5: Higher quality of institutions strengthens the poverty-reducing effect of finance.

The remaining chapter is organized as follows: Sect. 1.2 provides a discussion on the relevant literature. The analytical framework of the study is provided in Sect. 1.3. The descriptions of data and estimation methods have been given in Sect. 1.4. Section 1.5 puts forward the discussion of empirical findings. Finally, Sect. 1.6 concludes the discussion with policy recommendations.

1.2 Literature Review

The literature on causes of poverty reduction suggests that economic growth is an important strategy to eradicate poverty. For example, Dollar and Kraay (2002), in a cross-country data of 92 countries, found support to the proposition that the average income of the poorest bottom quintile increases with the growth of the average income of society. Similarly, Adams (2004) found poverty-decreasing effect of economic growth using a sample of 50 countries. In contrast, some studies do not find empirical support to confirm the poverty-reducing effect of economic growth. For example, Eastwood and Lipton (2002) replicated the study of Dollar and Kraay (2002) for a sample of 23 countries. They found the evidence that growth does not necessarily reduce poverty. They showed that that there are many episodes when high economic growth is neither pro-poor nor anti-poor. They argue that poverty effect of growth depends upon the degree of initial inequality. They found that economic growth, especially agriculture growth, adversely affected the poor in the presence of higher initial inequality.

Another important cause of poverty is the capital market failure that restricts the poor from borrowing and making investment. Theoretical literature predicts the negative impact of financial development on poverty. Schumpeter (1911) argues that financial intermediaries facilitate savings allocation that in turn enhance productivity and growth and ameliorate poverty. Similarly, Stiglitz (1994) argues that poverty can be reduced by increasing the poor's access to formal finance through addressing the failures and imperfections of financial markets. The development of financial markets helps the poor by providing them the credit and services for consumption and investment. The empirical literature also provides favorable evidence of financial development on poverty. For instance, using a sample of 70 countries, Honohan (2004) showed that poverty decreases by 2.5–3% in response to 10 percentage point increase in private-credit-to-GDP ratio. Moreover, he found that the role of governance-related variables is also significant in reducing poverty. Similarly, Jalilian and Kirkpatrick (2005) showed that one percent increase in financial development causes 0.3% decrease in poverty.

Another study of Beck et al. (2007) investigated finance–poverty nexus using private-credit-to-GDP ratio as a measure of financial development and a sample of 72 countries from 1960 to 2005. The findings of their study exhibited that financial development helps to reduce inequality and poverty. Jeanneney and Kpodar (2008) used two proxies of financial development that are credit-to-GDP ratio and broad-money-to-GDP ratio (liquidity ratio) for a sample of 75 countries over the period 1966–2000. They found out that financial development reduces poverty through McKinnon conduit effect (money/GDP ratio). They argue that financial development is pro-poor while financial instability is anti-poor. Likewise, Akhter and Daly (2009) also find similar evidence in a panel data of 54 developing countries from 1993 to 2004. Their study confirms poverty-reducing effect of financial development while poverty-increasing effect of financial instability. Moreover, political instability and corruption also accentuate poverty.

Contrary, some studies doubt on the poverty-reducing effects of financial development. For example, Fulford (2011) points out that the literature highlighting the poverty-reducing effect of financial development does not consider dynamic effects of financial development on poor and simply focuses on short horizons. However, financial development initially reduces poverty by increasing consumption of the poor, however, after some time increases poverty by decreasing consumption of the poor. Similarly, Rewilak (2013) found mixed evidence on poverty–finance nexus using the extended data of Dollar and Kraay. He found that financial development did not reduce poverty in Latin America and Caribbean countries while reduced poverty in South Asia. In addition, the poverty-decreasing effect of financial development can be constrained by corruption in the financial sector and other political factors may divert the credit from the poor to the rich or to unproductive uses. Thus, it is also important to include the role of institutions to have a better understanding of finance–poverty nexus.

The literature on institution has widely recognized the positive association of institution with economic growth (Scully 1988; Knack and Keefer 1995; Dollar and Kraay 2003). For example, Scully (1988) found out that economies having strong rule of law, market allocation of resources, private property rights, and poetically open societies tend to grow three times faster than those not having such freedoms. Apart from favorable outcomes for economic growth, institutions also influence inequality. Chong and Calderon (2000a) showed that high-quality institutions reduced inequality in rich countries while increased inequality in poor countries. The possible reason of diverse effects of institutions on inequality is the difference in transaction costs between the rich and the poor countries. The poor countries face additional transaction costs at the initial stages of new institutional setup. For instance, to control for corruption, to implement new reforms, and to initiate better training and programs may require additional costs for which burden is shifted to informal sector of the economy which is the poor in effect. Using a sample of more than 100 countries over the period 1970–2000, Chong and Gradstein (2007) investigate the impact of institutions on inequality. They used corruption, law and order, bureaucratic quality, democratic accountability, and government stability as measures of institutions. Their empirical results show that the quality of institutions plays an important instrumental role in alleviating cross-country inequalities.

The extant literature has been paid least attention to the role of institutions to explain finance–poverty nexus. There are only few studies, which have investigated poverty effects of institutions. Using a sample of 49 counties over the period 1960–1990, Chong and Calderon (2000b) exhibited mixed effects of institutions on poverty. Corruption, law and order, and repudiation of contract as measures of intuitional quality do not appear significant and robust in reducing poverty, whereas bureaucratic quality and low risk of expropriation as measures of institutions significantly alleviate poverty. They conclude that overall institutions help to alleviate poverty. Some other empirical studies find favorable impacts of institutions on poverty. Gupta et al. (2002) conducted a cross-country analysis from 1980 to 1997 and found out that one standard deviation increase in corruption increases poverty by 1.6 percentage points and income inequality by 4.4 points. Using a sample of 71 countries over the period 1996–2008, Rizk (2012) finds poverty-reducing effects of governance.

Recently, another study by Perera and Lee (2013) found mixed evidence of intuitional development on poverty in a panel of nine economies of East and South Asia over the period 1985–2009. The empirical findings showed that the institutional measures of law and order and government stability have a significant role in reducing poverty. Contrary, improving control of corruption, bureaucratic quality, and democratic accountability increased poverty and inequality. Overall, the role of institutions turned out to be negative and significant in reducing inequality and poverty. The discussed extant literature shows that intuitional improvements as a whole alleviate poverty, though different measures of institutions are not equally important to reduce poverty. Similarly, financial development is also helpful to address the issue of poverty. However, the impact of financial development varies depending upon the measures used for financial development. The literature on finance and poverty nexus ignores the importance of quality of institutions. Similarly, the literature on institutions and poverty pays less attention to finance. In this study, we argue that both finance and institutions are important in a single model to have a better understanding of the finance–poverty nexus. In particular, we argue that institutions play a mediating role to strengthen the poverty-reducing effect of financial development.

1.3 Methodology

1.3.1 Empirical Model Specification

Following Dollar and Kraay (2002), poverty model is specified as follows:

$$\ln \text{Pov}_{it} = \alpha_{it} + \alpha_1 \ln \text{GINI}_{it} + \alpha_2 Y_{it} + \alpha_3 \ln X_{it} + \mu_{it} \quad (1.1)$$

where $\ln P$ is natural log of poverty which is measured with headcount ratio and poverty gap. The term Ineq represents inequality, which is measured with Gini coefficient. The notation Y_{it} shows growth rate of GDP per capita. The vector Z_{it} includes other control variables, which can affect poverty. It includes inflation, trade, remittances, government expenditures, and education. The parameters α_1 and α_2 measure elasticity of poverty with respect to income inequality and economic growth, respectively. The notations t and i indicate time span and number of countries, respectively.

The financial sector has an import role to explain poverty outcomes. The studies of Honohan (2004), Jalilian and Kirkpatrick (2005), and Jeanneney and Kpodar (2008) argue that one of the fundamental causes of poverty is the inability of a poor to save from his minimum earnings and to invest them into productive activities. Financial markets are not only the means of enhancing poor's access to formal modes of finance provision but yield efficient ways of savings, mobilizing, and allocating resources.

Adding measures of financial development to Eq. 1.1

$$\ln P_{it} = \alpha_{it} + \alpha_1 \ln \text{Ineq}_{it} + \alpha_2 Y_{it} + \alpha_3 \ln \text{FD}_{it} + \alpha_4 \ln Z_{it} + \mu_{it} \quad (1.2)$$

The term $\ln \text{FD}$ represents indicators of financial development. Following the literature, α_1 is expected to be positive; α_2 and α_3 are expected to be negative. The literature on finance and poverty indicates that the impact of financial development on poverty also depends on the measures used to proxy financial development. Therefore, we incorporate three different measures of financial development to assess their separate marginal effects. Equations 1.3 and 1.4 include credit and broad money as measures of financial development, respectively. Equation 1.5 includes financial inclusion as a measure of inclusive financial development.

$$\ln P_{it} = \gamma_{it} + \gamma_1 \ln \text{Ineq}_{it} + \gamma_2 Y_{it} + \gamma_3 \ln \text{Cred}_{it} + \gamma_4 \ln Z_{it} + \varepsilon_{it} \quad (1.3)$$

$$\ln P_{it} = \gamma_{it} + \gamma_1 \ln \text{Ineq}_{it} + \gamma_2 Y_{it} + \gamma_3 \ln \text{M2}_{it} + \gamma_4 \ln Z_{it} + \varepsilon_{it} \quad (1.4)$$

$$\ln P_i = \partial_i + \beta_1 \ln \text{Ineq}_i + \partial_2 Y_i + \partial_3 \ln \text{Fin.Inc}_i + \partial_4 \ln Z_{it} + \varepsilon_{it} \quad (1.5)$$

α_3 and $\beta_3 =$ The elasticity of poverty with respect to financial development. $\partial_3 =$ The elasticity of poverty with respect to financial inclusion. Note that in the case of inclusive financial development, empirical analysis is restricted only for cross-sectional analysis because of data unavailability for panel analysis.

The favorable outcomes of increased financial development for poverty may be repressed in the presence of widespread corruption and poor institutional infrastructure. The resource allocation may become inefficient and divert from productive purposes in the presence of weak institutional infrastructure. In particular, low-quality institutions are disadvantageous to the poor because they divert the benefits of financial development and growth from the poor to the rich. Therefore, a financial system embedded in the strong institutional setup is necessary to eliminate poverty. Tebaldi and Mohan (2010) argue that improving the quality of institutions is the only way that can help to escape from the poverty trap. Note that the score of indicators used to measure the quality of institutions ranges from the lowest quality to the highest quality of institutions. For example, the lowest value of corruption 0 indicates highest corruption (worse quality of institutions) and the highest value 6 indicates no corruption (best quality of institutions).

Now extending Eq. 1.3 to include institutional quality measures

$$\begin{aligned} \ln P_{it} = {} & \alpha_{it} + \alpha_1 \ln \text{Ineq}_{it} + \alpha_2 Y_{it} \\ & + \alpha_3 \ln \text{Cred}_{it} + \alpha_4 \text{Cor}_{it} + \alpha_5 \ln Z_{it} + \mu_{it} \end{aligned} \quad (1.3a)$$

$$\begin{aligned} \ln P_{it} = {} & \alpha_{it} + \alpha_1 \ln \text{Ineq}_{it} + \alpha_2 Y_{it} \\ & + \alpha_3 \ln \text{Cred}_{it} + \alpha_4 \text{Law}_{it} + \alpha_5 \ln Z_{it} + \mu_{it} \end{aligned} \quad (1.3b)$$

$$\ln P_{it} = \alpha_{it} + \alpha_1 \ln \text{Ineq}_{it} + \alpha_2 Y_{it} + \alpha_3 \ln \text{Cred}_{it} + \alpha_4 \text{Dem}_{it} + \alpha_5 \ln Z_{it} + \mu_{it} \tag{1.3c}$$

$$\ln P_{it} = \alpha_{it} + \alpha_1 \ln \text{Ineq}_{it} + \alpha_2 Y_{it} + \alpha_3 \ln \text{Cred}_{it} + \alpha_4 \text{BQ}_{it} + \alpha_5 \ln Z_{it} + \mu_{it} \tag{1.3d}$$

$$\ln P_{it} = \alpha_{it} + \alpha_1 \ln \text{Ineq}_{it} + \alpha_2 Y_{it} + \alpha_3 \ln \text{Cred}_{it} + \alpha_4 \text{GS}_{it} + \alpha_5 \ln Z_{it} + \mu_{it} \tag{1.3e}$$

$$\ln P_{it} = \alpha_{it} + \alpha_1 \ln \text{Ineq}_{it} + \alpha_2 Y_{it} + \alpha_3 \ln \text{Cred}_{it} + \alpha_4 \text{Ins}_{it} + \alpha_5 \ln Z_{it} + \mu_{it} \tag{1.3f}$$

In the literature, two broad measures are used separately, and therefore, we introduce separate equations for private credit and board money. Now adding institutional measures into Eq. 1.4

$$\ln P_{it} = \gamma_{it} + \gamma_1 \ln \text{Ineq}_{it} + \gamma_2 Y_{it} + \gamma_3 \ln \text{M2}_{it} + \gamma_4 \text{Cor}_{it} + \gamma_5 \ln Z_{it} + \varepsilon_{it} \tag{1.4a}$$

$$\ln P_{it} = \gamma_{it} + \gamma_1 \ln \text{Ineq}_{it} + \gamma_2 Y_{it} + \gamma_3 \ln \text{M2}_{it} + \gamma_4 \text{Law}_{it} + \gamma_5 \ln Z_{it} + \varepsilon_{it} \tag{1.4b}$$

$$\ln P_{it} = \gamma_{it} + \gamma_1 \ln \text{Ineq}_{it} + \gamma_2 Y_{it} + \gamma_3 \ln \text{M2}_{it} + \gamma_4 \text{Dem}_{it} + \gamma_5 \ln Z_{it} + \varepsilon_{it} \tag{1.4c}$$

$$\ln P_{it} = \gamma_{it} + \gamma_1 \ln \text{Ineq}_{it} + \gamma_2 Y_{it} + \gamma_3 \ln \text{M2}_{it} + \gamma_4 \text{BQ}_{it} + \gamma_5 \ln Z_{it} + \varepsilon_{it} \tag{1.4d}$$

$$\ln P_{it} = \gamma_{it} + \gamma_1 \ln \text{Ineq}_{it} + \gamma_2 Y_{it} + \gamma_3 \ln \text{M2}_{it} + \gamma_4 \text{GS}_{it} + \gamma_5 \ln Z_{it} + \varepsilon_{it} \tag{1.4e}$$

$$\ln P_{it} = \gamma_{it} + \gamma_1 \ln \text{Ineq}_{it} + \gamma_2 Y_{it} + \gamma_3 \ln \text{M2}_{it} + \gamma_4 \text{Ins}_{it} + \gamma_5 \ln Z_{it} + \varepsilon_{it} \tag{1.4f}$$

Since inclusive financial development is essential to help the poor of Muslim countries, we also add institutional measures into Eq. 1.5

$$\ln P_i = \partial_i + \beta_1 \ln \text{Ineq}_i + \partial_2 Y_i + \partial_3 \ln \text{Fin.Inc}_i + \partial_4 \text{Cor}_{it} + \partial_5 \ln Z_{it} + \varepsilon_i \tag{1.5a}$$

$$\ln P_i = \partial_i + \beta_1 \ln \text{Ineq}_i + \partial_2 Y_i + \partial_3 \ln \text{Fin.Inc}_i + \partial_4 \text{Law}_{it} + \partial_5 \ln Z_{it} + \varepsilon_i \tag{1.5b}$$

$$\ln P_i = \partial_i + \beta_1 \ln \text{Ineq}_i + \partial_2 Y_i + \partial_3 \ln \text{Fin.Inc}_i + \partial_4 \text{Dem}_{it} + \partial_5 \ln Z_{it} + \varepsilon_i \tag{1.5c}$$

$$\ln P_i = \partial_i + \beta_1 \ln \text{Ineq}_i + \partial_2 Y_i + \partial_3 \ln \text{Fin.Inc}_i + \partial_4 \text{BQ}_{it} + \partial_5 \ln Z_{it} + \varepsilon_i \tag{1.5d}$$

$$\ln P_i = \partial_i + \beta_1 \ln \text{Ineq}_i + \partial_2 Y_i + \partial_3 \ln \text{Fin.Inc}_i + \partial_4 \text{GS}_{it} + \partial_5 \ln Z_{it} + \varepsilon_i \tag{1.5e}$$

$$\ln P_i = \partial_i + \beta_1 \ln \text{Ineq}_i + \partial_2 Y_i + \partial_3 \ln \text{Fin.Inc}_i + \partial_4 \text{Ins}_{it} + \partial_5 \ln Z_{it} + \varepsilon_i \tag{1.5f}$$

inst quality $_{it}$ = Institutional quality measured by the simple average of corruption index, law and order, democratic accountability, bureaucratic quality, and government stability. α_4, ∂_4 and γ_4 = The coefficients of institutional measures (Eqs. 1.3a–1.3f, 1.4a–1.4f and 1.5a–1.5f).

The available literature on finance and poverty exhibits that poverty effects of finance are ambiguous. To provide a better understanding of finance–poverty nexus, we add the mediating link of institutions. In cases where direct impact of financial development turns out to be insignificant or unfavorable for the poor, we add an interactive term of financial development and institutions.

Adding the interactive measure of financial development and different dimensions of institutions into Eq. 1.2

$$\ln P_{it} = \emptyset_{it} + \emptyset_1 \ln \text{Ineq}_{it} + \emptyset_2 Y_{it} + \emptyset_3 (\ln \text{FD}) * (\text{Ins})_{it} + \emptyset_4 \text{Ins}_{it} + \emptyset_4 \ln Z_{it} + \varepsilon_{it} \tag{1.6}$$

$\emptyset_3 =$ It is the coefficient of interactive terms of financial development and quality of institutions.

1.3.2 Econometric Methodology

The empirical strategy for this study proceeds as follows: To obtain baseline results, we apply Ordinary Least Squares (OLS) on models specified in Sect. 1.3.1. Since the issue of endogeneity can undermine the strength of results, we use instrumental variables approach for empirical analysis. To find suitable exogenous instruments, we rely on extant literature and try our best to use the best available instruments. We also use internal instruments using initial values in cross-sectional analysis and lag values in panel data analysis. In the case of panel data, we use Pooled OLS, Fixed Effects, Random Effects, and General Method of Moments. A brief discussion on the strengths and weakness of different estimators is given below. The regression using Pooled OLS is restrictive because its specification is based on the assumption of constant intercept and coefficients. Its specification is given as follows:

$$\begin{aligned} \ln P_{it} = {} & \alpha_0 + \alpha_1 \ln \text{Ineq}_{it} + \alpha_2 Y_{it} + \alpha_3 \ln \text{FD}_{it} \\ & + \alpha_4 \text{Ins}_{it} + \alpha_5 \ln Z_{it} + \mu_{it} \end{aligned} \tag{1.7}$$

To allow the variation of cross section-specific intercepts, the available option is Fixed Effects model. It accounts country-specific effects by allowing each country having its own intercept. It is specified as follows:

$$\begin{aligned} \ln P_{it} = {} & \alpha_i + \alpha_1 \ln \text{Ineq}_{it} + \alpha_2 Y_{it} + \alpha_3 \ln \text{FD}_{it} \\ & + \alpha_4 \text{Ins} + \alpha_5 \ln Z_{it} + \mu_{it} \end{aligned} \tag{1.8}$$

where i represents intercept of different countries used in the analysis. It may vary depending on the country-specific characteristics of each country. The Fixed Effects model allows varying intercept across cross sections but it is time invariant. However, in panel data, if we write α_{it} it indicates time variant intercept of each country. We can also use dummy variables approach to allow intercept to change across country over time. In this case, Eq. 1.7 can be written as follows:

$$\ln P_{it} = \beta_0 + \beta_1 D_{1i} + \beta_2 D_{2i} + \cdots + \beta_n D_{ni} + \alpha_1 \ln \text{Ineq}_{it} + \alpha_2 Y_{it} + \alpha_3 \ln \text{FD}_{it} + \alpha_4 \text{Ins}_{it} + \alpha_5 \ln Z_{it} + \mu_{it} \tag{1.9}$$

The Fixed Effects model is also referred as Least Squares Dummy Variable (LSDV) model. To avoid dummy variables trap N-1 dummies are used in N cross sections. The major advantage of using Fixed Effects model is that it captures country-specific factors such as natural and geographical factors, which do not vary over time. However, the disadvantage of using this approach is loss of degree of freedom because the use of many dummy variables consumes a lot of degree of freedom.

The Random Effects model is suggested as an alternative model, which expresses ignorance through error term. Error Component Model (ECM) assumes that intercept of a single cross-sectional unit is randomly drawn from a larger population with a constant mean value of the intercept. The country-specific intercept is then taken as the deviation from the mean value. The term α_{0i} is written as

$$\alpha_{0i} = \alpha_0 + \varepsilon_i \, i = 1, 2 \cdots \text{n} \tag{1.10}$$

where ε_i is a random error term with zero mean and constant variance σ_ε^2. This error term reflects individual differences in the intercept of each country. Substituting Eq. 1.10 into Eq. 1.9, we obtain

$$\ln P_{it} = \alpha_0 + \alpha_1 \ln \text{Ineq}_{it} + \alpha_2 Y_{it} + \alpha_3 \ln \text{FD}_{it} + \alpha_4 \text{Ins}_{it} + \alpha_5 \ln Z_{it} + \mu_{it} + \varepsilon_i \tag{1.11}$$

or

$$\ln P_{it} = \alpha_0 + \alpha_1 \ln \text{Ineq}_{it} + \alpha_2 Y_{it} + \alpha_3 \ln \text{FD}_{it} + \alpha_4 \text{Inst}_{it} + \alpha_5 \ln Z_{it} + \omega_{it} \tag{1.12}$$

$\omega_{it} = \varepsilon_i + \mu_{it}$ is a composite term having ε_i cross-sectional error component, and μ_{it} is a cross-sectional and time series error component. The assumptions of ECM are that individual error components are uncorrelated with each other and are uncorrelated across both time and cross-sectional units. We apply Hausman test to make a choice between Fixed Effects and Random Effects models.

1.3.3 Endogeneity

The assumption of zero conditional mean in the case of OLS is violated in three cases. First, the issue of endogeneity is likely to arise when explained variable and explanatory variable are determined simultaneously. Second is the issue of omitted variables bias, and third is the measurement error in the explanatory variables. There are different factors, which cause these three problems; however, they have a common solution that is the use of instrumental variable technique.

In this study, the problem of endogeneity is likely to arise because of simultaneous linkages between poverty, finance, and quality of institutions. Whereas a better quality of institutions and financial sector help to alleviate the burden of poverty, it is also likely that widespread poverty provides grounds for the reforms of financial sector and institutions. Therefore, the parameter estimates obtained using OLS can give biased results. To address this problem, we use instrumental variables techniques such as 2SLS and GMM. A comprehensive discussion on the theory of instruments used is provided in Sect. 1.5.

1.4 Data and Descriptive Analysis

In this study, we employ both cross-sectional and panel data sets to explore the linkages between poverty, finance, and the quality of institutions. The data is selected for all OIC countries from 1984 to 2012. Since some OIC countries do not have sufficient observation for variables of analysis, the final sample of study is restricted to 32 countries (Table 1.1).

Table 1.1 Data sources and variable definitions

Variables	Definitions	Sources
Poverty (headcount index)	It is defined as the percentage of population living below $1.25 a day at 2005 international prices	[4]
Poverty gap	It is defined as the mean shortfall from the poverty line. It is $1.25 a day (PPP) (%)	[4]
Gini coefficient	It is a measure of income inequality which ranges from 0 (perfect equality) to 1 (perfect inequality)	[4]
Economic growth	It is measured as GDP per capita at constant 2005 international $	[1]
Private credit	It is domestic credit to private sector by banks (% of GDP)	[1]
Broad money (M2)	It represents broad money as % of GDP. This ratio shows the real size of the financial sector	[1]
Corruption	ICRG index 0–6 scale; where 0 indicates high degree of corruption and 6 indicates no corruption	[3]
Law and order	ICRG index 0–6 scale; where 6 indicates high degree of law and order.	[3]
Democratic accountability	ICRG index 0–6 scale; where 6 indicates high degree of democracy.	[3]
Bureaucratic Quality	ICRG index 0–4 scale; where 4 indicates high degree of bureaucratic quality	[3]
Government stability	ICRG index 0–12 scale; where 0 indicates very high risk and 12 indicates very low risk	[3]
Inflation	It is GDP deflator (annual %)	[2]
Government expenditures	General government final consumption expenditure (% of GDP)	[1]
Population	Population growth rates	[1]
Remittances	This variable is measured as personal remittances, received (% of GDP)	[1]
Trade	It is the sum of exports and imports (% of GDP)	[1]
Colonial origin	A value of 1 is assigned if the country belongs to a particular colony and 0 otherwise	[5]
Ethno-Linguistic	It is ethno-linguistic fragmentation	[7]
Absolute latitude	It is a dummy variable	[7]
Black market exchange rate	It is an exchange rate that differs from the official exchange rate set by a government	[6]
Legal origin	It is a dummy variable. The legal origin of a country can be British, French, German, Socialist or Scandinavian	[5]
Financial inclusion	It is an index comprising three indicators of financial inclusion: (1) adults share with an account at a formal financial institution, (2) adults saving in the past year, (3) adults originating a new loan in the past year	[8]

Sources [1] World Bank, World Development Indicators online database (2013), [2] International Financial Statistics online database (2013), [3] ICRG (2013), [4] PovcalNet database (2014), [5] Klerman et al. (2009), [6] Gwartney et al. (2006), [7] La Porta et al. (1999)

Table 1.2 Descriptive statistics. *Source* Author's calculation

Variables	Observations	Mean	Std. dev.	Min	Max
Headcount ratio	32	29.71	26.48	0.55	71.62
Poverty gap	32	11.95	12.53	0.12	33.90
Inequality	32	39.92	5.85	29.84	52.88
Economic growth	32	0.016	0.015	−0.01	0.04
Private credit	32	23.29	21.39	3.17	108.9
Broad money (M2)	32	41.92	28.11	11.96	118.5
Financial inclusion	27	13.92	9.96	1.33	41.67
Corruption	32	2.44	0.56	1.23	3.54
Law and order	32	3.15	1.22	1.39	8.53
Democracy	32	2.88	0.83	1.48	4.44
Bureaucracy quality	32	1.52	0.55	0	2.67
Government stability	32	7.76	1.07	5.88	11.05
Government expenditures	32	13.63	4.96	4.71	30.74
Inflation	32	30.96	57.54	2.57	262.8
Remittances	32	4.24	4.76	0.31	19.17
Trade	32	66.90	35.76	28.66	187.6
Education	32	10.24	9.58	0.82	40.33
Institutions	32	3.55	0.55	2.46	5.20

Table 1.3 Correlation matrix. *Source* Author's calculation

Variables		(1)	(2)	(3)	(4)	(5)	(6)	(7)	(8)	(10)	(11)	(12)
Poverty	(1)	1.00										
Inequality	(2)	0.28	1.00									
Growth	(3)	−0.28	−0.25	1.00								
Credit	(4)	−0.52	−0.06	0.28	1.00							
M2	(5)	−0.73	−0.13	0.32	0.75	1.00						
Institutions	(6)	−0.69	0.06	0.24	0.53	0.52	1.00					
Corruption	(7)	−0.37	0.47	−0.06	0.20	0.29	0.67	1.00				
Law and order	(8)	−0.55	−0.03	0.14	0.40	0.41	0.83	0.48	1.00			
Democracy	(9)	−0.25	0.20	0.10	0.36	0.45	0.41	0.34	0.10	1.00		
Bureaucracy	(10)	−0.56	0.05	0.13	0.61	0.46	0.69	0.49	0.40	0.39	1.00	
Govt. stability	(11)	−0.48	−0.23	0.35	0.21	0.16	0.62	0.17	0.49	−0.21	0.27	1.00

1.4.1 Descriptive and Statistical Analysis

Table 1.2 describes descriptive statistics of cross-sectional data. The lowest level of poverty, 0.55, belongs to Albania while the highest level of poverty, 71.62, belongs to Mozambique. Malaysia has the maximum level of financial development, that is credit/GDP is 108.91, and Sierra

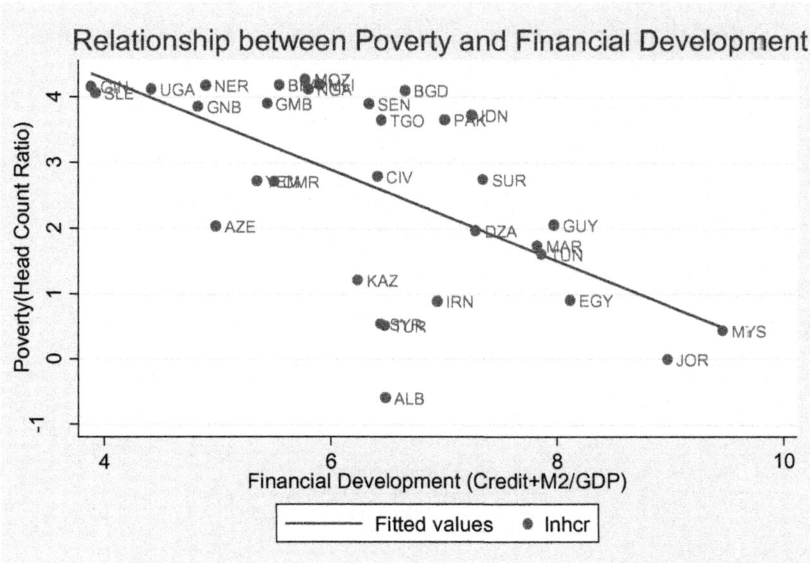

Fig. 1.1 Relationship between poverty and financial development (private credit)

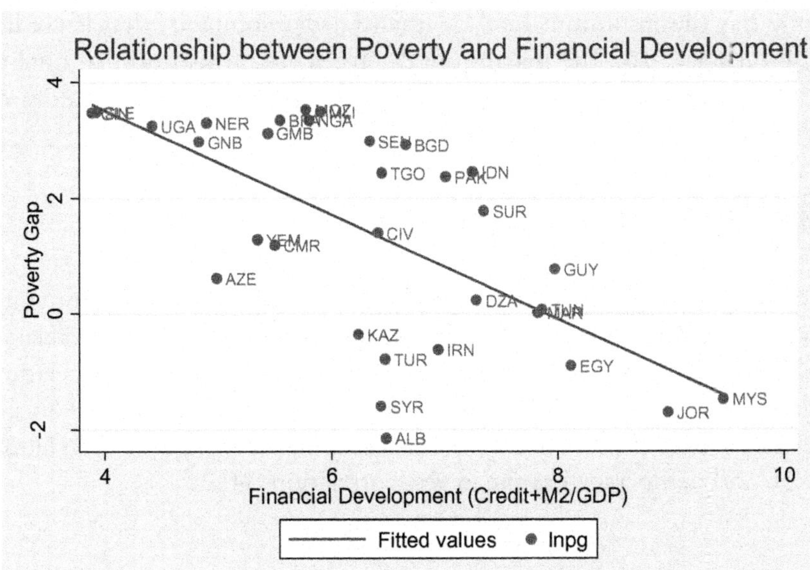

Fig. 1.2 Relationship between poverty and financial development (broad money)

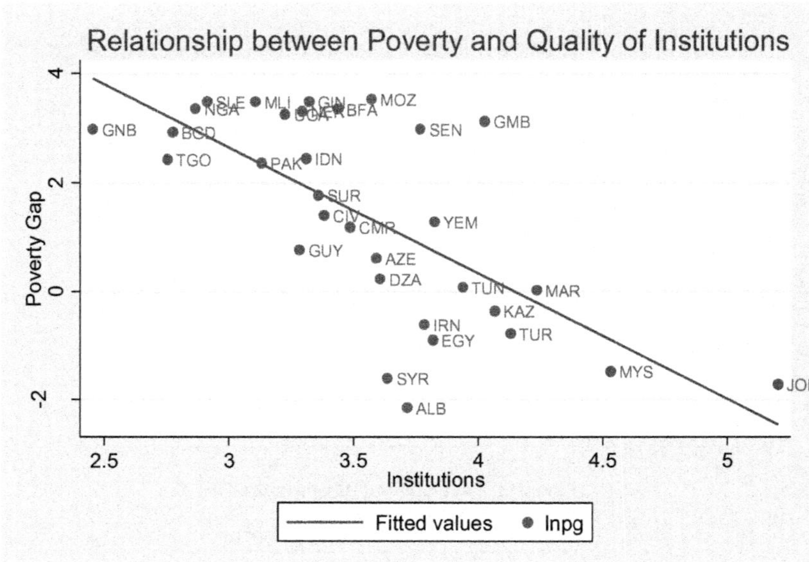

Fig. 1.3 Relationship between poverty and institutions

Leone has the minimum level of financial development, that is credit/GDP ratio is 3.16. The maximum average score of institutional quality is 5.02 for Jordan, while Guinea-Bissau shows the minimum values of institutional quality that is 2.45.

1.4.2 Correlation Analysis

The measures of financial development show a negative correlation with poverty. Similarly, the quality of institutions is also negatively correlated with poverty. It is evident from Table 1.3 that the highest correlation −0.72 corresponds to M2/GDP and poverty. The institutional measures show that the quality of bureaucracy has the highest correlation −0.56 and democracy has the lowest correlation −0.24.

1.4.3 Graphical Analysis

Figure 1.1 shows the relationship of financial development (credit+M2/GDP) with poverty measured using headcount ratio, while Fig. 1.2 shows the relationship of financial development with poverty gap. Both figures show that financial development helps to alleviate poverty

Table 1.4 Link test and Ramsey RESET test

Dep. variable poverty	Equation	Coefficients	Std. error	T-stats	Prob. value > *t*
Hat	3.6	1.105,421	0.1,700,013	6.50	0.000
Hat-square	3.6	−0.424,983	0.0,596,045	−0.71	0.482
Constant	3.6	0.0,549,798	0.1,978,438	0.28	0.783
Hat	4.6	1.119,018	0.1,561,363	7.17	0.000
Hat-square	4.6	−0.0,464,162	0.0,524,871	−0.88	0.384
Constant	4.6	0.0,570,221	0.1,844,384	0.31	0.759

Ramsey RESET test using powers of the fitted values of the dependent variable. Ho: model has no omitted variables $F(3, 23) = 1.17$ Prob $> F = 0.3433$ (Eq. 3.6); $F(3, 23) = 0.82$ Prob $> F = 0.4941$(Eq. 4.6)
Ramsey RESET test using powers of the independent variables. Ho: model has no omitted variables $F(15, 11) = 0.74$ Prob $> F = 0.7106$ (Eq. 3.6); $F(15, 11) = 0.82$ Prob $> F = 0.6436$ (Eq. 4.6)

Table 1.5 Multicollinearity tests

Independent variables	VIF	1/VIF	VIF	1/VIF
	Equation 3.6		Equation 4.6	
Inequality	1.06	0.939,247	1.14	0.879,145
Eco. growth	2.32	0.430,743	2.74	0.365,547
Private credit to GDP	2.01	0.498,463		
M2			2.61	0.383,311
Institutions	1.75	0.573,038	1.74	0.576,151
Average institutional quality index	1.32	0.759,623	1.59	0.628,733
Mean VIF	1.69			1.96

Table 1.6 Shapiro–Wilk tests of normal data

Variable	Equation	Observations	*W*	*V*	*Z*	Prob > *z*
Residual	3.6	135	0.99167	0.886	−0.273	0.60759
Residual	4.6	135	0.99167	0.886	−0.273	0.60759

Table 1.7 Hausman test: fixed effects model vs. random effects model

Equations	χ^2	Probability value > χ^2
Hausman test on Eq. 3.6	11.51	0.021
Hausman test on Eq. 4.6	53.32	0.000

irrespective of the measure of poverty. Moreover, Fig. 1.3 shows the negative relationship of poverty with the quality of institutions.

1.4.4 Data Diagnostic Tests

If a regression model is not specified correctly, it may lead to unbiased and inefficient results, which may leave us with incorrect analysis of the data. We have applied following data diagnostic tests.

1.4.4.1 Model Specification Test

To check the correct specification of our focused Eqs. 1.4f and 1.5f, we applied LINK test and Ramsey Regression Equation Specification Error Test (RESET) test. Since *p*-values of the squared terms in the LINK test and Ramsey RESET test are greater than 0.5, we infer that our models are specified correctly (Table 1.4).

1.4.4.2 Multicollinearity Test

To check the multicollinearity, we have applied Variance Inflation Factor (VIF) test. VIF is equal to the inverse of $1 - R^2 \left(\mathrm{VIF} = \frac{1}{1 - R^2}\right)$. We can observe in Table 1.5 that there is no evidence of multicolliniarity because the VIF for all independent variables and their mean value is fairly small.

Table 1.8 Cross-section regressions of poverty on financial development and institutions

Variables	(1)	(2)	(3)	(4)	(5)	(6)	(7)
GINI	3.023**	5.123***	2.996***	3.022**	3.148**	2.705**	3.410***
	(1.181)	(1.143)	(1.046)	(1.239)	(1.195)	(1.211)	(1.045)
Eco. growth	−1.680***	−1.468***	−1.546***	−1.680***	−1.587***	−1.578***	−1.356***
	(0.242)	(0.211)	(0.219)	(0.252)	(0.266)	(0.258)	(0.238)
Pvt. credit/GDP	−0.0182	0.0190	0.140	−0.0186	0.0790	−0.0338	0.167
	(0.271)	(0.226)	(0.246)	(0.282)	(0.295)	(0.270)	(0.245)
Corruption		−1.166***					
		(0.321)					
Law and order			−0.419***				
			(0.142)				
Democracy				0.001			
				(0.243)			
Bureaucracy					−0.385		
					(0.449)		
Govt. stability						−0.204	
						(0.185)	
Institutional development							−1.122***
							(0.368)
Constant	1.742	−4.678	1.803	1.747	0.963	3.843	1.576
	(4.587)	(4.219)	(4.064)	(4.756)	(4.698)	(4.954)	(4.030)
Observations	32	32	32	32	32	32	32
R^2	0.752	0.834	0.813	0.752	0.759	0.763	0.816

Note Standard errors in parentheses ***$p < 0.01$, **$p < 0.05$, *$p < 0.1$

1.4.4.3 Normality Test

To check the normality of the residuals obtained from Eqs. 1.4f and 1.5f, we have applied Shapiro–Wilk test of normality. Table 1.6 shows that the null hypothesis (residuals are normally distributed) is accepted at 1% level of significance.

1.4.4.4 Hausman Test: Fixed Effects Model vs. Random Effects Model

Table 1.7 reports the results of Hausman Test. The null hypothesis is that Random Effects are efficient and consistent with the alternative hypothesis that Fixed Effect will always be consistent. The probability values of 0.021 and 0.00 indicate that our null hypothesis of random effect is appropriate and were rejected at 1 and 5% level of significance, respectively. Thus, Fixed Effects model is more appropriate.

1.5 Empirical Results and Discussion

1.5.1 Cross-Sectional Analysis

The results reported in Table 1.8 show that elasticity of poverty with respect to economic growth is negative and significant at one percent level of significance. This finding is consistent in all columns of Table 1.8. The parameter estimate of economic growth implies that 1% increase in economic growth leads to about 1% reduction in poverty, keeping all other variables constant. In contrast, the elasticity of poverty with respect to income inequality is positive and significant at 5% level of significance in all regressions. These findings are consistent with Dollar and Kraay (2002), Adams (2004), and Majeed (2015).

The empirical results indicate that monetization effect (broad money) is stronger than credit effect. Thus, financial development does help the poor but its effect is sensitive to the measure used to proxy financial development. This is consistent with the literature on finance and poverty. The direct impact of private credit on poverty is insignificant; however, when it is interacted with the quality of institutions (column 4), its impact turns out be significant with a negative sign. This finding reveals that the impact of financial development depends on the quality of institutions. In Muslim countries where the quality of institutions is better, the finance is pro-poor. To assess the sensitivity of baseline line results, we also use poverty gap as a measure of poverty. The results reported in columns (5–8) confirm that baseline findings are not sensitive to the measures of poverty.

Since the issue of reverse casualty can undermine the strength of results and may give biased analysis, to address this problem we used a variety of internal and external instruments following La Porta et al. (1999), Acemoglu et al. (2001), Klerman et al. (2009), and Tebaldi and Mohan (2010). The empirical literature on institutions suggests that

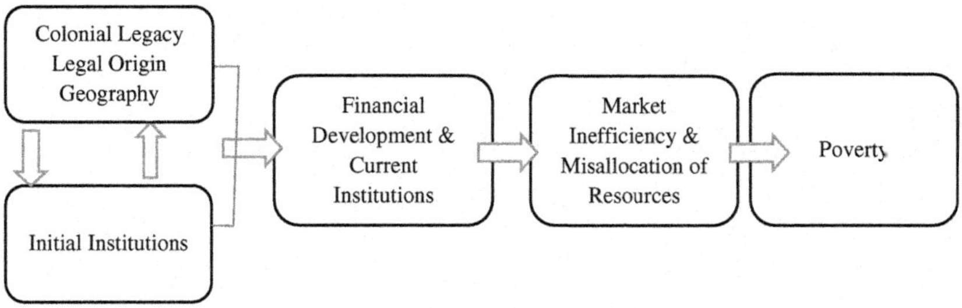

Fig. 1.4 Legal and colonial origin, finance and poverty

much of institutional differences are explained by the historical and geographical factors (La Porta et al. 1999; Acemoglu et al. 2001; Klerman et al. 2009). Geographical, colonial, and institutional indicators are closely linked with each other. For instance, Acemoglu et al. (2001) highlighted that European formed diverse institutional policies in different colonies. The colonies having the issues of infectious diseases, such as malaria, were considered disadvantageous by European. They discouraged the creation of institutions, which promote property rights, and they used these colonies as extractive states.

European set up property rights and European-type institutional infrastructure in geographical advantageous colonies that is which are advantageous with a better environment. Acemoglu et al. (2001) argue that initial institutional setup provides the basis for current institutions and economic performance. In the same way, La Porta et al. (1999) emphasize on historical factors such as the legal origin to explain institutional framework. The geographic specific factors such as distance from the equator and ethno-linguistic heterogeneity are also considered important factors in the establishment of present institutions. The historical and geographical factors not only determine the quality of present institutions but also are used as instrumental variables for financial development. For instance, Levine (1999) has used legal original to instrument financial development to determine its effect on economic growth. Figure 1.4 summarizes the discussion on instruments of institutions and financial development.

From an empirical standpoint, the concepts and ideas discussed above can be written in the form of following regression equations.

$$\text{Finance}_{it} = \gamma_{it} + \gamma_1 \text{legal}_{it} + \gamma_2 \text{colonial}_{it} + \gamma_3 Z_{it} + \omega 1_{it} \tag{1.13}$$

$$\text{Institutions}_{it} = \delta_{it} + \delta_1 \text{legal}_{it} + \delta_2 \text{colonial}_{it} + \delta_3 Z_{it} + \omega 2_{it} \tag{1.14}$$

Equations 1.13 and 1.14 are the first-stage regression equations for 2SLS, where legal is the legal origin: English, French or Socialist law, is taken from La Porta et al. (1999), and is measured by a set of dummy variables that identifies 1 if the country has a particular legal system and 0 otherwise.

We use a dummy variable to incorporate the instrument of colonial region where a value of 1 is assigned to a country when it belongs to a particular colony and 0 otherwise. The data of colonial origin is obtained from Klerman et al. (2009). The row vector ω given in both equations represents other instruments such as initial values of endogenous variables, absolute latitude ethno-linguistic fragmentation, and black market exchange rates. The data on latitude and ethno is derived from La Porta et al. (1999), while the data on black market exchange rate is derived from Gwartney et al. (2006). That said, we specify second-stage equation for 2SLS, which uses the estimated values of financial development and institutions generated from first-stage regressions.

$$\ln P_{it} = \alpha_{it} + \alpha_1 \text{Ineq}_{it} + \alpha_2 Y_{it} + \alpha_3 \text{financial development}_{it} + \alpha_4 \text{institutions}_{it} + \mu_{it} \tag{1.15}$$

Table 1.9 presents the results obtained from the first-stage regression of 2SLS where we have regressed all endogenous variables on their exogenous instruments. It is evident from the column (1) of Table 5.2 that 70% of the variation in financial development (private credit) has been explained by historical and geographical instruments. Similarly, the other measure of financial development (broad money) depends on historical and geographical instruments, and approximately, 86% of the

Table 1.9 2SLS first-stage regression of endogenous variables on exogenous variables

Variables	(1)	(2)	(3)	(4)	(5)	(6)	(7)	(8)
	Credit	M2/GDP	Corruption	Law	Demo	Bureau	Gov. stab	Institutions
Initial credit	0.0290***							
	(0.00763)							
Initial M2		0.0150***						
		(0.00281)						
Initial corruption			0.358***					
			(0.0786)					
Initial law and order				0.618***				
				(0.178)				
Initial democracy					0.396***			
					(0.0807)			
Initial bureaucracy						0.376**		
						(0.173)		
Initial govt. stability							0.335***	
							(0.0878)	
Initial institution								0.485***
								(0.0890)
Legal origin-	1.805***	0.693**	0.411	2.323***	−0.266	0.907**	0.251	0.948***
English[a]	(0.523)	(0.271)	(0.299)	(0.744)	(0.346)	(0.316)	(0.795)	(0.251)
Legal origin-	0.735**	0.414	0.591***	0.875***	2.034***	0.975***	−0.720	0.639***
French[a]	(0.293)	(0.241)	(0.102)	(0.231)	(0.174)	(0.217)	(0.489)	(0.0569)
Colonial origin-	−0.241	−0.571**	−0.255	1.348**	−2.312***	−0.578***	0.804	0.0634
French[b]	(0.234)	(0.217)	(0.285)	(0.487)	(0.461)	(0.191)	(0.740)	(0.178)
Colonial origin-	−1.331***	−0.864***						
British[b]	(0.314)	(0.226)						
Colonial origin-	−0.196	−0.427*	−0.153	1.687**	−2.496***	−0.308	1.035	0.224

(continued)

Table 1.9 (continued)

Variables	(1)	(2)	(3)	(4)	(5)	(6)	(7)	(8)
	Credit	M2/GDP	Corruption	Law	Demo	Bureau	Gov. stab	Institutions
Other F. C[b]	(0.352)	(0.231)	(0.285)	(0.586)	(0.414)	(0.210)	(0.765)	(0.213)
Colonial origin-	−0.384*	−0.750***	−0.489**	0.792**	−1.746***	−0.320	−0.0772	−0.348***
Not-Colonized	(0.212)	(0.242)	(0.212)	(0.309)	(0.303)	(0.251)	(0.542)	(0.0887)
Ethno-linguistic	−0.894**	−0.620***	−0.319	−1.732**	−0.859**	−0.681*		−0.865***
	(0.321)	(0.196)	(0.265)	(0.703)	(0.402)	(0.375)		(0.286)
Absolute latitude	−0.155	0.0276	0.626	0.735	−0.434	0.790	2.757**	0.880***
	(0.583)	(0.490)	(0.407)	(0.725)	(0.872)	(0.646)	(1.138)	(0.273)
Black Market			0.0642	0.145	0.190	0.0355	−0.0215	0.0907*
			(0.0577)	(0.152)	(0.124)	(0.139)	(0.101)	(0.0513)
Constant	2.197***	3.383***	0.668	−1.274	1.083	0.235	5.163***	0.778
	(0.263)	(0.318)	(0.536)	(1.548)	(1.181)	(1.169)	(1.299)	(0.459)
Observations	30	30	26	26	26	26	28	26
R^2	0.70	0.86	0.69	0.75	0.72	0.60	0.70	0.82

Note Standard errors in parentheses $^{***}p < 0.01$, $^{**}p < 0.05$, $^{*}p < 0.1$

Notes For Table 5.2:[a] Socialist law is omitted category. [b]Other former colony is omitted category. "Other F. C." in the Colonial origin column means former colony of other French civil law country (e.g., former portuguese or Spanish colony) (Klerman et al. 2009)

Table 1.10 2SLS second-stage regression of poverty on financial development (private credit) and institutions

Variables	(1)	(2)	(3)	(4)	(5)	(6)	(7)
Inequality	2.173**	2.227*	1.143	1.563	1.702	1.396	1.355
	(1.039)	(1.237)	(1.065)	(1.223)	(1.207)	(1.344)	(1.105)
Eco. growth	−1.326***	−1.377***	−1.392***	−1.354***	−1.383***	−1.415***	−1.224***
	(0.223)	(0.242)	(0.216)	(0.268)	(0.250)	(0.294)	(0.243)
Pvt. credit/GDP	−0.0979	0.0821	0.297	−0.0500	0.0892	−0.0699	0.234
	(0.286)	(0.314)	(0.301)	(0.317)	(0.331)	(0.326)	(0.311)
Corruption		−0.715*					
		(0.410)					
Law and order			−0.454***				
			(0.158)				
Democracy				−0.283			
				(0.289)			
Bureaucracy					−0.590		
					(0.442)		
Govt. stability						−0.0689	
Corruption						(0.288)	
Institutional Development							−0.985**
							(0.405)
Constant	3.954	5.256	8.433*	7.018	6.371	7.820	8.736*
	(4.023)	(4.656)	(4.138)	(4.750)	(4.691)	(5.796)	(4.345)
Observations	30	26	26	26	26	26	26
R^2	0.726	0.774	0.814	0.752	0.761	0.742	0.798

Note Standard errors in parentheses $^{***}p < 0.01$, $^{**}p < 0.05$, $^{*}p < 0.1$

Table 1.11 2SLS second-stage regression of poverty on financial development (M2) and institutions

Variables	(1)	(2)	(3)	(4)	(5)	(6)	(7)
Inequality	2.142	1.878	0.928	1.197	1.350	0.616	1.021
	(1.436)	(1.443)	(1.431)	(1.534)	(1.480)	(1.786)	(1.430)
Eco. growth	−1.333***	−1.206***	−1.219***	−1.340***	−1.311***	−1.287***	−1.069***
	(0.148)	(0.153)	(0.162)	(0.175)	(0.207)	(0.212)	(0.191)
Financial inclusion	−0.233	−0.734**	−0.478***	−0.482	−0.452	−0.669*	−0.568*
	(0.231)	(0.338)	(0.288)	(0.332)	(0.315)	(0.352)	(0.317)
Corruption		−0.858**					
		(0.340)					
Law and order			−0.376***				
			(0.0933)				
Democracy				−0.210			
				(0.314)			
Bureaucracy					−0.446		
					(0.420)		
Govt. stability						−0.232	
Corruption						(0.259)	
institutional							−0.882***
Development							(0.269)
constant	4.369	7.680	9.773*	9.037	8.275	12.44	10.54*
	(5.413)	(5.398)	(5.216)	(5.843)	(5.553)	(7.592)	(5.505)
Observations	30	26	26	26	26	26	26
R^2	0.731	0.810	0.822	0.768	0.775	0.769	0.816

Note Standard errors in parentheses ***$p < 0.01$, **$p < 0.05$, *$p < 0.1$

variation of current institutions is explained by these instruments. In all regressions, it can be seen that current levels of financial development and institutions are highly affected by their initial values. It implies that countries having initial better financial system and institutions tend to have better financial and institutional system (Tebaldi and Mohan 2010).

Furthermore, the results of first-stage regression show that countries that belong to English legal origin are associated with good financial and institutional system. Contrary, countries belonging to French legal system may have better or poor financial and institutional system depending on the measures used to measure financial development.

As far as the colonial legacy is concerned, the countries having British or French colonial origin tend to have weak institutions and financial development. Moreover, the results show that ethno-linguistic fractionalization exerts a significant impact on financial development and

Table 1.12 2SLS second-stage regression of poverty on financial development (inclusion index) and institutions

Variables	(1)	(2)	(3)	(4)	(5)	(6)	(7)
Inequality	2.142	1.878	0.928	1.197	1.350	0.616	1.021
	(1.436)	(1.443)	(1.431)	(1.534)	(1.480)	(1.786)	(1.430)
Eco. Growth	−1.333***	−1.206***	−1.219***	−1.340***	−1.311***	−1.287***	−1.069***
	(0.148)	(0.153)	(0.162)	(0.175)	(0.207)	(0.212)	(0.191)
Financial inclusion	−0.233	−0.734**	−0.478***	−0.482	−0.452	−0.669*	−0.568*
	(0.231)	(0.338)	(0.288)	(0.332)	(0.315)	(0.352)	(0.317)
Corruption		−0.858**					
		(0.340)					
Law and order			−0.376***				
			(0.0933)				
Democracy				−0.210			
				(0.314)			
Bureaucracy					−0.446		
					(0.420)		
Govt. stability						−0.232	
Corruption						(0.259)	
Institutional							−0.882***
Development							(0.269)
Constant	4.369	7.680	9.773*	9.037	8.275	12.44	10.54*
	(5.413)	(5.398)	(5.216)	(5.843)	(5.553)	(7.592)	(5.505)
Observations	30	26	26	26	26	26	26
R^2	0.731	0.810	0.822	0.768	0.775	0.769	0.816

Note Standard errors in parentheses $^{***}p < 0.01$, $^{**}p < 0.05$, $^{*}p < 0.1$

institutions suggested by La Porta et al. (1999). Finally, institutions are weak in those countries, which are located close to the equator (absolute latitude near to zero) and have greater ethnic and linguistic heterogeneity.

Results of the second-stage regression are reported in Tables 1.10, 1.11, 1.12 and 1.13. In all tables, we have used the estimated values of financial development and institutional measures obtained from the first-stage regressions. Table 1.10 displays the results when we regressed poverty on the estimated value of financial development (private credit/GDP) and alternative measures of institutional quality obtained from first-stage regression. We found weak evidence of poverty-reducing effect of private credit as all regressions show insignificant effect of private credit on poverty. Moreover, sign of coefficient on private credit is not consistent. In contrast, the impact of quality of institutions on poverty is significant and negative. Overall improvement in institutional quality

Table 1.13 2SLS second-stage regression of poverty on financial development (private credit) and institutions: interactive effects

Variables	(1)	(2)	(3)	(4)	(5)	(6)	(7)
Inequality	2.173**	2.325*	1.258	1.660	1.802	1.313	1.520
	(1.039)	(1.271)	(1.063)	(1.231)	(1.185)	(1.337)	(1.098)
Eco. growth	−1.326***	−1.359***	−1.430***	−1.353***	−1.358***	−1.401***	−1.272***
	(0.223)	(0.245)	(0.216)	(0.268)	(0.245)	(0.280)	(0.235)
Pvt. credit/GDP	−0.0979	0.721	0.728*	0.231	0.531	0.266	1.351**
	(0.286)	(0.560)	(0.389)	(0.437)	(0.465)	(0.848)	(0.634)
Corruption*credit		−0.247***					
		(0.148)					
Law and order*credit			−0.123***				
			(0.0430)				
Democracy*credit				−0.0959			
				(0.0990)			
Bureaucracy*credit					−0.251***		
					(0.149)		
Govt. stability*credit						−0.0418	
						(0.101)	
Intuitional Quality*credit							−0.295**
							(0.119)
Constant	3.954	2.963	6.768	5.840	4.803	7.468	4.833
	(4.023)	(5.187)	(4.118)	(4.916)	(4.754)	(4.936)	(4.360)
Observations	30	26	26	26	26	26	26
R^2	0.726	0.771	0.814	0.752	0.772	0.743	0.800

Note Standard errors in parentheses ***$p < 0.01$, **$p < 0.05$, *$p < 0.1$

by one unit reduces poverty by 0.98%. In columns 2–7 (Table 1.10), we estimate the impact of institutional measures individually that is corruption, law and order, democratic accountability, bureaucratic quality, and government stability are assessed one by one. The overall impact of institutional quality is checked by taking the simple average of these measures following Chong and Calderon (2000a, b). All measures of the intuitional quality have negative relationship with poverty, reduction in the corruption, stable and accountable governments, and improvements in rule and law are helpful in reducing poverty.

Table 1.11 repeats the same regressions when we use broad money/GDP to proxy financial development. It can be seen that in all regressions coefficient of broad money/GDP is highly significant and sufficiently large varying between 0.58 and 0.86%. As before, all measures of good institutional quality have a negative relationship with poverty. We arrive at the conclusion that financial and institutional developments play an important role in alleviating poverty.

Table 1.14 Pooled OLS results of poverty, financial development, and institutions

Variables	(1)	(2)	(3)	(4)	(5)	(6)
Inequality	2.210**	1.498*	1.000	1.060	0.945	1.586**
	(0.968)	(0.792)	(0.836)	(0.813)	(0.803)	(0.783)
Eco. growth	−7.753**	−3.546	−5.259	−5.818*	−1.101	−2.446
	(3.476)	(3.189)	(3.375)	(3.308)	(3.492)	(3.102)
Pvt. credit/GDP	−0.802***	−0.615***	−0.884***	−0.709***	−0.902***	−0.568***
	(0.161)	(0.165)	(0.161)	(0.173)	(0.151)	(0.157)
Corruption	−0.470**					
	(0.183)					
Law and order		−0.377***				
		(0.0850)				
Democracy			−0.142			
			(0.114)			
Bureaucracy				−0.512***		
				(0.188)		
Govt. stability					−0.193***	
					(0.0616)	
Institutional development						−0.877***
						(0.165)
Constant	−1.981	0.0882	1.900	1.593	3.140	0.112
	(3.443)	(2.961)	(3.114)	(3.047)	(3.031)	(2.855)
Mean VIF	1.35	1.19	1.07	1.19	1.11	1.21
Linktest	−0.08	−0.001	−0.25	−0.32	−0.022	−0.08
	(0.470)	(0.98)	(0.04)	(0.07)	(0.03)	(0.26)
Ovtest	0.74	0.77	1.72	2.61	3.80	0.66
	(0.53)	(0.51)	(0.17)	(0.05)	(0.01)	(0.58)
Observations	132	130	132	132	132	132
R^2	0.303	0.370	0.276	0.308	0.320	0.400

Note Standard errors in parentheses ***$p < 0.01$, **$p < 0.05$, *$p < 0.1$

Table 1.12 reports the results using financial inclusion as a measure of financial development. The role of financial inclusion is consistently negative in all regressions implying that inclusive financial development is important to tackle the problem of poverty in the Muslim world.

Table 1.13 presents the results incorporating the mediating role of institutions to explain poverty outcomes of the Muslim world. Since financial development in terms of private credit did not show significant poverty-reducing impact, we interact this term with the quality of institutions to assess whether it is only difference of a measure or the mediating role of institutions is also important to explain its insignificance. All columns (2–7) of Table 1.13 indicate that independent impact of private credit is not poverty reducing while its impact in the presence of high quality of institutions is poverty reducing.

Table 1.15 Pooled OLS results of poverty, financial development, and institutions

Variables	(1)	(2)	(3)	(4)	(5)	(6)
Inequality	1.141	0.731	0.135	0.363	0.250	1.144
	(0.895)	(0.734)	(0.765)	(0.739)	(0.740)	(0.753)
Eco. growth	−8.150***	−4.896*	−6.378**	−6.619**	−3.845	−4.064
	(3.067)	(2.872)	(2.985)	(2.908)	(3.134)	(2.872)
M2/GDP	−1.535***	−1.364***	−1.672***	−1.460***	−1.587***	−1.234***
	(0.199)	(0.206)	(0.203)	(0.202)	(0.190)	(0.210)
Corruption	−0.330**					
	(0.166)					
Law and order		−0.282***				
		(0.0777)				
Democracy			0.00759			
			(0.106)			
Bureaucracy				−0.414**		
				(0.162)		
Govt. stability					−0.128**	
					(0.0569)	
Institutional development						−0.643***
						(0.162)
Constant	4.701	5.666*	7.987***	7.117**	8.240***	5.087*
	(3.339)	(2.893)	(2.984)	(2.899)	(2.899)	(2.879)
Observations	132	130	132	132	132	132
R^2	0.434	0.481	0.416	0.445	0.438	0.480

Note Standard errors in parentheses ***$p < 0.01$, **$p < 0.05$, *$p < 0.1$

Our results show that finance and institutions help to alleviate poverty incidence in the Muslim world. Financial development is beneficial to the poor but in a corrupt society, the benefits of financial development can be diverted from the poor to the rich or toward unproductive purposes. Thus, to ensure the favorable outcomes of financial development for the poor, it is necessary to build strong and sound institutional framework.

1.5.2 Panel Data Analysis

Tables 1.14, 1.15 and 1.16 report pooled OLS results. Table 1.14 shows results with private credit as a measure of financial development. Parameter estimates on private credit and institutional development turn out to be significant with negative signs confirming that both financial development and strong institutional framework help to ameliorate poverty. The results show that increasing control of corruption,

Table 1.16 Pooled OLS results of poverty, finance, and institutions: sensitivity analysis

Variables	(1)	(2)	(3)	(4)	(5)	(6)	(7)
Inequality	1.986**	1.690*	2.311***	2.556***	1.961**	3.184***	2.507***
	(0.783)	(0.861)	(0.789)	(0.788)	(0.849)	(0.791)	(0.824)
Eco. growth	−2.446	2.717	−2.941	0.0223	−3.739	−2.933	−3.630
	(3.102)	(3.210)	(3.072)	(3.139)	(3.356)	(2.921)	(3.136)
Pvt. credit/ GDP	−0.568***	−0.505***	−0.618***	−0.423***	−0.517***	−0.723***	−0.503***
	(0.157)	(0.171)	(0.157)	(0.161)	(0.168)	(0.153)	(0.160)
Institutions	−0.877***	−0.850***	−0.905***	−0.715***	−0.884***	−0.748***	−0.765***
	(0.165)	(0.179)	(0.164)	(0.171)	(0.192)	(0.159)	(0.174)
Education		−0.0163**					
		(0.00670)					
Inflation			−0.0140**				
			(0.00683)				
Trade				−0.883***			
				(0.309)			
Remittances					−0.0312		
					(0.0287)		
Population						0.406***	
						(0.0972)	
Government Expenditures							−0.734*
							(0.392)
Constant	0.112	2.172	−0.630	0.523	0.246	−11.12***	−0.571
	(2.855)	(3.264)	(2.842)	(2.781)	(3.037)	(3.800)	(2.850)
Observations	132	113	132	132	126	132	132
R^2	0.400	0.459	0.420	0.437	0.415	0.473	0.417

Note Standard errors in parentheses ***$p < 0.01$, **$p < 0.05$, *$p < 0.1$

improving law and order situation, enhancing the quality of bureaucracy, and stability of government all are important institutional dimensions, which significantly reduce poverty.

Table 1.15 also confirms the same finding when financial development is measured with broad money. Table 1.16 shows benchmark results with the inclusion of standard control variables suggested in the literature such as education, trade, and remittances. It is clear that benchmark findings remain intact after controlling the additional control variables. Table 1.17 reports results using Fixed Effects econometrics technique. Since Hausman test does not support Random Effects technique, we only report Fixed Effects result. It is clear that institutions help to eradicate poverty. Finally, Table 1.18 reports results using GMM technique. The results remain same after using instruments in Table 1.18. To check the validity of the instruments, we use

Table 1.17 Fixed Effects results of poverty, financial development, and institutions

Variables	(1)	(2)	(3)	(4)	(5)	(6)
Inequality	2.968***	3.074***	3.111***	3.077***	3.130***	3.144***
	(0.694)	(0.658)	(0.667)	(0.673)	(0.654)	(0.662)
Eco. growth	2.219	1.647	2.047	1.890	2.634	1.966
	(1.721)	(1.615)	(1.617)	(1.661)	(1.613)	(1.627)
Pvt. credit/GDP	−0.654***	−0.524***	−0.633***	−0.626***	−0.599***	−0.554***
	(0.130)	(0.134)	(0.130)	(0.135)	(0.127)	(0.134)
Corruption	0.0566					
	(0.0923)					
Law and order		−0.156**				
		(0.0630)				
Democracy			0.00850			
			(0.0656)			
Bureaucracy				−0.0420		
				(0.0962)		
Govt. stability					−0.0648**	
					(0.0300)	
Institutional development						−0.214**
						(0.0995)
Constant	−6.800***	−6.863***	−7.266***	−7.066***	−6.890***	−6.785***
	(2.565)	(2.473)	(2.523)	(2.528)	(2.464)	(2.488)
Observations	132	130	132	132	132	132
Number of id	32	32	32	32	32	32

Note Standard errors in parentheses $***p < 0.01$, $**p < 0.05$, $*p < 0.1$

Hansen's J-test of the over-identifying restrictions. Under the null hypothesis, the instruments are uncorrelated with the error term. The p-values of the Hansen J-Statistics show that we are unable to reject the null hypothesis that our instruments are uncorrelated with the error terms for all regressions, implying that the instruments are valid.

1.6 Conclusion

Eliminating poverty has become the biggest challenge for the present world. In particular, the Muslim world is observing high rates of poverty. For years, development practitioners and policy makers considered increasing economic growth as the main strategy to eradicate poverty. However, many high episodes of high economic growth rates cannot ensure eradication of poverty. In effect, increasing growth rates cause more inequalities rather than reducing poverty. This has shifted economists' attention toward searching other avenues of reducing poverty.

Table 1.18 GMM results of poverty, financial development, and institution

Variables	(1)	(2)	(3)	(4)	(5)	(6)	(7)
Inequality	1.017	2.082*	1.607	0.931	1.243	1.007	0.0593**
	(0.994)	(1.214)	(1.029)	(1.062)	(0.982)	(0.945)	(0.0264)
Eco. growth	−3.438	−10.93***	−3.391	−5.170	−5.816	0.117	−1.666
	(3.923)	(3.783)	(4.323)	(4.249)	(4.428)	(4.233)	(4.154)
Pvt. credit/GDP	−0.845***	−0.853***	−0.571***	−0.905***	−0.699***	−0.885***	−0.488***
	(0.147)	(0.145)	(0.170)	(0.156)	(0.162)	(0.132)	(0.168)
Corruption		−0.550***					
		(0.189)					
Law and order			−0.431***				
			(0.0858)				
Democracy				−0.133			
				(0.117)			
Bureaucracy					−0.559***		
					(0.160)		
Govt. stability						−0.254***	
Corruption						(0.0604)	
Institutional Development							−1.054***
							(0.182)
Hansen's J χ^2	0.009	1.11	0.022	0.19	0.78	0.01	0.06
	(0.92)	(0.29)	(0.88)	(0.67)	(0.38)	(0.97)	(0.62)
Wald χ^2	39.49	96.55	120.06	63.68	73.34	98.65	144.29
	(0.000)	(0.000)	(0.000)	(0.000)	(0.000)	(0.000)	(0.000)
Constant	1.207	−1.068	−0.260	2.182	0.940	3.326	5.455***
	(3.853)	(4.401)	(3.998)	(4.076)	(3.850)	(3.526)	(1.040)
Observations	130	129	127	129	129	129	129
R^2	0.25	0.30	0.37	0.28	0.31	0.32	0.40

Note Standard errors in parentheses ***$p < 0.01$, **$p < 0.05$, *$p < 0.1$

The recent research has identified several merits of financial development and high quality of institutions. A lot of research has provided evidence that financial development and institutional infrastructure help to promote growth and to ameliorate inequality. However, the literature has been paid least attention to an equally important issue that is alleviating poverty through the development of financial sector and institutional infrastructure. The available literature on financial development and poverty provides mixed effects. The empirical studies conclude that the effect of financial development on poverty varies depending upon the measures used for financial development. However, these studies do not consider the role of quality of institutions in explaining poverty outcomes. In particular, the mediating role of institutions to explain poverty finance nexus is ignored.

The present study attempts to fill the gaps in the literature by incorporating the role of institutions and finance in a single model for a large set of Islamic countries from 1884 to 2012. To the best of our knowledge, the finance–poverty nexus incorporating the role of institutions is not analyzed into the literature. In particular, this analysis is missing in the case of the Muslim world. The empirical analysis of this study is based on three measures of financial development that is credit to private sector, broad money, and an index of financial inclusion. The quality of institutions is measured using five indicators of corruption, law and order, government stability, democratic accountability, and bureaucratic quality.

The empirical findings of the study confirm that finance is an important channel through which poverty outcomes can be explained. In most of the estimation methods, the effect of financial development on poverty turns out to be negative. In a comparative analysis, liquidity effect turns out to be more significant than the effect of private credit. The poor of OIC countries benefit from the development of banking sector because it facilitates economic transaction and helps the poor by providing opportunities for saving and investment. Furthermore, increasing private credit facilities help the poor to invest in productive purposes and enhance their living standards.

Moreover, the empirical results show that the quality of institutions significantly helps to eliminate poverty and strengthen the ability of financial sector to alleviate poverty. The role of corruption in increasing poverty incidence is robustly significant. The stability of government and strong rule of law are important dimensions of institutional setup that helps to eliminate poverty in the Muslim world.

The findings of this study recommend that poverty reduction strategies need to support those policies that improve inclusive development of financial sector. Such policies may focus on easing poor's access to credit and also provide information and guidelines for profitable investments. Moreover, rules and conditions applicable to extension must be less strict for the poor. Since the role of institutions is central in ameliorating poverty in the Muslim world, policy makers need to design such policies which focus on improving the quality of institutions. In particular, such policies need to be implemented that ensure control of corruption and strengthen the rule of law to provide justice.

References

Acemoglu, D., Johnson, S., & Robinson, J. (2001). The colonial origins of comparative development: An empirical investigation. *American Economic Review, 91*(5), 1369–1401.

Adams, R. H. (2004). Economic growth, inequality and poverty: Estimating the growth elasticity of poverty. *World Development, 32*(12), 1989–2014.

Akhter, S., & Daly, K. (2009). Finance and poverty: Evidence from fixed effect vector decomposition. *Emerging Markets Review, 10*(3), 191–206.

Beck, T., Demirguc-Kunt, A., & Levine, R. (2007). Finance, inequality and the poor. *Economic Growth, 12*(1), 27–49.

Chong, A., & Calderon, C. (2000a). Institutional quality and distribution of income. *Economic Development and Cultural Change, 48*(4), 761–786.

Chong, A., & Calderon, C. (2000b). Institutional quality and poverty measures in a cross-section of countries. *Economics of Governance, 1*(2), 123–135.

Chong, A., & Gradstein, M. (2007). Inequality and institutions. *The Review of Economics and Statistics, 89*(3), 454–465.

Dollar, D., & Kraay, A. (2002). Growth is good for the poor. *Economic Growth, 7*(3), 195–225.

Dollar, D., & Kraay, A. (2003). Institutions, trade, and growth. *Monetary Economics, 50*(1), 133–162.

Eastwood, R., & Lipton, M. (2002). Pro-poor growth and pro-growth poverty reduction: Meaning, evidence, and policy implications. *Asian Development Review, 18*(2), 22–58.

Fulford, S. (2011). *Financial access, precaution, and development: Theory and evidence from India* (Working Paper Department of Economics). Boston, MA: Boston College.

Gupta, S., Davoodi, H., & Alonso-Terme, R. (2002). Does corruption affect income inequality and poverty? *Economics of Governance, 3*(1), 23–45.

Gwartney, J., Lawson, R., & Easterly, W. (2006). *Economic freedom of the world: 2006 annual report*. Vancouver: Fraser Institute.

Honohan, P. (2004). *Financial development, growth and poverty: How close are the links?* (World Bank Policy Research Working Paper No. 3203). Washington, DC: World Bank.

IMF. (2013). *International financial statistics yearbook*. Washington, DC: International Monetary Fund.

International Country Risk Guide. (2013). *A business guide to political risk for international decisions*. New York: The PRS Group.

Jalilian, H., & Kirkpatrick, C. (2005). Does financial development contribute to poverty reduction? *Journal of Development Studies, 41*(4), 636–656.

Jeanneney, S. G., & Kpodar, K. (2008). *Financial development and poverty reduction: Can there be a benefit without a cost?* (IMF Working Paper No. WP/08/62). Washington, DC: International Monetary Fund.

King, R. G., & Levine, R. (1993). Finance, entrepreneurship and growth. *Journal of Monetary Economics, 32*(3), 513–542.

Klerman, D. M., Mahoney, P. G., Spamann, H., & Weinstein, M. I. (2009). *Legal origin and economic growth*. (Unpublished draft dated April 30).

Knack, S., & Keefer, P. (1995). Institutions and economic performance: Cross-country tests using alternative institutional measures. *Economics and Politics, 7*(3), 207–227.

La Porta, R., Lopez-de-Silanes, F., Shleifer, A., & Vishny, R. (1999). The quality of government. *Law, Economics and Organization, 15*(1), 222–279.

Levine, R. (1999). Law, finance, and economic growth. *Financial Intermediation, 8*(1), 8–35.

Majeed, M. T. (2015). Poverty effects of remittances: A comparative analysis. *Journal of International Development, 27*(1), 1–14.

Perera, L. D., & Lee, G. H. (2013). Have economic growth and institutional quality contributed to poverty and inequality reduction in Asia? *Journal of Asian Economics, 27,* 71–86.

Rewilak, J. (2013). Finance is good for the poor but it depends where you live. *Journal of Banking and Finance, 37*(5), 1451–1459.

Rizk, R. (2012). Governance and its impact on poverty reduction: Is there a role for knowledge management? *International Journal of Innovation and Knowledge Management in Middle East and North Africa, 1*(1), 81–104.

Schumpeter, J. (1911). *The theory of economic development*. Cambridge, MA: Harvard University Press.

Scully, G. W. (1988). The institutional framework and economic development. *Journal of Political Economy, 96*(3), 652–662.

Stiglitz, J. (1994). The role of the state in financial markets. *Proceeding of the World Bank Annual Conference on Development Economic*, 19–52.

Tebaldi, E., & Mohan, R. (2010). Institutions and poverty. *Development Studies, 46*(6), 1047–1066.

World Bank. (2013). *World development indicators 2013*. Washington, DC: World Bank.

2

Financial Intermediation, Development, and Access to Finance in an Islamic Environment

Charilaos Mertzanis

Abstract Micro survey data from 36,135 firms in 41 Islamic countries are used to address two questions: first, what are the firm-specific and country-level predictors of financing constraints of firms and, second, whether there are differences between low- and high-income Islamic countries. The firm-specific characteristics are shown to predict financing constraints of firms. Differences are documented between low- and high-income Islamic countries. Firm age, size, sector of activity, export and ownership status of firms appear to be robust predictors of access to finance in low-income countries, whereas only a few of these determinants are found to be significant in high-income Islamic countries. Finally, country-level indicators that measure economic development,

The Abraaj Group Chair in Private Equity, The American University in Cairo, AUC Avenue, PO Box 74, New Cairo, Egypt. Email: charilaos.mertzanis@aucegypt.edu. An earlier version of the paper was presented in the 10th International Conference of Islamic Economics and Finance, Doha, March 23–25, 2015.

C. Mertzanis (✉)
American University in Cairo, Cairo, Egypt
e-mail: charilaos.mertzanis@aucegypt.edu

© The Author(s) 2017

M. Zulkhibri and A. G. Ismail (eds.), *Financial Inclusion and Poverty Alleviation*,
Palgrave Studies in Islamic Banking, Finance, and Economics,
https://doi.org/10.1007/978-3-319-69799-4_2

income distribution, and financial infrastructure also affect the role of firm-specific characteristics on financial constraints.

Keywords Financial intermediation • Access to finance • Institutions
Islamic countries

2.1 Introduction

Early development theory emphasized the role of wealth concentration and income inequality in the early stages of a country's economic development (Kuznets 1955; Kaldor 1957). Early empirical evidence from most OECD countries supported the Kuznets hypothesis. However, since the 1970s the view that income inequality is growth-enhancing was further challenged by new empirical evidence, which found a negative correlation between the average rate of growth and measures of inequality (Alesina and Rodrick 1994; Alesina and Perotti 1996; Persson and Tabellini 1994). New development theory turned its attention to finance and placed credit and capital market imperfections at its core (Aghion and Bolton 1997; Banerjee and Newman 1993; Galor and Zeira 1993, Rajan and Zingales 2003). Lack of access to finance was seen as a critical factor preventing the absorption of financial services that was necessary for firm growth and generating persistent income inequality or poverty traps.

The associated policy conclusion was simple: Given financial market imperfections, growth can be fostered by proper wealth redistribution that would result from the effective removal of financial market imperfections. This new approach to development finance was supported by new empirical evidence, which suggests a significant and robust relationship between financial depth and growth (Demirgüc-Kunt and Maksimovic 1998; Rajan and Zingales 1998; Beck et al. 2000; Levine 2005). Empirical evidence also suggests that financial depth is particularly beneficial for the poor, reducing income inequality (Beck et al. 2004; Honohan 2007).

While financial depth indicators have been variously identified (liquid liabilities to GDP, private credit to GDP, stock market capitalization to GDP, etc.), only recently, financial access indicators have been developed. For example, Beck et al. (2007) collected data on branch and ATM penetration, the number of deposit and loan accounts, and the average size of these accounts relative to income per capita for up to 99 countries. They showed that these indicators are imperfectly correlated with financial depth indicators, suggesting that there is not a one-to-one relationship between depth and access. Indeed, firms in countries with broader access to such facilities reported lower barriers to credit, even after controlling for financial depth. These results suggest that access matters independently of financial depth.

In an effort to measure why large proportions of the population in many developing countries have inadequate access to financial services, Beck et al. (2007, 2006) surveyed the largest commercial banks for a large sample of countries to document price and non-price barriers associated with deposit, credit, and payment services. They showed large cross-country variations in hurdles associated with physical access (services being delivered in fewer and less convenient ways), eligibility (documents and other requirements to process services), and affordability (minimum balance requirements and fees). Further, in more competitive, open, and transparent economies characterized by improved contractual and informational frameworks and physical infrastructure, access to bank finance was higher. Moreover, domestic banking systems with a large share of foreign banks, access to finance, and associated costs were lower. On the other hand, in countries with predominantly government-owned banks, customers paid lower fees but also faced greater approval restrictions. Aggregate indicators on bank penetration were further used to predict the proportion of households that use financial services, thus highlighting the extent of financial inclusion. In a cross-country study, Peachey and Roe (2004) showed that the penetration of micro-financial institutions (MFIs) to financially needy people varied considerably. Combining data from different sources and household surveys, Honohan (2007) presented estimates of the share of households with access to financial services for over 150 countries, which showed substantial differences. As a result, Demirgüc-Kunt et al. (2008) argued that access to finance is not only pro-growth, but also pro-poor.

While these findings have important implications for policy reforms to expand access to financial services, they have also revealed the constraints posed by the lack of adequate data on access to financial services. While theory focuses on the importance of broader access, i.e., financial inclusion, there is relatively little empirical evidence linking access to finance to investment behavior and development outcomes, and little guidance for policies on how best to promote access. Developing indicators of access to financial services have been a first step in filling this gap. Before access can be improved, it must be measured. Until recently, there has been little systematic information on who is served by the financial sector in developing countries, which financial institutions or services are the most effective in supporting access for the poor households and small enterprises, or what practical and policy barriers there may be to the expansion of access. Better data are important in advancing financial inclusion, and recently, there have been significant efforts in this direction.

Today, about 70% of the adult population in emerging economies still has no access to basic financial services (WBG Global Financial Development Report 2014). A large part of that comes from countries with predominantly Muslim population. About 700 million of the world's poor live in predominantly Muslim-populated countries; about 25% of the adults residing in the Organization of Islamic Cooperation (OIC) member countries have an account in formal financial institutions, which is below the global average of about 50%; and only 9% of Muslim adults have savings accounts as compared with 18% of non-Muslim adults in the world (Demirgüç-Kunt et al. 2013). In addition, financial intermediation in the Islamic world increases considerably. Islamic banking and financial institutions (IBFIs) are currently found in over 75 countries, comprising almost a third of IMF member countries, and controlling assets with an average annual growth of 15% since the 1990s. IBFIs are projected to reach US$4 trillion in economic activity by 2015, holding 40–50% of total Muslim savings—a population that is further projected to reach 1.5 billion over the next 10 years.

However, the financial activities of IBFIs are considerably bifurcated into two competing areas of content and form: the first represents a theoretical challenge to conventional economic thinking, particularly as it relates to the aversion of debt and the accrual of interest that binds monetary policy with social responsibility considerations; the second corresponds to the conflicting activity of IBFIs as agents that reify and perpetuate existing capitalistic conventions toward a clientele with considerable non-capitalistic social values. In such environment, financial contracting is variably affected by the promotion of risk-sharing contracts that provide an alternative to conventional debt-based financing and the use of specific instruments for wealth redistribution among the members of society. Thus, the demand and possibly the supply of financial services in an Islamic environment are affected by the more complex, religion-based behavior toward different financial services and instruments.

Notwithstanding the importance of the common religious precepts underlying financial behavior, Islamic countries' attitudes toward finance diverge further due to considerable differences among themselves. While Shari'ah-compliance imposes obligations on various aspects of economic interactions, such compliance is permeated by both the strong conventional finance attitudes of a large part of the population and the divergent cultures and social structures of the various Islamic countries.

Given these growing trends in the Islamic world, it is very important to explore the latter's approach to financial inclusion and economic development. While Islamic finance focuses on historically developed financial instruments and services, the availability of financing vehicles available to the poor is still at very early stages (CGAP 2009). Islamic finance addresses the issue of financial inclusion, first, through the promotion of risk-sharing contracts which provide a viable alternative to conventional debt-based financing and, second, through specific instruments of redistribution of the wealth among the society.

The peculiarities of Islamic finance highlight the role of socioeconomic development in explaining the degree of financial access. Low levels of socioeconomic development are often associated with lower demand for and supply of financial services. Based on the indicators reported in Demirgüç-Kunt et al. (2008), Fig. 2.1 shows the constellation of the Islamic countries with respect to their access to finance. Substantial differences emerge regarding access to finance among Islamic countries. Further, Fig. 2.2 shows the correlation between access to finance and socioeconomic development as approximated by the

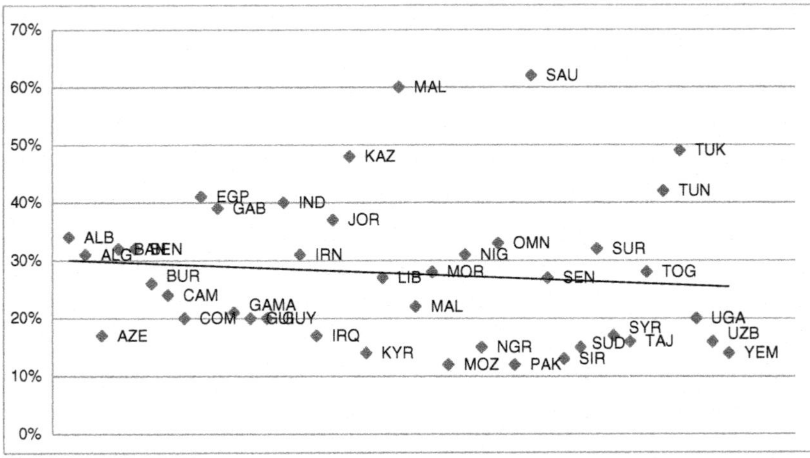

Fig. 2.1 Access to finance in Islamic countries (percent). *Source* World Bank, finance for all (2008)

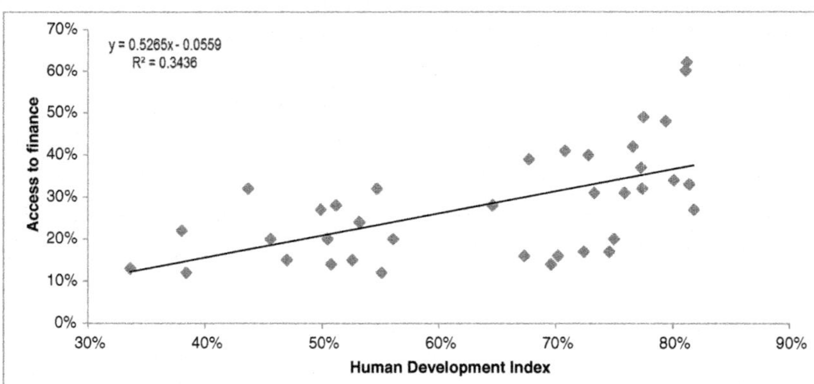

Fig. 2.2 Access to finance and human development of Islamic Countries (percent). *Source* World Bank, finance for all (2008); UN Human Development Report (2008)

United Nations' Human Development Index—HDI (UNDP 2014). The correlation coefficient between these two variables is 0.52 and is significant at the 1% level. In general, countries with greater access to social services and a better quality of life are countries that have also developed a stronger financial culture in which the use of financial services through formal markets becomes indispensable. As expected, Fig. 2.2 shows that developed countries display the highest values of both the HDI and the indicator of access to finance. Most emerging markets are above the fitted line, suggesting that, ceteris paribus, there is potential for improving access given their degree of development.

In this chapter, the focus is on the extent to which firms in a sample of Islamic countries have access to finance. A firm-specific data survey, based on private-sector firm responses, is used to analyze the impact of firm-specific and country-specific factors on the extent to which firms in the sample of Islamic countries face constraints to finance. Further, the analysis examines the impact of those factors at different levels of economic, financial, institutional, and human development of the sample countries. The chapter contributes to the existing literature on financing constraints in several ways. First, it focuses specifically on Islamic countries and considers the impact of differences in their development level by dividing the sample countries into two subgroups of more-developed and less-developed ones. Second, it utilizes the most recent version of data collected by the microenterprise surveys conducted by the World Bank. Third, it contributes to the debate on the proper classification of firms as between financially constraint and unconstrained ones by taking into consideration the impact of economic and human development indicators, thereby introducing additional behavioral elements in the theory. Finally, it considers more explicitly the impact of financial development and the prevalent financial intermediation conditions.

The results broadly confirm relevant empirical evidence. However, occasionally and in some important respects, the results also differ from those in other countries. This calls for further analysis of the nature of financial intermediation in the Islamic world, as well as for the future inclusion of social and cultural factors in the analysis. The policy implications are that grouping of firms by age, size, and ownership structure is therefore a better choice when considering the effect of macroeconomic factors such as economic, financial, institutional, and human development on firms' financing constraints.

The chapter is organized as follows. Section 2.2 presents a review of the related literature and the background for the study. Section 2.3 describes the data and the empirical methodology used for the analysis. Section 2.4 explores the predictive power of firm-specific characteristics. Section 2.5 provides additional robustness checks by controlling for the impact of country-level factors reflecting the countries' level of economic, financial, and human development, as well as the prevalent financial intermediation structure in the whole sample and the subgroups of Islamic countries. Finally, Sect. 2.6 concludes the chapter.

2.2 Related Literature

Access to finance is found to be a key determinant of a firm's ability to operate and expand. The relevant literature analyzes financing constraints by focusing on the relation between financing availability and investment. For example, Levine (2005) shows that better access to financing enhances the firms' ability to finance their expansion projects and allocate resources efficiently. On the basis of between- and within-country regressions on firm perceptions regarding financing, Carlin et al. (2006) find that small firms complain about access to finance while large firms complain about everything else, raising the question of whether firm perceptions are in fact true indicators of actual access to finance. Kinda et al. (2011) use a sample of developing countries and show that satisfactory access to financing contributes significantly to the productive performance of firms.

The empirical analysis assumes that the availability of finance depends crucially on the characteristics of firms as well as on country-level factors. The characterization of a firm as financially constrained is complex. The theory assumes that the firm is considered to be financially constrained if it does not have sufficient internal resources to finance investment opportunities, and the cost of getting external financing is high. Fazzari et al. (1988) used the annual Value Line database of US manufacturing firms during 1969–1986 to identify the presence of financial constraints based on the differential sensitivity of corporate investment to cash flow. They argued that the higher the dividend payout ratio, the less constrained the firm. Thus, information to test for financing constraints of firms can be obtained from those firms' financial statements. Along with this argument, Korajczyk and Levy (2003) studied the effect of macroeconomic conditions on capital structure and classified firms by their dividend level. However, Kaplan and Zingales (1997, 2000) question the validity of Fazzari et al. (1988) cash flow-based classification scheme. They offered a different classification based on the availability of and the demand for funds (especially debt) using quantitative and qualitative information from firms' annual reports. Their results are confirmed by Cleary (1999) who finds that firms with higher creditworthiness are extremely sensitive to internal funds availability than less creditworthy firms. Fazzari et al. (2000) reacted by pointing out that this approach confuses financially constrained with financially distressed firms, the latter being the result of the phase of the business cycle. Moyen (2004) contributes to this debate by investigating different classification schemes (dividends payout policy, firms' cash flow, investment, Cleary's index). She finds that depending on the chosen firm classification criterion, cash flow sensitivity of financially constrained firms could be either higher or lower than that of financially unconstrained ones. More generally, Bond et al. (2005) pointed out that investment-cash flow sensitivities could also indicate misspecification in the underlying investment models. Firms' financing constraints are studied by Vermeulen (2002) and Pal and Ferrando (2006) using financial statements information and profit and loss accounts. Vermeulen (2002) proposes the financial gap as a criterion of financially constrained firm classification. The firm is defined as credit constrained when its financing gap is positive, and the firm is not able to access external financing. Despite a positive financing gap, firms are considered relatively constrained if they can afford expensive external finance. Firms are considered unconstrained if they either have a negative financing gap or are able to attract relatively cheap external finance. Other classification criterial, based on asymmetry of information costs, include business-group affiliation (Hoshi et al. 1991), the presence of bond ratings (Whited 1992), the degree of shareholder concentration, or the pattern of insider trading (Oliner and Rudebusch 1992).

On the basis of review articles, Devereux and Schiantarelli (1990) and Schiantarelli (1995) argue that a single classification indicator is insufficient to decide whether a firm is credit constrained or not. Pal and Ferrando (2006) propose five criteria of classification of financially constrained firms: total investment, financing gap, financial debt, new shares issuance, and average interest payments on debt relative to interest rates charged in the local credit markets. They argue that the use of several interrelated variables allows for the placement of a firm into the constrained, relatively constrained or unconstrained group utilizing all available information. For example, negative total investment (reduction in fixed assets) signals that a firm has experienced financing constraints since it liquidates fixed assets. A positive financing gap indicates that the firms' total investment is higher than the current cash flow and that the firm needs external financing. If total investments and the financing gap are both positive, firms need external financing. Firms are sorted out into unconstrained and relatively constrained categories based on the price they pay to obtain necessary financing. Those firms, which are able to increase leverage at a lower price than the country-specific retail interest rate, are defined as unconstrained. If the price is higher, a firm falls into the relatively constrained category. Firms, which under these conditions are not attracting financing, are defined as absolutely constrained.

Focusing on multiple classification criteria, Devereux and Schiantarelli (1990), Oliner and Rudebusch (1992), and Schiffer and Weder (2001) have highlighted the role of firm age and size as significant predictors of financing constraints. They showed that perceived constraints to financing are higher for small firms than for large firms. Kuntchev et al. (2013) and Hallward-Driemeier and Aterido (2007) found that small-size firms have significantly less access to the financial system and tend to finance a smaller share of their investment through formal credit. Schiffer and Weder (2001) found that smaller firms hold more intense perceptions of financing constraints than do larger firms. Additional classification criteria include ownership structure, stakeholder relationships, legal status, sectoral origin, export-oriented production, etc. Sembenelli and Schiantarelli (1996) show that foreign-owned firms may have easier access to various external sources of financing. Harrison and McMillan (2003) suggest that state-owned firms are expected to report lower financing constraints since in many countries they receive direct budgetary support. Hoshi et al. (1991) show that information and incentive problems among firms with different types of relationships and affiliations with banks affect financing and investment activity. Studies on venture capital suggest that younger firms are more financially constrained because of information asymmetries associated with financiers' access to relevant information, which could help build long-term relationships. Yet further, Oliner and Rudebusch (1992) show that firms that are listed on a stock exchange are facing lower financing constraints due to fewer information asymmetries as a result of increased transparency requirements. Finally, Dollar et al. (2006) show that in developing countries the link between access to finance and the likelihood of being an exporter is stronger, and they find a positive association between a firm's export status and its access to finance.

The main problem of the empirical literature is that the classification of firms as financially constrained is highly supply-side driven and dependent on the methodology used to identify whether a firm experiences financing constraints or not. All the studies considered above use an exogenous classification of firms and take a supply-side perspective. This makes the results highly sensitive to the point of sample separation because it could be problematic to decide which group a firm belongs to since the severity of financial constraints faced by the firm is not directly observable.

One approach to understand the extent of financing constraints is to take a demand-driven behavioral perspective. As Claessens (2006) points out, the analysis on financial inclusion seems to have reached a tipping point in terms of the extent to which provision of more and differentiated financial products can be used to stimulate access to and use of financial services. Thus, an understanding of the absorption of financial services must rest more squarely on such factors as the level of socioeconomic development of countries. The exclusion of people from finance is normally part of a wider social exclusion, which involves level of education, type of employment, training, etc.

This supply-side approach has focused on different aspects of accessibility that is making financial services both available and affordable and designing products in a reliable and flexible manner. Further, the supply-side approach focuses on the role of prescriptive regulation aiming at protecting consumers and ensuring that emerging financial markets and microfinance institutions integrate well into the traditional financial system. In spite of the ongoing conscious effort to improve access to finance, financial exclusion still remains high in developing economies. Thus, an increasing body of financial inclusion research has turned to demand-side factors. Bauer et al. (2012) and Kostov et al. (2012) study firms' perceptions regarding their access to finance by focusing on how self-discipline, based on present bias theory (current vs. future preference) and financial perceptions, behavior and attitudes, contribute to financial access and inclusion. Kon and Storey (2003) argue that whether a firm would find it prudent to apply for a loan or make use of financial services can be partly explained by the concept of 'discouraged borrower', based on the psychological component of application cost. The authors show that a good borrower—discouraged borrower—may not apply for a loan to a bank because of a possible rejection. The rejection may be the result of borrowers' lack of knowledge/information about their own capabilities and inadequacies, of negative perceptions, attitudes, and behavior which are largely premised on personal (known) adverse prior experience with a financial institution, of traditional idiosyncratic and covariate risk of poor people and, perhaps, and of insufficient financial or political connections. This means that the borrower's perception about the likely outcome of an application is imperative for achieving the targets of financial inclusion. Levenson and Willard (2000) argue that the implications of this discouragement to access to finance may be more important than Stiglitz and Weiss (1981) credit rationing hypothesis. Research of demand-side factors along with behavioral lines continues. Alternatively, Baddeley (2011) argues that unforeseen exogenous factors such as the ongoing social conflicts may be a determinant of financing constraints as those conflicts generate financial strains particularly if they are associated with an increase in military expenditure and arms imports.

Turning now into the country-level factors affecting financing constraints of firms, these focus on financial and developmental institutions and macroeconomic conditions. In the law and finance tradition, Demirgüç-Kunt and Maksimovic (1998) found that financing constraints are lower in countries with more efficient legal systems. After controlling for all other determinants, the efficiency of a country's legal system appeared to be important predictor of financing constraints of firms. Beck et al. (2005) suggest that country-level financial and other development institutions are instrumental in mitigating the constraining impact of financing constraints. Beck et al. (2006) argue that overall institutional development tends to be a prominent country-level predictor of a firm's constraints to financing. Further, Leaven (2003) argues that financial liberalization is a strong factor in reducing the financing constraints to firms. On the basis of firms' responses from 35 developing countries, Clarke et al. (2006) found that the participation of foreign banks improves accessibility of firms to external financing. Kuntchev et al. (2012) found that in countries with high private credit to GDP ratios, firms are less likely to be credit constrained. Love (2003) finds a strong negative relationship between the sensitivity of investment to the availability of internal funds and an indicator of financial market development, and concludes that financial development reduces the effect of financing constraints on investment. Laeven (2003) and Gelos and Werner (2002) find that financial liberalization relaxes financing constraints of firms, in particular for smaller firms. Finally, Love and Martinez Peria (2012) found that low market competition reduces firms' access to finance and that the impact of competition on access to finance depends on the operational environment of financial institutions.

This chapter provides an analysis of access to finance based on an account of both firm-specific and country-level factors. It adopts a multiple criteria approach to deciding between constrained and unconstrained forms. Thus, firm-specific characteristics, such as age, size, sector of activity, external audit, ownership structure, and internal fund financing, are explicitly considered. Moreover, country-level factors relating to economic, financial, institutional, and human development are also considered as control factors. Further, the chapter also explores the role of firms' perceptions and behavior regarding their access to finance. The latter relationship underlies the choice of data used in the analysis. This data are obtained from the World Bank's Enterprise Surveys of firms. These carefully conducted surveys account for firms' perceptions on access to finance and provide in-depth information on access to different financial services and allow the evaluation of the impact of this access. A shortcoming of these enterprise surveys is that there are often doubts regarding their representativeness for a specific country. Indeed, the responses of firms are private unaudited information. These concerns that could only be addressed by using firm census data, which are not, however, available for most developing countries. In this chapter, financing constraints should be taken to represent self-reported perceptions of firms and not actual constraints.

2.3 Data and Methodology

The source of data for this study is the Enterprise Surveys (ESs) conducted by the World Bank. The ES is an ongoing World Bank project since 2005, which involves the collection of both objective data based on firms' experiences and enterprises' perception of the environment in which they operate. The data are based on firm-specific surveys and have evolved into a mature stage that uses a standardized methodology of implementation, sampling, and quality control in most client-countries of the World Bank. The Enterprise Surveys currently cover over 130,000 firms carried out during 2005–2013 in 125 countries, of which 113 have been surveyed following a standardized methodology, which allows comparisons across countries and over time. The ES represents a sample of the non-agricultural, formal, private economy with a strong emphasis on building panel data to make it possible to track changes in the business environment over time. The ES facilitates linking firm performance and other firm characteristics with the business environment while assessing the constraints to private-sector growth and job creation faced in a particular country. The ES has included some high-income countries as comparators mostly as an exception since the mandate of the World Bank Group focuses on the developing world. The ES data are collected in several waves and contain repeated cross-sections for the countries in our sample. Because the goal is to isolate within-country variation in access to finance across time, all sample countries have survey data for at least two years.

The ES questionnaire covers the following topics: Firm characteristics (age, firm legal status, gender of the owner), quality and availability of infrastructure and related services, sales and supplies, competition, capacity utilization, land and permits, crime, finance (percentage of investments financed through bank loans, percentage of working capital financed through trade credit, the type of collateral used to secure a bank loan), business-government relations, and labor. It also provides a ranking of constraints, covering the most important of 15 potential constraints to conduct business, as well as performance, covering constraints such as cost of labor and cost of raw materials.

The ES is composed of representative random samples of firms from the manufacturing and service sectors, including retail, wholesale, IT, construction, transport, and communication. Samples have broad within-country coverage typically centralized in the major centers of economic activity of a country. Every ES is based on sampling frames that are evaluated at the onset of every project. Special attention is placed on questionnaire translation, and in every country, pretesting and pilot interviews are conducted prior to main field work to reduce measurement errors. Measurement error may be present regarding some sensitive questions, such as those regarding corruption and performance results. Also, some information may be intentionally underreported due to fears of repercussions and/or due to the sensitive nature of the questions. However, the ES questionnaire has been gradually adjusted to minimize this risk. Questions are simple and direct; respondents are specially assured of the confidentiality of their answers. Survey data in the developing world may suffer also a coverage bias. This bias emerges from dealing with outdated or unclean firm information. The ES uses the most updated and complete sampling frames for each economy, and efforts are undertaken to purge alien elements from the frame prior to the selection of the sample.

The basic data sample used in this analysis includes 36,135 firms from 41 Islamic countries covered by the ES between 2006 and 2014.

The survey does not cover some Islamic countries of the Middle East and North Africa, Africa, and Asia. Further, some important Islamic countries are omitted for either they were not covered by the ES or the relevant data were coded with a different methodology that is not compatible with the rest of the sample. An important strength of the data is its broad coverage of small and medium firms. The ES stratifies firm size consistently into: small (5–19 employees), medium (20–99), and large (100 and more) firms.

The dependent variable is ACCESS. Based on the ES explanations, the categorical variable ACCESS reflects the firms' perceptions of financing constraints during the fiscal year referenced in each survey. It is the answer of firms to the question: 'How problematic is financing for the operation and growth of your business?' The answer varies between 0 (no constraint), 1 (minor constraint), 2 (moderate constraint), 3 (major constraint), and 4 (very severe constraint). However, it is possible that these answers may not capture all reality as well as that some firms may report financing constraints while they are not actually constrained by them but only facing temporary liquidity distress. Therefore, one must be cautious of this behavioral bias and interpret the results carefully.

Average values of ACCESS per country are reported in Table 2.1. The data show large divergence. Firms operating in Burkina Faso (2.977) consider access to finance as the biggest obstacle to their operations, while firms operating in Kosovo (0.492) consider it as a least important obstacle among the whole sample of Islamic countries. The average value for the whole sample is 1.411, which shows that access to finance is a considerable obstacle for the firms operating in Islamic countries.

The independent variables include firm-specific characteristics that reflect the impact of the firm's nature and operation. They include: age, size, sector of business activity; legal status; the location of business operations; export status; and auditing of accounts. They also include ownership structure.

Moreover, country-level variables are used to control for the impact of national economic and non-economic factors. These control variables capture unobservable differences between countries and are included to account for any spurious relationships and better measure the impact

Table 2.1 Access to finance as an obstacle to business operations (mean value). *Source* World Bank Enterprise Surveys

Country	Number of Firms	Mean value	St.Dev.
Afghanistan	945	1.874	1.865
Albania	664	0.788	1.920
Azerbaijan	770	1.130	1.938
Bangladesh	2946	1.718	1.293
Benin	150	2.340	1.828
Bosnia & Herzegovina	721	1.405	1.342
Burkina Faso	394	2.977	1.186
Cameroon	363	2.402	1.335
Chad	150	2.073	1.806
Djibouti	266	0.996	1.511
Egypt	2897	1.480	1.813
Gabon	179	1.179	2.315
Gambia	174	1.793	1.448
Guinea	223	2.552	1.422
Guinea Bissau	159	2.912	1.384
Indonesia	1444	0.330	2.797
Iraq	756	2.022	1.717
Jordan	573	1.972	1.342
Kazakhstan	1144	0.946	2.232
Kosovo	472	−0.492	4.486
Kyrgyz Rep.	505	1.329	1.624
Lebanon	561	1.704	1.493
Mali	850	2.211	1.818
Mauritania	387	2.166	1.523
Morocco	407	1.189	1.672
Niger	150	1.893	2.060
Nigeria	4567	1.278	2.030
Pakistan	2182	1.102	1.816
Senegal	1107	2.204	1.564
Sierra Leone	150	1.953	1.095
Sudan	662	1.236	1.137
Suriname	152	1.993	1.182
Tajikistan	719	0.954	2.198
Tanzania	1232	1.798	2.312
Togo	155	2.148	1.858
Tunisia	592	1.144	1.368
Turkey	2496	0.671	1.695
Uganda	1325	1.807	1.985
Uzbekistan	756	0.893	1.467
West Bank & Gaza	434	1.954	1.548
Yemen	830	0.755	3.089
Total	36,135	1.411	2.014

of any single firm-specific variable beyond the effects of others. Thus, the regression estimates represent within-country variation in the relationship between the various exogenous indicators and financing constraints. In other words, each individual firm is not large enough to affect country-level measures of those development indicators. The control variables include quantitative measures of country economic development, financial development, and human development. The latter is captured by UNDP's human development index (HDI), which is a composite measure of social variables, i.e., schooling, life expectancy, inequality, etc. Further, control variables include measures of financial intermediation and structure. These country-level control variables capture unobservable differences between countries and are included to account for any spurious relationships and better measure the impact of any single firm-specific variable beyond the effects of others. Thus, the regression estimates represent within-country variation in the relationship between the various exogenous development indicators and financing constraints. In other words, each individual firm is not large enough to affect country-level measures of those development indicators. The Appendix describes in detail all the variables in the chapter.

Since the dependent variable is a categorical variable, an ordered probit model is used for estimating the regression (Greene 2012). The disturbance parameter is assumed to follow a normal distribution, and the standard maximum likelihood estimator is therefore used. Since omitted country characteristics might cause error terms to be correlated for firms within countries, clustered error terms are allowed. In a second step, economic, financial, institutional, and human development indicators are introduced in the analysis to obtain more robust results regarding the impact of firm-specific characteristics on firms' financing constraints. In general, the model assumes that the firm's underlying response can be described by the following Eq. 2.1:

$$\Upsilon_{ij} = \alpha + X_1'\beta_1 + X_2'\beta_2 + \varepsilon_{ij} \tag{2.1}$$

where $\Upsilon_{i,j}$ (ACCESS) is the underlying probability that firm i in country j perceives access to finance to be no, low, moderate, major, or severe constraint; $X_1'\beta_1$ is the vector of firm-specific variables; $X_2'\beta_2$ is the vector of country-level control variables; and $\varepsilon_{i,j}$ is a disturbance parameter that is assumed to follow a normal distribution. Unobservable differences between countries are captured by including country fixed effects coefficient.

Note that when analyzing categorical data with a probit model, an equivalent statistic to the OLS R^2 does not exist to evaluate the goodness-of-fit. The model estimates are maximum likelihood estimates arrived at through an iterative process. They are not calculated to minimize variance, so the OLS approach to goodness-of-fit does not apply. The goodness-of-fit of probit models is therefore approximated by several 'pseudo' R^2 measures, which also range from 0 to 1, with higher values indicating better model fit. However, these measures cannot be interpreted as one would interpret an OLS R^2 given that the different pseudo R^2 can arrive at very different, often very low, values. Wooldridge (2002) suggests that, if the dependent variable in probit models involves only binary responses, McFadden's pseudo R^2 estimates could have an analogous interpretation with the R^2 estimates of the OLS regression.

2.4 Analysis of Results

Summary statistics of the variables are shown in Table 2.2. The responses show that a significant percentage of firms are facing financing constraints. On average, access to finance tends to be a very severe problem of business operation for 11.3% of firms, a major problem for 18.3% of firms, and a moderate problem for 20.6% of firms in the total sample, a total of 50.1%. About half of the firms in the whole sample of countries have indicated that access to finance is a problem. Further, in the sample of Islamic countries, about 54.2% of all firms are small firms, 30.6% are medium firms, and 15.2% are large firms. Moreover, 23.4% of total firms are in the retail and wholesale sector, about 8.1% are in construction and transport sector, about 10.2% are in the services sector, about 11.9% are in the food sector; and the remaining firms mostly belong to other manufacturing sectors. About half of the firms are limited-liability companies. Moreover, on average, private ownership

Table 2.2 Descriptive statistics of variables. *Source* World Bank Enterprise Surveys

VARIABLE	Firms	Mean	S.D.	Min	0.25%	Median	0.75%	Max
ACCESS	34134	1.41	2.01	0.00	0.00	2.00	3.00	4.00
AGE	36095	3.01	0.89	0.69	2.56	2.89	3.26	7.61
SIZE	36135	1.61	0.74	1.00	1.00	1.00	2.00	3.00
SECTOR	36072	15.06	9.54	1.00	5.00	16.00	22.00	100.00
LEGAL	35937	2.91	0.98	1.00	2.00	3.00	3.00	6.00
LOCATION	28910	2.64	1.24	1.00	2.00	2.00	3.00	5.00
EXPORT	36028	6.97	22.34	0.00	0.00	0.00	0.00	100.00
OWNPRV	36132	88.87	29.49	0.00	100.00	100.00	100.00	100.00
OWNFOR	36124	5.23	20.51	0.00	0.00	0.00	0.00	100.00
OWNGOV	36124	0.79	7.25	0.00	0.00	0.00	0.00	100.00
OWNOTH	36122	3.51	17.63	0.00	0.00	0.00	0.00	100.00
OWNDOM	36113	80.83	29.76	0.00	60.00	100.00	100.00	100.00
AUDIT	35937	1.36	1.58	0.00	1.00	2.00	2.00	2.00
GDPCAP	36135	3090.9	3196.2	299.2	929.6	1668.3	3314.5	13611.5
GINI	36135	36.76	6.34	27.80	30.80	36.20	39.80	52.90
HDI	36135	0.58	0.12	0.30	0.49	0.56	0.69	0.86
FINDEV	34819	28.98	19.86	2.05	14.61	27.66	34.93	98.64
FINDEP	32397	37.52	28.41	4.44	19.06	29.68	49.49	199.71
FORASS	11601	33.98	35.21	0.00	4.00	17.00	50.00	100.00
SPREAD	24577	6.79	3.29	1.52	4.61	6.65	7.21	19.16
BCONCN5	32571	71.25	16.69	17.73	60.54	71.07	85.78	99.99
ZSCORE	35504	15.00	12.91	−4.55	4.68	12.34	19.71	50.01
BOONE	34995	−0.05	0.04	−0.12	−0.08	−0.06	−0.03	0.15
HSTAT	11115	64.86	226.77	0.32	0.42	0.57	0.77	909.83
LERNER	29975	0.25	0.11	0.07	0.17	0.24	0.30	0.52
VOICACC	36135	−0.71	0.50	−2.08	−1.04	−0.74	−0.26	0.33
POLSTAB	36135	−1.21	0.84	−2.69	−2.01	−1.19	−0.50	0.75
GOVEFF	36135	−0.68	0.43	−1.53	−1.01	−0.69	−0.46	0.37
REGQUAL	36135	−0.54	0.45	−1.63	−0.86	−0.60	−0.32	0.42
RULLAW	36135	−0.73	0.45	−1.95	−1.07	−0.72	−0.44	0.39
CONTRCORR	36135	−0.79	0.41	−1.64	−1.05	−0.90	−0.60	0.11

Table 2.3 Correlation among firm-specific variables

PWCORR	ACCESS	AGE	SIZE	SECTOR	LEGAL	LOCATION	EXPORT	OWNPRV	OWNFOR	OWNGOV	OWNOTH	OWNDOM	AUDIT
ACCESS	1												
AGE	−0.059*	1											
SIZE	−0.064*	0.143*	1										
SECTOR	0.003	−0.070*	−0.144*	1									
LEGAL	0.049*	−0.024*	−0.155*	0.031*	1								
LOCATION	0.015*	−0.045*	0.011	−0.032*	−0.072*	1							
EXPORT	−0.022*	0.019*	0.309*	−0.164*	−0.079*	0.039*	1						
OWNPRV	0.065*	−0.051*	−0.096*	−0.038*	−0.008	0.055*	−0.074*	1					
OWNFOR	−0.027*	0.008	0.136*	−0.001	−0.023*	−0.059*	0.119*	−0.646*	1				
OWNGOV	−0.011*	0.039*	0.102*	0.026*	−0.024*	0.045*	0.019*	−0.210*	0.025*	1			
OWNOTH	−0.011	−0.021*	−0.041*	0.048*	0.030*	−0.020*	0.005	−0.546*	−0.031*	0.029*	1		
OWNDOM	0.054*	−0.084*	−0.293*	0.410*	−0.026*	−0.017*	−0.153*	0.124*	−0.085*	−0.054*	0.052*	1	
AUDIT	0.124*	−0.117*	−0.119*	−0.002	0.031*	0.016*	−0.048*	0.073*	−0.046*	0.003	0.007	0.093*	1

Note the symbol * indicates significant correlation at the 5% level

of firms is 88.9%, foreign ownership is 5.2%, government ownership is low at 0.79%, while the largest shareholder has an 80.8% stake. The data indicate that ownership structure is considerably concentrated in the sample of countries.

Further, Table 2.3 presents the pairwise correlations between the firm-specific variables. Prima facie evidence shows negative correlation between firm size, ownership and export status and access to finance, while it shows a positive correlation between firm sector of activity, legal status, and location of operation with access to finance. The results do not show severe multicollinearity between the firm-specific control variables. Therefore, all of these variables can be included in regression analysis.

Taking a multivariate analysis, a quantitative assessment is provided of the determinants of financing constraints through the application of probit analysis. Several series of maximum likelihood regression models (A.1–A.11) were estimated sequentially, and the regression results are reported in Table 2.4. In the benchmark model, the results are presented according to the order at which firm-specific characteristics are estimated individually and collectively for the entire sample of firms and for each one of the high-income and low-income Islamic countries. The results report the estimated probability that a firm describes access to finance as major obstacle for its business operation depending on its characteristics.

The results of the ordered probit regression models for the whole sample suggest that, taken individually, a firm's age, size, location of operations, and export status are negative significant predictors of firms' access to finance: Thus, higher values of those firm characteristics imply lower financing constraints of firms. Further, limited-liability companies and companies that their accounts audited are positively associated with financing constraints of firms. The sector of activity surprising is not a significant predictor of firms financing constraints. Moreover, private ownership, foreign ownership, and dominant owners are positive significant predictors of firms' financing constraints. Higher ownership stakes are associated with higher financing constraints. Government ownership appears to be a rather insignificant factor.

Table 2.4 Impact of firm-specific characteristics (by development level)

ACCESS	A.1	A.2	A.3	A.4	A.5	A.6	A.7	A.8	A.9	A.10	A.11
									All countries	High–income countries	Low–income countries
AGE	−0.049***								−0.026***	−0.064***	0.010
	(−7.56)								(−3.85)	(−6.73)	(0.96)
SIZE		−0.139***							−0.084***	−0.103***	−0.065***
		(18.73)							(−9.84)	(−7.97)	(−4.86)
SECTOR			0.00						−0.001	0.001	−0.002***
			(0.10)						(−1.03)	(0.07)	(−1.71)
LEGAL				0.081***					0.075***	0.030***	0.088***
				(14.17)					(12.02)	(3.49)	(9.67)
LOCATION					−0.010*				0.161	−0.066***	0.065***
					(−1.99)				(1.40)	(−8.21)	(9.52)
EXPORT						−0.002***			−0.001***	−0.001***	−0.001*
						(−9.38)			(−3.83)	(−3.06)	(−1.76)
OWNPRV							0.002***		0.002***	0.003***	0.001***
							(9.60)		(7.32)	(7.81)	(2.95)
OWNFOR							0.001***		0.001***	0.001***	0.001
							(2.81)		(2.92)	(2.45)	(1.22)
OWNGOV							−0.001		0.001	−0.003***	0.005***
							(1.32)		(0.38)	(−2.56)	(3.34)
OWNDOM							0.002***		0.002***	0.001***	0.001***
							(12.43)		(7.90)	(3.56)	(4.43)
AUDIT								0.055***	0.038***	0.045***	0.024***
								(13.10)	(8.37)	(7.45)	(3.52)
Obs	34134	34134	34071	33937	28886	34045	34102	33964	28464	14661	13803
Pseudo R^2	0.003	0.003	0.002	0.002	0.002	0.001	0.002	0.002	0.008	0.011	0.007

Note Dependent variable is ACCESS. An ordered probit model is used. Symbols ***, **, * indicate significant correlation at the 1%, 5%, and 10% level, respectively. Z values in parentheses

When all firm-specific characteristics are included in the analysis, the results remain about the same. Only the location of firms' operation turns out to be insignificant. Similar conclusions carry over when the analysis considers separately the effect in the high-income. However, in the low-income group of Islamic countries, the results present an expected shift: Firm age and foreign ownership turn insignificant, while government ownership turns out to be a significant predictor of financing constraints.

These findings are only partly in line with other relevant empirical findings. In general, firm-specific characteristics, such as age, ownership dispersion, export-oriented activity, are significant determinants of financing constraints of firms in the sample Islamic countries. These results are in line with those of Devereaux and Schiantarelli (1990) and Beck et al. (2006), who find that young firms are more sensitive to the cash flow-investment link, thus they are more financially constrained, and they go against those of Oliner and Rudebusch (1992), who find insignificant sensitivity. Also, these results are in line with those of Harrison and McMillan (2003) and Beck et al. (2006), who find that domestically, owned firms are more sensitive to the cash flow-investment link. However, in less-developed Islamic countries, firm age and foreign ownership do not appear to matter much in understanding firms' financing constraints. It appears that in the latter countries the problem of access to finance is not significantly related to the firms' reputation and history or to the presence of foreign shareholders. Local institutions financial structures are probably the main cause of it. On the other hand, government ownership does matter, reflecting presumably the considerably larger extent of state ownership and the more active role of government in decision-making.

In order to see the regional impact of firm-specific characteristics on firms' access to finance constraints, Eq. (2.1) is re-estimated for each of the UN-classified regions: Africa (AFR), Europe and Central Asia (ECA), Middle East and North Africa (MNA), East Asia and the Pacific (EAP), and other Special Arrangement Regions (SAR). Table 2.5 presents the results of the benchmark regression model. The results present considerable differences as regards the predictive power of firm-specific characteristics. It appears that the dominant owners, the auditing of

Table 2.5 Impact of firm-specific characteristics (by region)

	Africa	East Asia and the Pacific	Europe and Central Asia	Middle East and North Africa	Special arrangement regions
AGE	−0.035***	−0.023	0.056***	−0.007	−0.124***
	(−3.37)	(−0.61)	(3.27)	(−0.42)	(−6.46)
SIZE	−0.120***	0.054	0.025	−0.101***	−0.026
	(−6.71)	(1.29)	(1.37)	(−5.48)	(−0.95)
SECTOR	−0.006***	−0.009***	0.003*	−0.003**	0.002
	(−5.02)	(−2.30)	(1.77)	(−2.43)	(0.85)
LEGAL	0.005	0.050	−0.034***	0.053***	0.082***
	(0.43)	(1.58)	(−2.70)	94.34)	(3.20)
LOCATION	−0.063***	0.046	0.034***	0.081***	−0.082***
	(−4.99)	(1.31)	(3.56)	(9.65)	(−2.96)
EXPORT	−0.003***	−0.001	0.001	−0.001	−0.002***
	(−4.09)	(−0.55)	(0.48)	(−1.32)	(−3.06)
OWNPRV	0.004***	−0.001	0.001	0.004***	0.007***
	(12.92)	(−0.82)	(0.21)	(4.93)	(5.02)
OWNFOR	0.001**	0.001	0.001	0.002***	0.001
	(2.43)	(−0.03)	(−0.06)	(2.58)	(0.68)
OWNGOV	−0.001	−0.002	0.001	0.003	−0.002
	(−0.36)	(0.48)	(−0.28)	(1.19)	(−0.27)
OWNDOM	0.001***	0.002	0.001***	0.001***	0.001
	(3.35)	(0.07)	(2.77)	(3.010	(1.26)
AUDIT	0.045***	0.080***	0.029***	0.010	0.053***
	(5.42)	(3.02)	(3.56)	(0.88)	(4.90)
Obs	9021	1428	7120	7217	3526
Pseudo R^2	0.0166	0.0071	0.003	0.01	0.0186

Note Dependent variable is ACCESS. An ordered probit model is used. Symbols ***, **, * indicate significant correlation at the 1%, 5%, and 10% level, respectively. Z values in parentheses

accounts, sector of activity, location, and legal status remain significant predictors of firms' financing constraints in most international regions, but firms' age, size, export status, and ownership are significant only in few of the regions. Given that firms located within the Islamic countries of each region exhibit considerably different characteristics and that they are operating under considerably different economic, social, and cultural environments that interact with firm characteristics in various ways, then a richer picture of the impact of the firm-specific characteristics can only be obtained if the impact of broad economic and

Table 2.6 Marginal effects of firm-specific characteristics (by development level)

ACCESS	dy/dx		
	All countries	High-income countries	Low-income countries
AGE	0.001***	0.002***	0.001
	(3.77)	(6.46)	(−1.01)
SIZE	0.003***	0.004***	0.003***
	(8.78)	(7.03)	(4.69)
SECTOR	0.001	0.001	0.001*
	(1.03)	(0.07)	(1.70)
LEGAL	−0.003***	−0.001***	−0.004***
	(−11.12)	(−3.39)	(−8.43)
LOCATION	0.001	0.003***	−0.003***
	(1.40)	(7.54)	(−8.46)
EXPORT	0.002***	0.001***	0.001*
	(3.79)	(2.76)	(1.67)
OWNPRV	0.001***	0.001***	0.001***
	(−7.04)	(−7.06)	(−2.72)
OWNFOR	0.001***	0.002***	0.001
	(2.91)	(−2.47)	(−1.14)
OWNGOV	0.002	0.001***	0.001***
	(−0.37)	(2.28)	(−3.40)
OWNDOM	0.002***	0.001***	0.002***
	(−7.65)	(−3.35)	(−4.36)
AUDIT	−0.002***	−0.002***	−0.001***
	(−7.66)	(−7.87)	(−4.26)
Obs	28464	14661	13803

Note Dependent variable y is ACCESS. The delta method is used to calculate marginal effects, dy/dx. Symbols ***, **, * indicate significant correlation at the 1%, 5%, and 10% level, respectively. Z values in parentheses

financial conditions as well as social and cultural factors at the national level is properly accounted for. Economic and financial development along with national social and cultural factors, including religiosity and religion, affect decision-making and the nature of financial contracting which in turn affects the supply of and demand for finance and thereby firms' financing constraints.

In order to test for the economic significance of the results of the probit regression analysis and hence the expected policy intervention impact, the marginal effects of firm-specific characteristics are estimated. These effects show the marginal discrete change in the dependent variable (ACCESS) following a value change in each categorical or numerical firm-specific characteristic (dy/dx). The marginal effects for the whole sample and for each of the two subgroups of countries are reported in Table 2.6. They show that a unit or category change in firm age, size, sector of activity, legal and export status, private domestic, and foreign ownership exert a meaningfully effect on firms' perceptions regarding obstacles to finance. For most of the latter characteristics, the impact is variously significant in the whole sample and each of the two subgroups of Islamic countries. Overall, only some of the firm-specific characteristics used in this analysis appear to have a meaningful economic impact.

2.5 Discussion and Robustness Checks

There may be concerns that the results obtained above depend on the firm-specific characteristics of the sample countries. After all, different countries have different, more- or less-developed institutions, different societal structures, and characterized by different cultural and behavioral norms. Therefore, it is possible that, by accounting for the impact of different country-level factors, the firms' characteristics become either more or less effective in easing firms' financing constraints. In order to test these conjectures, a series of additional robustness tests are taken into account for the impact of various national economic and non-economic conditions. Equation 2.1 is re-estimated to include the impact of a country's economic and human development as well as its financial development and financial intermediation conditions. The variables are described in the Appendix.

2.5.1 Impact of Economic and Human Development

The level of economic and human development of countries has an impact on the financing constraints of firms. In order to check for this conjecture, Eq. 2.1 is expanded to include regressors capturing the impact of economic and human development of the sample countries. Table 2.7 presents the results of the benchmark regression model after

Table 2.7 Impact of economic development (by development level)

ACCESS	All countries	High-income countries	Low-income countries
AGE	−0.036***	−0.058***	0.011
	(−5.23)	(−6.05)	(1.12)
SIZE	−0.072***	−0.078***	−0.052***
	(−7.78)	(−5.91)	(−3.92)
SECTOR	−0.001**	−0.002***	−0.002**
	(−2.15)	(−2.54)	(−2.14)
LEGAL	0.038***	0.028***	0.057***
	(5.88)	(3.14)	(6.09)
LOCATION	0.021***	−0.029***	0.080***
	(3.82)	(−3.35)	(11.20)
EXPORT	−0.001***	−0.001	0.001
	(−2.42)	(−1.41)	(0.29)
OWNPRV	0.003***	0.002***	0.002***
	(10.60)	(4.80)	(5.60)
OWNFOR	0.001***	−0.001**	0.001***
	(3.83)	(−2.16)	(2.40)
OWNGOV	−0.001	−0.005***	0.004***
	(−0.55)	(−4.46)	(2.71)
OWNDOM	0.001***	0.001***	0.001*
	(3.24)	(2.83)	(1.77)
AUDIT	0.034***	0.046***	0.020***
	(7.44)	(7.40)	(2.90)
GDPCAP	0.001***	0.001***	0.001***
	(−16.39)	(−21.34)	(−8.43)
GINI	0.004***	0.033***	−0.014***
	(4.01)	(15.93)	(−6.89)
HDI	−0.422***	0.281***	−1.261***
	(−5.19)	(2.78)	(−6.24)
Obs	28464	14661	13803
Pseudo R^2	0.0153	0.0267	0.014

Note Dependent variable is ACCESS. An ordered probit model is used. Symbols ***, **, * indicate significant correlation at the 1%, 5%, and 10% level, respectively. Z values in parentheses

controlling for economic development (GDPCAP), income inequality (GINI), and human development (HDI) for the whole sample and for each of the two groups of high-income and low-income Islamic countries. The results show that economic development, income inequality, and human development are significant predictors of firms' financing constraints. Higher levels of economic development as well as inequality in the distribution of income imply higher financing constraints of firms. It seems that faster economic growth is associated with higher needs for finance of firms, which cannot be accommodated. Further, increasing income inequality tends to intensify financing constraints most likely by distorting the efficient allocation of finance. On the other hand, higher levels of human development imply lower financing constraints of firms. Human skill and knowledge matter for determining the extent to which firms face financing constraints. The Economist (2011) argued that higher levels of human development lead to improved financing by lowering corruption and bureaucracy. These results are in line with those of Beck et al. (2006) who found a significant role for economic development, and those of Reinhart et al. (2010) who stressed the significant role of human development, in a smaller sample of countries and subject to different model structures. After controlling for economic and human development levels, most firm-specific characteristics remain significant predictors of firms' financing constraints, except perhaps for the export status of firms and firm age, which remain significant according to the model used. However, the sign of some of the firm-specific characteristics changes in low-income countries. It seems that further analysis is needed to explain their influence under more complex economic and non-economic conditions prevalent in those countries.

2.5.2 Impact of Financial Development and Financial Intermediation Conditions

The financial conditions and the level of financial development of countries are also considered to have an impact on the financing constraints of firms. They represent important supply-side factors in the availability of finance. In order to check for this conjecture, Eq. 2.1 is expanded to include regressors capturing the impact of the overall level of financing liquidity and aspects of the financial intermediation environment. Table 2.8 presents the results of the benchmark regression model after controlling for the level of financial development (FINDEV), the size of the system's financing capacity (FINDEP), the extent of foreign

Table 2.8 Impact of financial conditions (by development level)

ACCESS	Panel A			Panel B		
	All countries	High-income countries	Low-income countries	All countries	High-income countries	Low-income countries
AGE	0.033	−0.013	0.100***	−0.030***	−0.061***	−0.015
	(1.27)	(−0.40)	(2.26)	(−2.91)	(−3.90)	(−1.06)
SIZE	−0.013	0.059	−0.114***	−0.106***	−0.070***	−0.102***
	(−0.44)	(1.62)	(−2.21)	(−6.45)	(−2.93)	(−4.30)
SECTOR	−0.009***	−0.010***	−0.005	−0.006***	−0.007***	−0.004***
	(−3.52)	(−3.20)	(−1.10)	(−5.61)	(−3.91)	(−2.71)
LEGAL	0.040*	0.072***	0.009	0.082***	0.107***	−0.027
	(1.67)	(2.62)	(0.19)	(6.40)	(5.09)	(−1.60)
LOCATION	0.103***	0.024	0.139***	−0.049***	0.008	0.051***
	(5.74)	(0.75)	(6.12)	(−4.51)	(0.34)	(3.55)
EXPORT	0.001	−0.001	0.005***	−0.002***	−0.002***	−0.001*
	(1.38)	(−1.12)	(3.08)	(−3.72)	(−3.24)	(−1.85)
OWNPRV	0.001	−0.001	0.001	0.000	0.003***	0.002***
	(−0.46)	(−0.58)	(−0.13)	(0.31)	(4.15)	(3.82)
OWNFOR	−0.001	0.001	−0.002	−0.002***	−0.001	−0.001
	(−0.92)	(0.28)	(−0.74)	(−3.13)	(−1.10)	(−0.89)
OWNGOV	0.002	−0.004	0.003	0.007***	0.001	0.007***
	(0.72)	(−1.23)	(0.80)	(3.27)	(0.27)	(3.15)
OWNDOM	−0.001	0.000	−0.002	0.003***	0.003***	0.001
	(−0.97)	(0.24)	(−1.60)	(6.80)	(6.41)	(0.45)
AUDIT	0.025*	0.067***	−0.015	0.042***	0.037***	0.030***
	(1.72)	(2.92)	(−0.88)	(5.71)	(3.83)	(2.51)
FINDEV	−0.003**	−0.007**	0.001*			
	(−1.92)	(−2.06)	(1.67)			
FINDEP	−0.027***	0.001*	0.00111			
	(−6.52)	(1.87)	(0.13)			
FORASS	0.013***	0.001	0.001			
	(5.24)	(1.15)	(01.4)			
SPREAD	0.102***	0.001	0.001			
	(5.03)	(0.17)	(0.98)			
BCONCN				0.005***	0.017***	0.036***
				(3.70)	(7.20)	(10.32)
ZSCORE				0.009***	−0.072***	0.007***
				(7.98)	(−9.65)	(3.08)
BOONE				−5.943***	9.75***	−1.455
				(−9.69)	(8.70)	(−1.01)
HSTAT				0.044	−15.822***	1.622***
				(0.40)	(−9.93)	(2.72)
LERNER				0.610***	0.001	−3.569***
				(6.28)	(0.15)	(−5.42)

(continued)

Table 2.8 (continued)

ACCESS	Panel A			Panel B		
	All countries	High-income countries	Low-income countries	All countries	High-income countries	Low-income countries
Obs	2933	1902	1031	9540	4659	4381
Pseudo R^2	0.0164	0.0065	0.0261	0.028	0.0504	0.026

Note Dependent variable is ACCESS. An ordered probit model is used. Symbols ***, **, * indicate significant correlation at the 1%, 5%, and 10% level, respectively. Z values in parentheses

ownership of domestic bank assets (FORASS), the concentration of the banking system (BCONCN), the competition within the banking system (LERNER, BOONE, HSTAT), and the cost of financial intermediation (SPREAD), for both the whole sample and each subgroup of Islamic countries. The results show that financial development and financial intermediation conditions are significant predictors of firms' financing constraints, except perhaps for the low-income countries. Higher levels of financial development and liquidity in the financial system imply lower financing constraints of firms. In contrast, foreign ownership of bank assets has the opposite effect.

On the other hand, the results show that financial intermediation conditions matter in alleviating firms' financing constraints. Higher bank concentration implies higher financing constraints of firms in the whole sample and the two subgroups. The same appears to hold in the case of bank competition, except for low-income countries. These results are partly only in line with other relevant empirical findings, such as Beck et al. (2006) who found a significant role for financial development, using a less homogeneous sample of countries. They are also in line with Love and Martinez Peria (2012) who found that low bank competition diminishes firms' access to finance. After the inclusion of financial system controls, firm size and sector of activity, legal status, audit, and location of operation remain in most models significant predictors of financing constraints. The predictive power of the other characteristics changes in accordance with the model used. It seems that the consideration of financial conditions has a significant impact on the financing of the different firms that awaits for more detailed analysis for it to be better understood in the Islamic world. Again, the consideration of social and cultural factors is an obvious way to go.

2.6 Conclusions

Access to finance has been found to be one of the most binding constraints on firms' growth. In this chapter, drawing in the relevant literature and a data set based on World Bank's Economic Surveys, certain firm characteristics are identified and explored as determinants of firms' financing constraints in a sample of Islamic countries. The latter represent a large and growing portion of world population and output and in recent decades, a parallel mode of finance, Islamic finance, based on different values and contracting habits, has become a sizable economic activity. In order to test the predictive ability of firm characteristics on financing constraints under different socioeconomic environments, the sample of countries is split between high- and low-income ones. The main contribution of the chapter is to examine firms' access to finance in an Islamic environment drawing on a recent and comprehensive data set based on firms' Surveys and properly including the impact of national development factors. However, as this data represent firms' views and perceptions regarding their access to finance, the quantitative analysis is bound by the limitations of existing methods concerning categorical variables.

In line with most relevant empirical findings, firms' age, size, and ownership predict firms' financing constraints in most of the models used. In contrast, sectoral origin, external audit of accounts, government ownership, and investment funding through internal funds have less significant predictive power, and their prediction power is conditional upon the model specification. Islamic countries do occasionally deviate from the norm observed in the rest of the world. Further, the results show that national levels of economic, financial, and human development do affect the predictive power of firm-specific characteristics in the sample Islamic countries. Further analysis is needed to understand the nature of financial intermediation and disentangle the complex interaction between conventional and Islamic financing of firms and the economy. Further analysis is also needed, along with the inclusion of social and cultural factors, to better understand the diversity in the severity of financing constraints facing firms operating in Islamic environments.

Appendix. Definition of Variables

See Table A.1

Table A.1 Definition of variables

Name	Description and source
AGE	Logarithm of the number of years since the year that the company was established, from the World Bank Enterprise Surveys
SIZE	Categorical variable is equal to 1 if the firm is small (5–19 employees), 2 if the firm is medium (20–99 employees), and 3 if the firm is large (> 99 employees), from the World Bank Enterprise Surveys
SECTOR	Categorical variable is equal to 1 if the firm is in manufacturing, 2 in retail-wholesale, 3 in services, and 4 in other sectors, from the World Bank Enterprise Surveys
EXPORT	Percent of the firm's total sales directly exported, from the World Bank Enterprise Surveys
LEGAL	Categorical variable is equal to 1 if the firm is publicly listed, 2 if it is private limited-liability one, 3 if it is sole proprietorship, 4 if it is partnership, 5 if it is limited partnership, and 6 if other, form the World Bank Enterprise Surveys
LOCATION	Categorical variable is equal to 1 if the firm is located at the capital city, 2 if it is in city with more than 1 million people, 3 in a city with 0.25–1 million people, 4 in a city with 0.05–0.25 million people, and 5 in a city with less than 0.05 million people, form the World Bank Enterprise Surveys
AUDIT	Percent of firms with annual financial statement reviewed by external auditor last year, from the World Bank Enterprise Surveys
OWNPRV	The percentage of the firm owned by domestic private individuals, companies, or organizations, from the World Bank Enterprise Surveys
OWNFOR	The percentage of the firm owned by foreign private individuals, companies, or organizations, from the World Bank Enterprise Surveys
OWNGOV	The percentage of the firm owned by the state, from the World Bank Enterprise Surveys

Table A.1 (continued)

Name	Description and source
OWNDOM	The percentage of the firm's largest owner, from the World Bank Enterprise Surveys
GDPCAP	Logarithm of GDP per capita (current USD), from the World Bank Development Indicators. It is generally considered a measure of a country's level of economic development
GINI	Gini coefficient, from the World Bank Development Indicators. It is a measure of a country's income distribution, and it is generally considered an indicator of income inequality
HDI	Index ranging from 0 to 1, with higher values corresponding to higher human development, form the UNDP indicators. It is a summary measure of average achievement in key dimensions of human development: a long and healthy life, knowledge, and decent standard of living
FINDEV	Domestic credit to the private sector (% GDP), from the World Bank Development Indicators. It is generally considered a measure of a country's level of financial development
FINDEP	Financial system deposits as a percent of GDP, from the IMF International Financial Statistics
FORASS	Foreign bank assets as a percent of total domestic assets, from the IMF International Financial Statistics
SPREAD	Difference between the banks' lending and deposit rate, from the IMF International Financial Statistics
BCONCN	It measures the value of assets of the three largest commercial banks as a share of total commercial banking assets, so it is effectively a measure of bank concentration (%). Raw data are from Bankscope, but the ratio is published by the World Bank Global Financial Development Indicators
LERNER	The variable is approximated by the Lerner Index which is a measure of market power in the banking market, from the World Bank Global Financial Development Indicators. It is defined as the difference between output prices and marginal costs (relative to prices). Prices are calculated as total bank revenue over assets, whereas marginal costs are obtained from an estimated translog cost function with respect to output. Higher values of the Lerner index indicate less bank competition
ZSCORE	Index capturing the probability of default of a country's banking system, calculated as a weighted average of the z-scores of a country's individual banks (the weights are based on the individual banks' total assets). Z-score compares a bank's buffers (capitalization and returns) with the volatility of those returns

Table A.1 (continued)

Name	Description and source
BOONE	The Boone statistic is a measure of the degree of bank competition based on profit-efficiency in the banking market, from the World Bank Global Financial Development Indicators. It is calculated as the elasticity of profits to marginal costs. An increase in the indicator implies a deterioration of the competitive conduct of financial intermediation
HSTAT	The H-statistic is a measure of the degree of bank competition based on internal organization in the banking market, from the World Bank Global Financial Development Indicators. It measures the elasticity of banks revenues relative to input prices. Under perfect competition, the H-statistic equals 1. Under monopoly, the H-statistic is less than or equal to 0. Under monopolistic competition, the H-statistic is between 0 and 1

References

Aghion, P., & Bolton, P. (1997). A theory of trickle-down growth and development. *Review of Economic Studies, 64*(2), 151–172.

Alesina, A., & Perotti, R. (1996). Income distribution, political instability and investment. *European Economic Review, 40*(6), 1203–1228.

Alesina, A., & Rodrik, D. (1994). Distributive politics and economic growth. *Quarterly Journal of Economics, 109*(2), 465–490.

Baddeley, M. (2011). Civil war and human development: Impacts of finance and financial infrastructure. CWPE 1127, https://doi.org/10.17863/CAM.5240. University of Cambridge.

Banerjee, A. V., & Newman, A. F. (1993). Occupational choice and the process of development. *Journal of Political Economy, 101*(2), 274–298.

Bauer, M., Chytilova, J., & Morduch, J. (2012). Behavioral foundations of microcredit: Experimental and survey evidence from rural India. *American Economic Review, 102*(2), 1118–1139.

Beck, T., Demirguc-Kunt, A., & Levine, R. (2004). *Finance, inequality, and poverty: Cross-country evidence* (NBER Working Paper No. 10979).

Beck, T., Demirgüç-Kunt, A., Laeven, L., & Maksimovic, V. (2006). The determinants of financing constraints. *Journal of International Money and Finance, 25*(6), 932–952.

Beck, T., Demirgüç-Kunt, A., & Levine, R. (2007). Finance, inequality and the poor: Cross-country evidence. *Journal of Economic Growth, 12*(1), 27–49.

Beck, T., Demirgüç-Kunt, A., & Maksimovic, V. (2005). Financial and legal constraints to firm growth: Does firm size matter? *The Journal of Finance, 60*(1), 137–177.

Beck, T., Levine, R., & Loayza, N. (2000). Finance and the sources of growth. *Journal of Monetary Economics, 58*(1), 261–300.

Bond, S., Harhoff, D., & Van Reenen, J. (2005). Investment, R&D and financial constraints in Britain and Germany. *Annales d' Economie et de Statistique, 79/80*, 433–460. http://www.jstor.org/stable/20777584.

Carlin, W., Schaffer, M., & Seabright, P. (2006). *Where are the real bottlenecks? A Langrangian approach to identifying constraints on growth from subjective survey data* (CERT Discussion Paper no. 2006/04). Edinburgh: Center for Economic Reform and Transformation.

CGAP. (2009). *Measuring access to financial services around the world.* Washington, DC: World Bank.

Claessens, S. (2006). Access to financial services: A review of the issues and public policy objectives. *World Bank Research Observer, 21*(2), 207–240.

Clarke, G. R. G., Robert Cull, María Soledad Martínez Pería. (2006). Foreign bank participation and access to credit across firms in developing countries. *Journal of Comparative Economics, 34*(4), 774–795.

Demirgüç-Kunt, A., Beck, T., & Honohan, P. (2008). *Finance for all?: Policies and pitfalls in expanding access.* Washington, DC: World Bank.

Demirgüç-Kunt, A., & Maksimovic, V. (1998). Law, finance and firm growth. *Journal of Finance, 53*(6), 2107–2137.

Demirguc-Kunt, A., Klapper, L., & Randall, D. (2013). *Islamic finance and financial inclusion: Measuring use of and demand for formal financial services among muslim adults* (Policy Research Working Paper Series 6642). Washington, DC: World Bank.

Devereux, M., & Schiantarelli, F. (1990). Investment, financial factors and cash flow from UK panel data. In G. Hubbard (Ed.), *Information, Capital Markets and Investment.* Chicago, IL: University of Chicago Press.

Dollar, D., Hallward-Driemeier, D., & Mengistae, T. (2006). Investment climate and international integration. *World Development, 34*(9), 1498–1516.

Fazzari, S., Hubbard, G., & Petersen, B. (1988). Financing constraints and corporate investment. *Brookings Papers on Economic Activity, 1988*(1), 141–195.

Fazzari, S., Hubbard, G., & Petersen, B. (2000). Investment-cash flow sensitivities are useful: A comment on Kaplan and Zingales. *Quarterly Journal of Economics, 115*(2), 695–705.

Galor, O., & Zeira, J. (1993). Income distribution and macroeconomics. *Review of Economic Studies, 60*(1), 35–52.

Gelos, R.G., & Werner, A. M. (2002). Financial liberalization, credit constraints, and collateral: Investment in the Mexican manufacturing sector. *Journal of Development Economics, 67*(1), 1–27.

Greene, W. H. (2012). *Econometric analysis* (7th ed.). Boston: Pearson.

Hallward-Driemeier, M., & Aterido, R. (2007). *Impact of access to finance, corruption and infrastructure on employment growth: Putting in a global context* (*Policy Research Working Paper No. 4792*). Washington, DC: World Bank.

Harrison, A., & McMillan, M. (2003). Does direct foreign investment affect domestic firm credit constraints? *Journal of International Economics, 61*(1), 73–100.

Honohan, P. (2007, January). *Cross-country variation in household access to financial services*. Washington, DC: The World Bank.

Hoshi, T., Kashyap, A., & Scharfstein, D. (1991). Corporate structure, liquidity and investment: Evidence from Japanese industrial groups. *Quarterly Journal of Economics, 106*(1), 33–60.

Kaldor, N. (1957). A model of economic growth. *The Economic Journal, 67*(268), 591–624.

Kaplan, S., & Zingales, L. (1997). Do investment-cash flow sensitivities provide useful measures of financing constraints? *Quarterly Journal of Economics, 112*(1), 169–215.

Kaplan, S., & Zingales, L. (2000). Investment-cash flow sensitivities are not valid measures of financing constraints. *Quarterly Journal of Economics, 115*(3), 705–712.

Kinda, T., Plane, P., & Veganzones-Varoudakis, M. (2011). Firm productivity and investment climate in developing countries: How does and manufacturing perform? *The Developing Economies, 49*(4), 429–462.

Kon, Y., & Storey, D. J. (2003). A theory of discouraged borrower. *Small Business Economics, 21*(1), 37–49.

Korajczyk, R. A., & Levy, A. (2003). Capital structure choice: Macroeconomic conditions and financial constraints. *Journal of Financial Economics, 68*(1), 75–109.

Kostov, P., Arun, T., & Annim, S. K. (2012). Determinants of access to finance: An investigation into the Mzansi intervention. *European Journal of Development Research, 24*(3), 397–412.

Kuntchev, V., Ramalho, R., Rodriguez-Meza, J., & Yang, J. (2012). *What have we learned from the enterprise surveys regarding access to finance by SMEs?* (World Bank. https://doi.org/10.1596/1813-9450-6670).

Kuntchev, V., Ramalho, R., Rodríguez-Meza, J., & Yang, J. (2013). *What have we learned from the enterprise surveys regarding access to finance by smes?* (World Bank Policy Research Working Paper No. 6670). Washington, DC: World Bank.

Kuznets, S. (1955). Economic growth and income inequality. *American Economic Review, XLV*(1), 128–156.

Laeven, L. (2003). Does financial liberalization reduce financing constraints? *Financial Management, 32*(1), 5–34.

Levenson, A. R., & Willard, K. L. (2000). Do firms get financing they want? Measuring credit rationing experienced by small business in the U.S. *Small Business Economics, 14*(2), 83–94.

Levine, R. (2005). Finance and growth: Theory and evidence. In P. Aghion & S. Durlauf (Eds.), *Handbook of Economic Growth* (Vol. 1A). Amsterdam: North Holland.

Love, I., & Martinez-Peria, M. S. (2012). *How bank competition affects firms' access to finance* (World Bank Policy Research Working Paper No. 6163). The World Bank.

Oliner, D., & Rudebusch, G. (1992). Sources of the financing hierarchy for business investment. *Review of Economics and Statistics, 74*(2), 643–654.

Pal, R., & Ferrando, A. (2006). *Financing constraints and firms' cash policy in the Euro area* (ECB Working Paper No. 642), June.

Peachey, S., & Roe, A. (2004). *Access to finance: A study for the world savings banks institute* (Research Report). Oxford Policy Management.

Persson, T., & Tabellini, G. (1994). Is inequality harmful for growth? *American Economic Review, 84*(3), 600–621.

Rajan, R., & Zingales, L. (1998). Financial dependence and growth. *American Economic Review, 88*(3), 559–587.

Rajan, R. G., & Zingales, L. (2003). The great reversals: The politics of financial development in the twentieth century. *Journal of Financial Economics, 69*(1), 5–50.

Reinhart, C., Rojas-Suarez, & Vazquez, F. (2010). *Financial access and the poor: The cross-country evidence.* Paris: Organisation for Economic Co-operation and Development.

Schiantarelli, F. (1995). Financial constraints and investment: A critical review of methodological issues and international evidence. In J. Peek &

E. Rosengren (Eds.), *Is bank lending important for the transmission of monetary policy?* Boston, MA: Federal Reserve Bank of Boston.

Schiffer, M., & Weder, B. (2001). *Firm size and the business environment: Worldwide survey results* (Discussion Paper No. 43). Washington, DC: International Finance Corporation.

Sembenelli, A., & Schiantarelli, F. (1996). *Form of ownership and financial constraints* (Working Paper No. 1629). Washington, DC: World Bank.

Stiglitz, J., & Weiss, A. (1981). Credit rationing in markets with imperfect information. *American Economic Review, 71*(3), 393–410.

United Nations Development Program. (2014). (*HDI*). http://hdr.undp.org/en/content/-index-hdi.

Vermeulen, P. (2002). *Investment and financing constraints: What does the data tell?* (EIFC Working Paper No. 25).

Whited, T. M. (1992). Debt, liquidity constraints, and corporate investment: Evidence from panel data. *The Journal of Finance, 47*(4), 1425–1460.

Wooldridge, J. (2002). *Econometric analysis of cross-section and panel data.* Cambridge, MA: MIT Press.

World Bank. (2014). *Global financial development report - financial inclusion.* Washington, DC: World Bank.

3

Financial Inclusion for Women: Impact Evaluation on Islamic Microfinance to Women's Empowerment in Indonesia

Umi Karomah Yaumidin, Diah Setiari Suhodo, Putri Irma Yuniarti and Achsanah Hidayatina

Abstract This chapter evaluates the impact of the Islamic microfinance institution toward the women empowerment. We surveyed approximately two hundred and forty women who had been involved in the microfinance of the Misykat program in the Dompet Peduli Ummat of Daarut Tauhid and BAZNAS in Bandung. The primary data collection was held in two sessions, starting from June to December 2014. The causal effect of the credit on empowerment was identified using quasi-experimental setting with proxy controls for latent heterogeneity between the control and the treatment groups. The study suggests that women involvement in the microfinance improves their position within the household through (i) access to independent income; (ii) control over savings and credit use; and

This report is submitted as part of responsibility as a grantee of East Asian Development Network research grants 2014/2015.

U. K. Yaumidin (✉) · D. S. Suhodo · P. I. Yuniarti · A. Hidayatina
Economic Research Centre, Indonesia Institute of Sciences,
Widya Graha building 4–5th floor, Jendral Gatot Subroto street No. 10,
Jakarta, Indonesia
e-mail: yaumidinuk@gmail.com

© The Author(s) 2017

M. Zulkhibri and A. G. Ismail (eds.), *Financial Inclusion and Poverty Alleviation*,
Palgrave Studies in Islamic Banking, Finance, and Economics,
https://doi.org/10.1007/978-3-319-69799-4_3

(iii) ability to bring productive asset to household economy. In addition, using the matching propensity score and the instrumental variable methods helps address the bias selection in a cross-sectional setting.

Keywords Islamic microfinance · Women empowerment · Zakah management · Poverty alleviation · Propensity score matching

3.1 Introduction

3.1.1 Background and Rationale

Indonesia's poverty rate has returned to a level similar to what it was prior to the financial crisis of 1997–1998. It has not fallen further partly because of slow economic growth. The higher rates of poverty continued for considerable periods. By 2005, the poverty rate has fallen to 16%, but has risen in 2006 to 17.7% (Yaumidin 2010). Various ways and financial resources have been deployed to accelerate the elimination of poverty in Indonesia. As a result, the number of poor started decline significantly, but in contrary, inequality has increased slightly in Indonesia, a country with abundant natural resources (Yaumidin 2013). Indonesia's government continues its efforts to reduce the gap by increasing inter-regional connectivity, infrastructure development, and human resource development through various programs.

Transformation of poverty alleviation program in Indonesia has begun by implementing conditional and unconditional cash transfers. These programs have been tested to empower the poor and vulnerable groups as well as to prevent the poor from falling below the poverty line. However, the result is very slow in reducing the number of poor people, which Indonesia not able to reach the goal of MDGs in reducing half of the poverty rate by 2015.

As a country with majority Muslim population, Indonesia leverages the potential of the Islamic financial system in its economic development. Islamic financial system development is inextricably associated with the interest of the government and development agencies to reduce poverty and improve welfare for a more balanced economic growth. Transformation also occurs in the utilization of *Zakat*, *Sadaqa*, and

Infaq, forms of charity to the needy Muslims—to revive the economy for groups of small and medium enterprises (SMEs). In Islam utilization of social protection was initiated further in the form of microfinance for the poor. The purpose of this initiative is to integrate Islamic finance in advancing social condition and reaching the unbankable group of people. For instance, the potential collection of *Zakat* in 2009 was Rp111,064 billion, while according to BAZNAS[1], the potential of *Zakat* collection should reach Rp100,000 billion each year. However, BAZNAS only successfully collected Rp1.2 billion of *Zakat* fund, or only 1.1% of the potential *Zakat* collection (Yaumidin 2011).[2]

BAZ and LAZ as institutions for *Zakat* management in Indonesia have implemented ideas to empower women. According to Mannan (2000), *Zakat* revenue can be spent for raising the productivity of the poor, such as financing various development projects in education, health care, safe water, and other social welfare activities that are designed exclusively for the benefit of the poor. It is expected that such programs can have a multiplier effect on welfare of the poor. However, it is intuitively plausible that an increase in income from *Zakat* investment might be expected to have a multiplier effect larger than an increase in income from non-*Zakat* funds investment. In addition to the leakage into saving, some portion of income over the successive rounds of income and spending would be siphoned off by other leakages such as taxes and imports, mostly in case of the income of the rich. Many economists agree that alleviating poverty in Indonesia using *Zakat* funds is limited. Recently, the distribution of *Zakat* for economically productive programs has been sporadic, inconsistent, subjective, as well as less coordination and comprehensive planning between *Zakat* institutions and the local governments.

Women's empowerment is not well defined. This terminology has different understanding from countries to countries and societies to societies. Conceptually, women empowerment is influenced by the gender system in the countries. For Indonesia, which have mixed education system (Islamic and conventional), it is believed that women have been becoming disempowered. However, some would argue that the rules of classical Islamic law could leave a woman financially better off (Landes 2013; Wee and Shaheed 2008).

According to the statistics, the number of women poverty is about 51% at national level (women poverty or a person who are categorized as *mustahik*) which is slightly higher than men poverty which is about 49% (Purwakananta and Abilawa 2010). It was argued that *Zakat* institutions of *Zakat* from government (BAZNAS) operate in all provinces, while institutions of *Zakat* from private sector (LAZNAS) are more concentrated in Java. It is more likely to utilize *zakat* fund to empower women through micro-credit in order to improve their economic conditions along with the man.

Therefore, the purpose of this chapter is to examine the impact of Islamic microfinance on women's empowerment. To gain a comprehensive understanding of the concept of women's empowerment in Islam, this chapter delves deeper into the understanding of this concept on groups of Muslim women. The information is gathered through focus groups' discussion, which are divided into two different stratified groups by economic strata and level of education. Having a clear understanding of women empowerment, further studies look at the impact of granting credit from *Zakat* fund, *infaq*, and alms resources to access to independent income; control over savings and credit use; and ability to bring productive asset to household's economy.

This study took sample in the city of Bandung, West Java province, Indonesia, with 200 respondents involving Muslim women who participated in the microfinance of Misykat program in DPU Daarut Tauhid and Bandung's BAZNAS into stratified random sampling. Primary data collection was held from June to December 2014. Propensity score matching and instrumental variable methods were used to convince us to address the selection bias in cross-sectional setting. The methodology used in this study follows Asim (2008), which provides more reliably estimates treatment effects within the constraints imposed by the data. The proposed methodology is both resource efficient and cost-effective, and easily to replicate. We modified some questions in the questionnaire section to capture Indonesia Muslim women characteristics.

3.1.2 Research Statement

This research examines a number of Muslim women to see the impact of Islamic microfinance on empowering them. Islamic finance offers comprehensive approach to the poor to get access of finance through redistributive instruments such as *Zakat*, *Sadaqa*, *Waqf*, and *Qard Hassan*. However, Islam puts women in the highest place and protects them from slavery and sexual harassment in the workplace. Islam permits women to work for their actualization, but they have no responsibility to fulfill households' expenses. Thus, in the majority Muslim countries, women participation in the workforce is less than in the non-Muslim countries. Currently, Muslim women in Indonesia are actively involved in microfinance programs in order to make their life better. This study intended to answer some questions regarding the impact of Islamic microfinance to influence women (Muslim) participation in the economy as well as in household decision. Therefore, the research statements of this study are as follows:

1. How does Muslim women perception on women empowerment through microfinance.
2. What are the impact of Islamic microfinance to their ability to get independence income, controlling the use of credit and saving usages, and their ability to bring productive asset in their household?
3. Is there any different impact of private microfinance and government microfinance women's empowerment?

3.1.3 Objectives

Women empowerment is one of the alternatives to raise poverty. Numbers of women believe that they may become an economic driver in their families as well as in nation. Some studies found that microfinance (microcredit) in Indonesia, to some extent, leads to women empowerment, but it also impedes women as women have more responsibilities to do reproductive, production, and social function. Indonesia has majority of Muslim women who restricted to Islamic lesson that women should not involve in production network or have more responsibilities to fulfill basic household necessities than men. However, there is limited study to see the influence of Islamic microfinance to empower Muslim women in Indonesia. Therefore, the purposes of this study are as follows:

1. Determine to what extent Muslim women understanding of women empowerments and Islam microfinance.
2. Measuring the impact of Islamic microfinance toward the ability of women to access independent income, controlling the use of saving and credit; and their ability to bring productive asset to household economy.
3. Comparing the performance of Islamic microfinance between government and private to influence women's empowerment.

3.2 Literature Review

3.2.1 Islamic Views on Poverty

Islam does not define a fixed criterion for poverty that applies to all; the concept of poverty in Islam is broader and covers more than just food and services. However, Islam has a key principle in achieving its ideal of redistributive justice that is the support and empowerment of the weak. This can be achieved most significantly through the financial empowerment of family units in the lowest classes of the society.

Moreover, numerous studies on the linkage of financial development with economic development suggest that degree of financial development is not related to the poverty features in the country (Mohieldin et al. 2011). Meanwhile, small and medium enterprises (SMEs) are believed as agents of economic development in most emerging market. However, development of SMEs faces many constraints, lack of access to credit, inadequate collateral, insufficient legal status, and high transaction costs, which are among the reasons why such enterprises experienced exclusion from the formal financial system. It is the reason why SMEs less participate in development program (Obaidullah and Latiff 2007). Therefore, enhancing the access to and the quality of basic financial services such as availability of credit, mobilization of savings, insurance, and risk management can facilitate sustainable growth and productivity, especially for small and medium scale enterprises (SMEs). In the global context, building financial inclusion systems, on the view of microfinance to combat poverty in developing countries, is important agenda that has to be implemented worldwide.

World Bank report on financial access shows that almost 50% of adult populations in emerging market still have no access to basic financial services, and great part of them come from countries with predominantly Muslim population (World Bank 2012). Meanwhile, Islam puts equal emphasis on spiritual and on worldly affairs (Chapra 1980). Social justice, inclusion, and sharing of resources between the haves and the have not are essential for economic development in Islamic economics system. Islam recognizes claims based on equality of liberty and opportunity, which are reflected in the degree of access to resources, the degree and extent of the ability of persons to actualize their potential liberty and opportunity, and the right of prior ownership. The right that the less able has in the wealth of those who have greater ability and opportunity to produce greater wealth is redeemed through the various levies (*Zakat*, *Khums*, *Sadaqa*, *Nafaqa*, and so on), the payment of which is not beneficence but a contractual obligation that must be met. *Zakat,* for instance, is one of the fundamentals of the social transfer payment in Islamic lesson that has direct economic implications.[3] *Zakat* requires Muslims to distribute part of their wealth to alleviate poverty and achieve economic emancipation for the poor (Ahmed 2004). However, Ahmad (2000) states that *Zakat* contributions by Muslims are neither part of the state's public revenues nor part of the sovereign revenue from taxes in the state budget.

3.2.2 Islamic Views on Women Empowerment

According to WEMC, the definition of women's empowerment should entail some analyses on power dynamics. In general, it has been defined as an increase ability to question, challenge, and eventually transform unfavorable gendered power relations, often legitimized in the name of 'culture' (Wee and Shaheed 2008). This study focused on Muslim context in the view of women empowerments and found that the imposition of the Islamists' monolithic vision promotes (1) a misconception that the aspiration and struggle for women's rights are aliens to Muslim contexts and (2) a cultural impoverishment that deprives women of alternative reference points for exercising agency and autonomy. Thus, this condition caused disempowerment of women in different form of multiple levels: (1) At the macro-level, national politico-religious groups, often allied with groups in other countries or with international networks, may seek to reshape laws and policies to conform with gender-inequitable notions; (2) at the meso-level, local politico-religious groups may also seek to do the same with local laws and policies, often in alliance with national and international groups and networks. In addition, patriarchal kinship-based groups may seek to perpetuate disempowering values and practices, in convergence with the politico-religious groups; and (3) at the micro-level, individuals may assert disempowering values and practices in interpersonal relationships to a greater degree, often encouraged by trends at meso- and macro-levels.

3.2.3 Microfinance and Women Empowerment

Current thinking on microfinance has broadened its definition from microcredit to provision of an array of financial services, such as savings, insurance, and remittances. It emphasizes that access to microfinance and not cost of microfinance should be under focus in designing and implementing poverty alleviation strategy. The strategy should aim at sustainability through a shift from a charity-based donor-dependent approach to a market-based for-profits approach emphasizing systemic efficiency, transparency, and restricting use of donor funds to capacity building. It also underscores inclusiveness and integration of microfinance with the formal financial system. While there is a consensus among thinkers and practitioners, the same does not imply or advocate a single and uniform approach to microfinance. Arguably, diverse channels are needed to get diverse financial services into the hands of a diverse range of people who are currently excluded. In the context of Muslim societies, building inclusive financial systems would most certainly require integration of microfinance with Islamic finance (Obaidullah and Latiff 2007).

The form of microfinance in Islamic finance is not limited to the form of rural or small banks. Current consensus among Islamic economists agreed that the feature of microfinance for the poor should utilize any Islamic levies as source of funds rather than collecting funds from third party. However, the product of financing that is used for microfinance may be the same as product financing from Islamic banks. It is because many elements of microfinance are consistent with the broader goals of Islamic finance. Both advocate entrepreneurship and risk sharing and believe that the poor should take part in such activities, focus on developmental and social goals as well as advocate financial inclusion, entrepreneurship, and risk sharing through partnership finance (Obaidullah and Latiff 2007). However, most of favorite products are based on *Mudarabah*, *Murabahah*, *Qard Hassan*, *Musharakah*, *Bay-al Salam*, and *Ijarah* financing (Kaleem 2007; Kholis 2008).

In the case of empowering the poor, there are number of studies conclude that microfinance is related to women's empowerment (Asim 2008). However, defining women's empowerment is debatable since the term 'empowerment' has related to gender system in the country (Wee and Shaheed 2008). A gender system is a system of constructing and regulating specific standards for males and females, as well as relations between them, in terms of relative hierarchy or relative equality. Intersecting with other forms of power relations and diverse gender systems produces varied spaces for women's initiatives and empowerment, accompanied by distinctive constraints, diverse sources of support, and dissimilar access to a range of resources.

Empowering women becomes important agenda for developing countries to catch up their economic development. However, such empowerment terms should be defined clearly and apt to with ideology, culture, and norm of society. As discussed above, financial inclusion should involve women participation, so that developing microfinance is the one way to empower women. There were numerous studies to estimate and predict the impact of microfinance to improve women's position in the household as well as in the societies (Table 3.1).

The successful performance of microfinance institution is largely associated with the utilization and the function of social networks of poor clients including the existence of trust (Chavez and Vega 1996; Robinson 2002; Martowijoyo 2007; Sanrego and Antonio 2013). Islamic microfinance is another institutional innovation being designed to have soundness of lending technology (based on Islamic teachings) of group lending model (GLM) that could ascertain the poor to have an access to the financial services (Sanrego and Antonio 2013).

In Indonesia, Grameen Bank model has been replicated and modified in many of Islamic microfinance programs. Most of the Islamic microfinance has been designed in the form of cooperative model. Such program in the cooperative organization has certain characteristic as community-based empowerment, microfinance services, participatory, or group-based lending and addressed particularly for women of the poor or low-income families.

Finally, we conclude that the literature surveyed suffices to provide theoretical foundations for empirically testing the link between microcredit and women's empowerment as figured out in Fig. 3.1. According to Asim (2008), microcredit is expected to improve the position of women within the household through (1) empowerment brought about by increases in independent income; (2) empowerment through 'control' over credit and savings decisions; and (3) increased worth of women within the family, stemming from their ability to bring a 'valuable' asset to the household economy. The focus on any one of these mechanism alone will fail to provide a complete perspective on women's empowerment. For empirical study that aims to evaluate the empowerment potential of credit, it is necessary to look at the 'outcomes' associated with the empowerment effect rather than looking only at the 'processes' through which those empowerment effects were generated.

3.3 Methodology

3.3.1 Methodological Framework

The research design was set up to carry out a quasi-experimental framework. Prospective or new client is used as a comparison or control group. The mature client (old participants whether active or inactive) was compared with the control group to ascertain impact of credit. Questionnaire design based on the conceptualization of women's empowerment is outlined in the conceptual framework.

Table 3.1 Previous study on the impact of microfinance microcredit to Women Empowerment. *Source* Author's own compilation

Title	Author	Year	Finding
Evaluating the impact of microcredit on women's empowerment in Pakistan	Salman Asim	October 2008	No difference between the levels of empowerment of treated and control units. Participation in the microcreditprogram is found to be insignificant in explaining all the outcome indicators of empowerment for the sampled households
Female empowerment: impact of a commitment savings product in the Philippines	Nava Ashraf, Dean Karlan, Wesley Yin	March, 2008	Positive impacts, particularly for women who have below median decision-making power in the baseline, and this leads to a shift toward female-oriented durables goods purchased in the household
The impact of group-based credit programs on poor households in Bangladesh: does the gender of participants matter?	Mark M. Pitt, Shahidur R. Khandker	October 1998	Program credit has a larger effect on the behavior of poor household in Bangladesh when the women are the program participants. Women borrower had annual household consumption expenditure increase higher than men borrower
Women's empowerment through microcredit: a case study of district Gujrat, Pakistan	Sarfraz Khan, Mirza Rizwan Sajid, Hafeez-ur-Rehman	September 2011	Positive impact of microcreditprogram introduced by PRSP in the rural Gujarat on women'swomen empowerment.

(continued)

Table 3.1 (continued)

Title	Author	Year	Finding
Effect of microfinance operations on poor rural households and the status of women	Asian Development Bank	September 2007	Project design can be improved further by including more gender-disaggregated targets and indicators in the project framework, and by providing explicit discussion of the participation of women in the design and implementation process
Pact's women's empowerment program In Nepal a savings and literacy led alternative to financial institution building	Jeffrey Ashe, Lisa Parrot	October 2001	Economic aspects of the program are for women, at fifth stage (microfinance plus saving and access to loans) in the development of their groups the empowerment variables ranked much higher

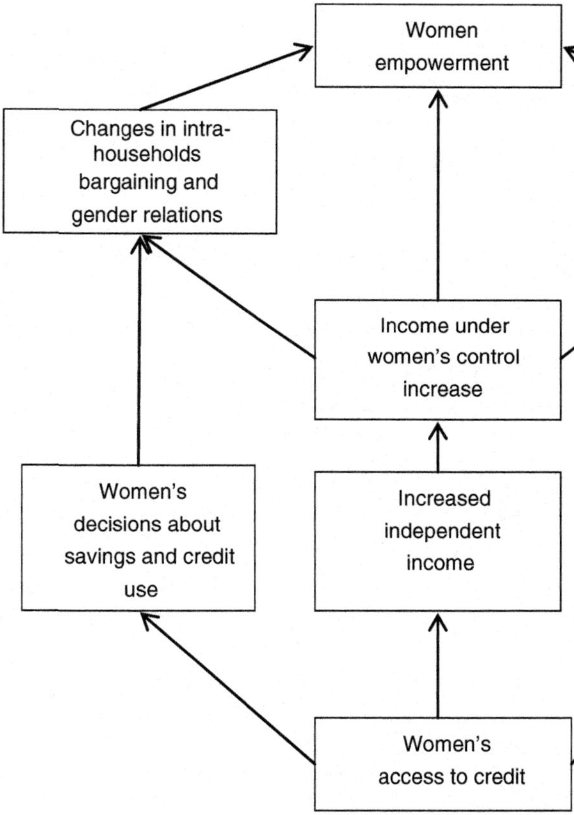

Fig. 3.1 Framework of women's empowerment through microcredit. *Source* Asim (2008)

Before we conduct experimental survey, we redefined the terms of 'women empowerment' through the exploratory evidence obtained from focus group discussion sessions and subsequent in-depth interviews to have the sense of 'women's empowerment' from Indonesia's Muslim women (see annexes for list of questions). We conducted FGD for two groups that classified based on level of education and economic strata. We divided women groups of MFI recipients into lower-medium education (from no graduate from elementary school to junior high school) and medium-higher education (graduated from senior high school to higher level). Based on the level of economic condition, we divided group as the recipients, who used MFI credit for consumption and have no business, and other group is MFI clients who use their loan for working capital and they have business. We also conducted participatory methods using focus group discussion to know how MFI management board perceives women empowerment. In addition, we also investigate how they manage their institutions.

3.3.2 Sample Design and Selection Procedures

Primary data are collected from 240 households in the south Bandung district (Fig. 3.2). The target population comprised all women registered with the Misykat program Dompet Peduli Ummat Daarut Tauhid (DPU-DT), Bandung, and Badan Amil *Zakat* Nasional (BAZNAS), West Java Province in the area of Bandung city.

A stratified random sample of 240 households was drawn from the population of 1800 female clients, with approximately 1000 DPU-DT and 800 BAZNAS clients. The sample of 240 clients with 192 clients

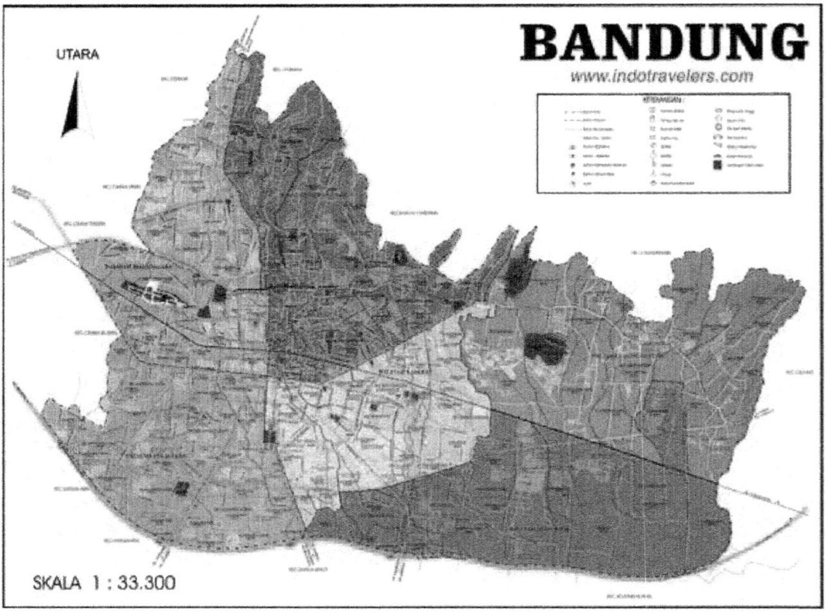

Fig. 3.2 Area of study. *Source* www.indotravelers.com

of DPU-DT and 84 BAZNAS clients represented the proportion of DPU-DT and BAZNAS clients in the population. The sample has further been divided into two groups.

1. The treatment groups are the mature clients: the minimum criteria for being counted as mature clients are that the respondents must have completed at least one loan cycle with the MFI.
2. The control groups are the prospective clients registered with the MFI in the month of the data collected (around May and June 2014), and/or they only receipt a loan for once a year as charity (without repay back the loan). The reason to select the prospective clients rather than non-clients as controller group is that there may be initial differences between clients and non-clients such as household income, entrepreneurial ability, and degree of female empowerment.

For about every two people in the treatment group, we have one person in the control group; thus, we have 144 treatment group respondent and 96 control group respondents in total. We assumed that treatment and control groups come from similar types of communities and have similar characteristic particularly in economic background and status.

3.3.3 Questionnaire Design

The questionnaire is designed to answer underlying research objective: how the impact of Islamic microfinance on indicators of women empowerment. It is designed to follow Asim (2008) with modification on the indicators of women empowerment, within the particular context of Indonesia.

The questionnaire captured series of questions relating to variables which indicate empower for women based on the theoretical views, i.e., children concerning, social mobility, and economic empowerment. Therefore, the questionnaire consisted of sections as follows;

1. Household Information (Adult).
2. Household Information (Children).

3. Household Information (Labor).
4. Credit profile of household.
5. Income/Expenditure/Saving/Debt/Asset Profile of HH.
6. Female Enterprise.
7. Attitude toward female enterprise/empowerment.

The questionnaire was designed to be generate qualitative information to reinforce the validity of research findings.

3.3.4 Method of Data Analysis

This study estimates the conditional demands for empowerment indicators *conditioned* on the individual's participation in the credit program. The reduced form systems of equations that we want to estimate are as follows:

$$C_t = \propto_c X_i + \pi Z_i + \varepsilon_i \tag{3.1}$$

$$Y_t = \propto_y X_i + \delta_y Z_i + \varepsilon_j \tag{3.2}$$

where C_i is the binary treatment measuring participation in the program, X_i is a vector of household and borrower's characteristics (age, education, children, etc.), Y_i is the conditional demand for women's empowerment outcomes (such as level of involvement in the decision making or ability to make decisions without someone's permission), Z_i is the set of exogenous instruments distinct from *X's* that affect C_i but not household behavior Y_i conditional on C_i, α_c, π, α_y, and δy are the parameters to be estimated, and ε_I and μ_I are errors representing unmeasured household level characteristics that determine participation in the program and outcomes, respectively. 'δy' is the parameter of interest that measures the impact of participation in the program on the outcome. The estimation problem arises because of the possible correlation between ε_I and ε_j due to the endogeneity of treatment. In the absence of exogenous instrument vector Z_i, strong assumptions are required to address concerns regarding endogeneity.

To measure and quantify the outcome variable Y, we quantify how decisions in the household are arrived. We allow our respondent to rank, in an ordinal manner, the extent to which her preferences are taken into account in intra household decisions. In the context of the urban women of Bandung city area, there are certain structural in equalities and prescribed social norms that reinforce the subservient position of women within the household. As this condition, we expect that access to credit will help women in contesting those prescribed gender rules. It can be measured by changes in the degree of female participation brought about by credit decision concerning household and women's welfare. We use ordered probit framework to capture these ordinal preferences in our estimation strategy as follows:

3.3.5 Regression Methods

To estimates and test hypothesis 1, we use the class of probit and bivariate probit models. The endogeneity of treatment in our specification necessitates making the following assumption:
Assumption 1: Ignorability treatment

Conditional on observed individual characteristic Xi, outcomes (Y^0, Y^1) are independent of the treatment T. This assumption implies conditional mean independence of outcomes:

$$\left[E\left(Y^0|X,T\right)=E\left(Y^0|X\right)\right] and \left[E\left(Y^1|X,T\right)=E\left(Y^1\ X\right)\right] \quad (3.3)$$

Assumption 2: Stable unit treatment value assumptions

Estimation strategy by imposing a linear relationship for conditional mean independence

$$\boldsymbol{E}\left(\boldsymbol{Y}^0|\boldsymbol{X}\right)=\boldsymbol{\gamma}_0+\boldsymbol{\beta}_0(\boldsymbol{X}-\overline{\boldsymbol{X}})$$

$$\boldsymbol{E}\left(\boldsymbol{Y}^1|\boldsymbol{X}\right)=\boldsymbol{\gamma}_1+\boldsymbol{\beta}_1(\boldsymbol{X}-\overline{\boldsymbol{X}}) \quad (3.4)$$

where X is the vector of covariates with the average value X in the treated population.

In this generic heterogeneous treatment effects model, we allow both the parameters of slope (β_0, β_1) and intercept term (γ_o, γ_1) to vary across the outcome regimes. This switching regression model can be reduced to a single equation giving the expected empowerment outcome Y conditional on X, T:

$$E(Y|X,T) = \mu_0 + \alpha T + \beta X + T(X - \overline{X})\delta \tag{3.5}$$

where $Y = (1-T)Y^0 + TY^1$ is the observed outcome (equal to Y^1 for participants in the treatment group and Y^0 for participants in the control group).

3.3.6 Propensity Score Matching

Propensity score matching has to ensure that the conditional probability of participation in the program is uniform between participants and matched comparators, Whereas in a randomized trial, the participants and non-participants are identical in terms of the distribution of all the characteristics, whether observed or not. Using a pooled sample of control and treatment groups, we estimate a flexible probit model by regressing treatment T_i on covariates Z_i and functions of covariates. The estimated parameters from this regression are used to predict $\widehat{P}(Z_i)$ the propensity score for treatment assignment.

$$\widehat{P}(Z_i) \equiv F\left(Z; \widehat{\gamma}\right) \tag{3.6}$$

where $\widehat{\gamma}$ is obtained from a probit regression of T_i on Z_i.

Propensity score matching uses the values of $\widehat{P}(Z_i)$ to select matching comparison units. The estimates of the program impact are highly sensitive to the choice of matching method used to construct comparison group (Smith and Todd 2005). However, Smith and Todd (2005) go on to demonstrate that the robustness of estimators can be enhanced by restricting the matches only to those units in the control and treatment group who have a common support in the distribution of propensity scores. We eliminate all the cases in the control and treatment group that lie outside the common support condition. We further check robustness of our estimates by using both kernel and radius matching methods.

3.3.7 Hypothesis

Hypotheses 1: Preference-Based Indicators of Empowerment
There are five different dimensions of empowerment: children-related decisions; health decisions; economic decisions; social mobility decisions; and major household purchases. This hypothesis empirically tests the immediate changes in gender relation brought about by participation in a microcredit program. If the position of the women within the household has improved after taking the loan, then the distribution power should change across some domains of decision making within the household.

Hypotheses 2: Autonomy-Based Indicators of Empowerment
This hypothesis tests whether microcredit is enabling women in contesting their way out of the prescribed norms of gender inequality embedded in the society. Intuitively, we would like to test whether microcredit will only empower women within the constraints of patriarchy imposed by the society and religions. We use another set of empowerment indicators where we ask the respondents whether they require someone's permission to make decision related to household purchase and children. We generate a dummy variable capturing their independence in decision making whenever they do not require someone's permission to make such decisions.

3.4 Result and Analysis

3.4.1 Development of Microfinance in Indonesia

Indonesia was one of the first countries to develop commercial microfinance in Asia, with regulated financial institutions providing the bulk of microfinance services throughout the archipelago. In addition to the success of commercial microfinance providers, Indonesia has also been a favorable ground for the development of numerous subsidized government programs, local- and community-based financial institutions, cooperatives, and NGOs (Citi Foundation 2009).

Indonesian microfinance is supported by a diverse set of institutions, originating from government, from voluntary sector agencies (both national and international), from the private sector, and from bi- and multi-lateral agencies. These institutions may be called as one of the initiators for setting up microfinance in Indonesia such as Pro-FI (the promotion of small financial institutions) project is supported by bank Indonesia and the German technical assistance agency, GTZ. It aims to improve the operations of two categories of microfinance providers: the 'People's Credit Banks' (BPR) and some non-bank microfinance institutions, especially the 'Village Credit Boards' (LPDs) in Bali. PERBARINDO, Permodalan Nasional Madani (PNM), Gerakan Bersama Pengembangan Keuangan Mikro Indonesia (GEMA PKM), Global Innovation Consulting (GIC), and many others gave high contribution to the development of microfinance, which operated by rural banks as well as non-bank financial institutions (Table 3.2).

In terms of numbers, BPR Shari'ah and Cooperative Shari'ah, which are operated based on Islamic lesson, are less than that of conventional. PNM as state-owned enterprises has mandate from government to engage in serving SMEs than micro-enterprises. PNM supports linkage program between commercial banks and BPRs, and between commercial banks and non-bank microfinance providers. PNM provides loans to non-bank microfinance providers through regional development

Table 3.2 Formed of microfinance in Indonesia. *Source* Bank of Indonesia (2013); Ministry of Cooperative and SMEs (2007)

	Number of bank	Number of worker	Total financing (Credit)	Note
BPR Syariah	160	4826	4,354,183	Oct. 2013
BPR conventional	1634		74,531,494	Oct. 2013
Cooperative conventional	203,701	438,541	8,118,959	Oct. 2013
Cooperative Syariah	3038		157,000	2007

banks (BPD), with saving mobilized by retail microfinance institution as a unique from of collateral. It has a special brief for the support of Shari'ah (Islamic) microfinance. Islamic banking is a significant force in the microfinance and financial sectors in Indonesia, in terms of volume of financial services provided and the number of outlets providing them.

Despite this proliferation of microfinance service providers, several studies have demonstrated that there is still an unmet demand for microfinance services, as a majority of rural households still do not have access to a source of funds from a semi-formal or formal institution. Non-access to funds may be due to regulations, or the limited revolving funds itself. Sometimes the lack of a well-managed financing institution also limits the access.

In the case of empowering the poor, there are number of studies concluded that microfinance is related to women's empowerment (Asim 2008). However, defining women's empowerment is debatable since the term 'empowerment' is related to gender system in the country (Wee and Shaheed 2008). A gender system is a system of constructing and regulating specific standards for males and females, as well as relations between them, in terms of relative hierarchy or relative equality. Intersecting with other forms of power relations, diverse gender systems produce varied spaces for women's initiatives and empowerment, accompanied by distinctive constraints, diverse sources of support, and dissimilar access to a range of resources.

3.4.2 Women Empowerment in the View of Women's Muslim

In this study, we conducted exploratory approach to obtain women perception on the terminology of women empowerment. We conducted focus group discussion for three times: First, we discussed with group of facilitator who have higher level of education and economic level; second, we discussed with members of microcredit who are less educated and have low level of economy; third, we discussed with the policy maker on the top level of management of *Zakat* management organization.

In the first discussion, we got impression that women in the view of Muslim should follow the Islamic laws. The taskforce and position between men and women are different, so they might not be the same in regard to implement responsibilities. However, they agree that women should have the same right in terms of conveying their opinion and as decision makers in their families.

Mrs. Aisyah from Amanah group stated that, '*women as a mother hold important role not only working in "the kitchen, toilet and bedroom", we should also include in the democratic processes in the household, particularly for educational aspect of our children. Although, my husband will pay the entire school tuition fee, but as a mother, I should take point on the right track.*'[4]

Similar to Mrs. Aisyah, Mr. Dasep who is the leader and senior mentor of the group declared that women are stronger to see future dimension of their children as well as control their husband's decision.

All of the FGD participants agreed that women can voice their opinion to their husband if they can make brilliant decision to solve their family problems. If they make wrong decision, their suggestion may not be followed in the future. To make women give brilliant suggestion, there are few aspects to be completed such as they must be educated. Education can be achieved not only from formal education but also from religious education, which can drive their morality to be good and apt to Islamic law that their husbands respect on it. In other word, women should have widely horizon in any matters of life. Educated them will not end up only in formal education, but they should be more active in their social live such as following religious or social organization in their communities. All of the participants in the focus group discussion tend to value empowerment similar to equality between men and women. However, they understand the process of empowerment. Equality post between wife and husband in their families is a result of this process.

One of the purposes of microfinance is reducing number of the poor by providing more access to financial institution, so they can empower themselves. Self-empowerment is the interaction that is able to assume an attitude of empowering herself by making good use of 'personal potential' in dealing with problems they faced (Charon 1979).

According to Sumardjo (1999), the characteristic of an empowered individual are:

1. Being able to comprehend herself and her potentials, being able to make planning (to anticipate the future change of condition);
2. Being able to direct herself;
3. Having power to negotiate;
4. Having bargaining power in doing a mutual cooperation and
5. Being responsible of her own action.

This indicates that an empowered individual is one who knows, understands, and has good motivation and opportunity, makes good use of the opportunity, has the energy, can cooperate, knows various alternatives, can make a decision, dares to take risk, can search for information, as well as having the ability to act in accordance with the situation. The process of empowerment should be done persistently and continuously so that it can lead them to prosperity.

In the case of mentors, most of the participants agreed that regardless of any rupiahs given by their husbands, the money should be able to supply all their household needs. They did not ask and push their husband to fulfill all their desires on something precious goods. However, *they emphasized that they may get full empowerment if they can control their husband's income over their own money. In other words, all husband's money should go as a wife's money, but if wife can earn some money from their own activities, this money should be as their own money and their husband could not control it.*

Some of them also argued that this thought may not be accepted by all men. Ms. Alifah stated that '*there is a time when my husband needs some of my money to pay the bill, it will be counted as a loan, and I always remain him to pay his loans.*' It is debatable to divide between wife's and husband's money. As mentioned by Ms. Ai who run her business together with her husband, '*If I have some more money from my own business, I always spent it for household needs, and never think that my husband has loan from me.*'

Mr. Dasep, one of the mentors of Misykat program, has different views: '*as a husband I have two income resources, my main income as a teacher is given to my wife, but secondary income from my band performance is used to my own necessities. However, I support my wife to have her own saving from her own income.'*

Compare to another Muslim women group who are not joined with Islamic microfinance, we got different views. This group has characteristic of low educated and income. They felt so afraid to speak out and share their opinion on women empowerment. They tend to ask their husband's permission before making their own decision. Some of them mentioned that their husband's families particularly their mother-in-law are always interfering their internal household. It seems that to define women empowerment is hard as they hold Islamic law partially. In the holy Quran, it was stated that 'Men is women leader' so that women shall be behind the men and seek approval from her husband in every decision making. This condition based on their story let them to be cheater and have problem with moneylenders who charge high interest rate for debt. In Bandung city, there are many money lenders that plunge the poor into deeper poverty.

It can be concluded that the group mentored and trained by *Misykat* program have affected the view on self-empowerment. The model of self-empowerment through a strong social capital, which is maintained well in togetherness, is able to grow personal spirit and make individual more productive; therefore, it improves individual competence. Self-empowerment gives positive values for individual, namely (a) promoting self-confidence; (b) opening and developing individual's entrepreneur; (c) opening job vacancies; (d) facilitating obtaining raw materials; (e) facilitating obtaining loans; (f) facilitating marketing because of the wide network; (g) improving work ethos; (h) improving skills/competence; and (i) having creative and innovative trait to reform.

3.4.3 Review on Islamic Microfinance

3.4.3.1 Misykat Program of DPU-DT (Dompet Peduli Ummat Daarut Tauhid)

Misykat (Microfinance Masyarakat—community-based microfinance) is one of the programs from Dompet Peduli Ummat Daarut Tauhid

Foundation.[5] This program was set up in 2004 but established four years later. This foundation developed the concept of channeling *Zakat* funds as revolving loan fund rather than charity program. However, some Islamic scholars do not agree to use this fund for loan as the function of *Zakat* as social protection and should be directly given to the beneficiaries as stated in the Qur'an.

In regard to reduce poverty rate, this foundation thought that the important thing to *Zakat* utilizations is not only put across funds to the beneficiaries, but also how to empower them so that they can come out from poverty. Thus, utilizing *Zakat* needs high skill, patient, and have to be serious. Basic concepts that this foundation implemented to its microfinance in regard to reduce poverty rate are as follows:

1. Capital is not everything. Islamic law thought that for Muslim there is no *Zakat* fund for people who is capable of working; thus, to anticipate the vulnerable people to under poverty line group, they need assessment to improve their business. According to this foundation, *Zakat* funds can be used for this purpose.
2. No charity, charity only helps the poor in short time, and they still be poor in the long time if there is no effort to empower them to be more active in the economy.
3. Awareness of their potentials, the first thing to do to help the poor is to beat their potential and developed it into optimum.
4. Access to wide market and networking.
5. Managing their household in terms of economics flow.
6. Mentoring and empowering need long process for planning, monitoring, and evaluation, so the role of mentors/facilitators is important to determine successful program.
7. Urge for professional mentor.
8. Need process and time not instant.
9. Motivation to work.

The source of *Zakat* funds is limited, but the number of poor people is huge; therefore, appropriate strategies are needed to cope with this problem. Some implications for this condition are as follows:

1. Charity systems do not work properly for poverty reduction.
2. *Zakat* Management Organization (ZMO) institutions have their own systematically strategy to combat poverty. They do not have to trap into populist program.
3. All empowerment programs are impossible to capture all poor people directly in the short time. Therefore, it could be involved in gradual program by conducting pilot project in priority region.
4. Empowering program should be only a trigger that does not use it as charity. Then, it should be counselled in management system from planning, organizing, and staffing to controlling.
5. Empowering program should be stimulated to open greater access to formal financial institution for the poor.

This shifting paradigm is not easy to be accepted for other Muslim. Therefore, this foundation requires restricted in requirement step to select the new member. They need high commitment from the member to follow the rule, which they set up based on Islamic lessons.

DPU Daarut Tauhid held *Misykat* (community-based microfinance), which provides microcredit to merchants who cannot afford in order to get closer to Allah, the economic and spiritual prosperity. The terms and conditions to be a *Misykat*'s members as should follow these requirements:

1. Women age 17–55 years, grouped into at least five people.
2. Each member must live in an area that could reach on foot and has lived there at least for six months.
3. Mandatory responsibility of the member is following the guidance from Daarut Tauhid that was held in weekly meeting. It consists of attending lectures, installment loans, saving money, and paying dues group.
4. In a group, its business may be heterogeneous or not the same.
5. Preferred members who already have a business (not starting from zero).

Misykat's type of financing is imposed jointly and severally with the 2–2–1 pattern. Out of five people in one group, two people were given first capital. If the first installment runs smoothly, then the next two newly will be given. It went on until the last person, who usually is the chairman of the group. This fee unsecured (non-physical) in the form of social cohesion or social tolerance. Therefore, when two people first loaned capital, three others learn to 'let go' and overseeing order not default installment so that they can later also directly loaned capital (Fig. 3.3).

Since its establishment in 2006, DT *Misykat* capital Jakarta has given nearly 300 people from a variety of sources of funding DPU-DT Jakarta, ranging from charity, and *Sadaqa/Infaq*. Friends who want to join so 'investors' can transfer funds to the account of productive.

Mrs. Alifah, one of the mentors told her story when she was joined microfinance. '*For the first time, I joined this microfinance as a member of a lending group from 2007 to 2010. The group chose me to manage our financial report. When our leader had a problem that caused her get a sack, I replaced her to be a leader as well as a mentor. Before I joined this MFI, I did not have a job, but after I got some entrepreneurship training from this MFI for more than four times then I tried to open a stall. After four years,*

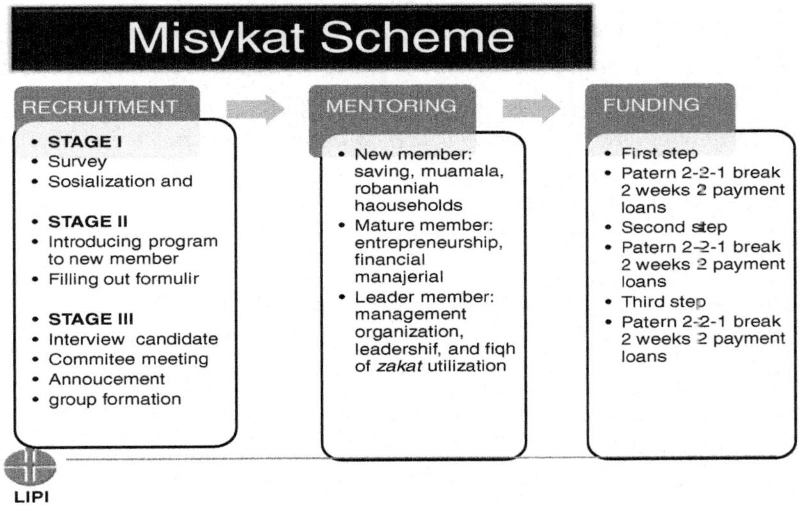

Fig. 3.3 Misykat scheme. *Sources* Dompet Peduli Ummat – Daarut Tauhid 2014

I have my own PAUD (Pendidikan Anak Usia Dini—pre-school building) for all children who their parents are clients of MFI.'

Another story has been told by Ms. Ai, she mentioned that before joined *Miyskat*, she was one of the board of 'Warna Sari' group, which is funded by the Indonesian Government Institution under BKKBN (National Board for Family Planning). The government gave them fund for 30 members. This program only lent money, and they have regular meeting about once in two or three month. In fact, the members were indiscipline in terms of paying the loan and following the group's rules. If there is a margin or profit from their business, they used it to develop their own organization. This model is difference with Misykat program. According to her, in Misykat, each member has responsibilities to attend weekly meeting and recitation. They also have two types of saving, mandatory saving and voluntary saving. This program also offers saving plan, which is useful to cover any unexpected expenses or large expenses such as for house leasing, paying school tuition fee, or other big plans for their own investments. The mentor should encourage the member to save their money before spending it to their necessary daily life.

In addition Ms. Lia also adds some information on how Misykat program can empower them through microcredit. '*There are some differences of lending process between other microfinance and Misykat program—DPU-DT. If we lend from cooperative (other microfinance), we just pay the installment and interest rate. In Misykat program, there is gathering in a week, mentoring program for the lender to manage their income so that they can saving the money and use the money appropriately. Members also learn much to understanding of contract.*'

3.4.3.2 *Zakat* Utilizations Program of BAZNAS

Relying on government budget without holding the private partner to alleviate poverty is hardly working to reach the MDG's goal. Poverty eradication should not only government in charge, but also all elements and entities in the countries. BAZNAS is one of the alternatives to get funding for poverty alleviation from privates as well as communities.

Zakat management has undergone significant change since enactment of Act No. 23 of 2011. This new Act mandated stronger integration of *Zakat* management in the country. In accordance with this Act, *Badan Amil Zakat Nasional (BAZNAS)* comprises three elements: Islamic scholars, professional, and Islamic communities leader. Eight of them should be from communities and 3 of them come from government. Presidential Decree no 14/2014 has completed this law to be implemented. However, the enactment of this law has caused controversy since it has stipulated *Zakat* management is the authority of the government and the public is only allowed to participate with a government authorization. This stipulation seemed to limit the number of *Zakat* management organizations. It can be said that through this law, government needs to strengthen *Zakat* management in order to mobilize its full potential, but on the other side government intends to control the *Zakat* management.

Zakat fund has been collected by BAZNAS in West Java Province in 2013, which is about 88% and the rest (12%) is from non-*Zakat* fund (alms) such as infaq and *Sadaqa*. This fund was increased dramatically from previous year. According to the board, they have just collected '*Zakat* Profession' rather than '*Zakat Maal*' from the civil servants. In every month, more than US$40,000 has been collected (Fig. 3.4).

Fig. 3.4 Collected *Zakat* fund by BAZNAS West Java Province 2013. *Source* BAZNAS West Java, 2013

In its operation, *Zakat* disbursement is allocated for any activities, which support an economic program such as small enterprise empowerment. This disbursement can be done directly by the *Unit Pengumpulan Zakat (UPZ-Zakat Distribution Unit)*, which is available in every counter of *BAZNAS* or *UPZ* partner. This economic program has been planned systematically in order to ensure that the benefits of this empowerment are not only for individual but also for their community. Therefore, it can encourage community development between *BAZNAS* partners and their community (Fig. 3.5).

In terms of disbursement *Zakat* system, *BAZNAS* have used three models to achieve the economic goals. The zero-level channel aims at direct empowerment through *mustahik*. The two-level channel uses coordinators to oversee the *mustahik* turnover; the three-level channel involves third parties and other coordinators.

Even when the recipient of *Zakat* is an individual, the usage of the money should not only be for consumption. Prophet Muhamad (pbuh) teaches us to distribute *Zakat* for productive activities would be advantageous not only for the *mustahik* but also for their community. Thus, the main purpose of *Zakat* allocation is that for poverty eradication.

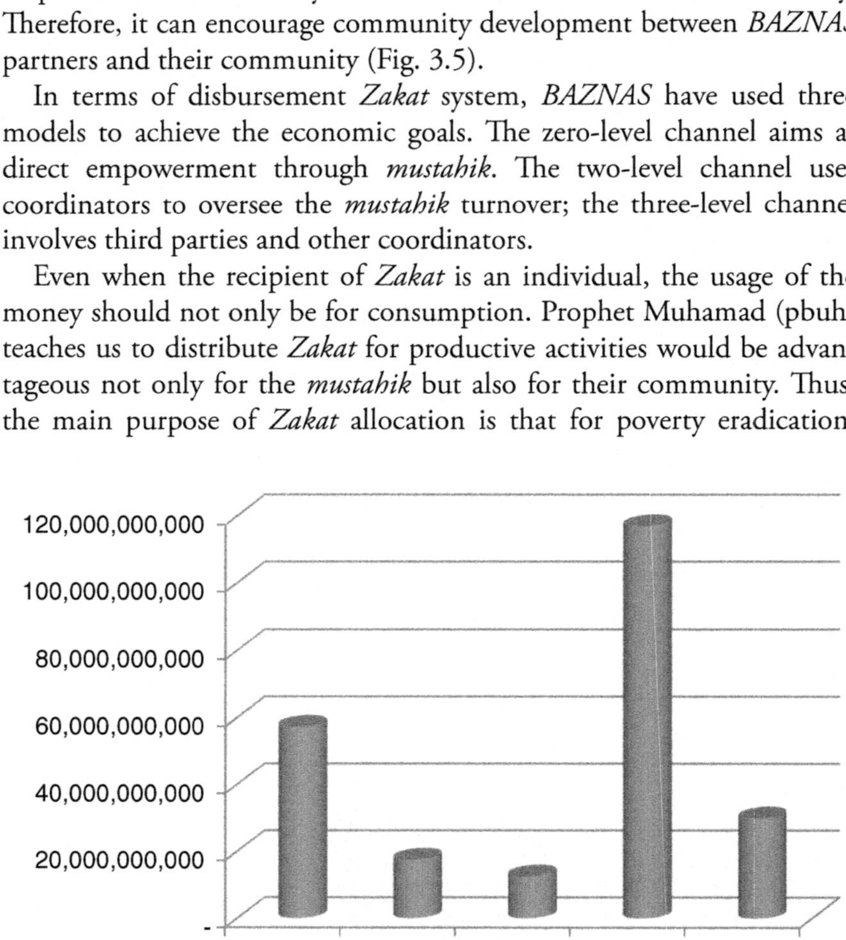

Fig. 3.5 *Zakat* disbursement and Utilization from BAZNAS West Java province 2013. *Source* BAZNAS West Java province, 2013

There have been some success stories in generating funds to alleviate poverty using *Zakat* fund through empowering the small-scale enterprises based on local initiative.[6] For Indonesia case, the disbursement of *Zakat* more likely follows some patterns.

3.4.4 Descriptive Analysis

The survey was carried out by a team of four female surveyors and was headed by the author for supervision during the implementation phase. This research was conducted in west and south city of Bandung. Surveyors were located from local areas and given one-day training to be familiarized with the questionnaire.

The surveyors had prior experience of field work and known the terrain of fieldwork. Their knowledge of the location helped us in hunting down the sampled clients including the dropout ones. If any problems were identified, the questionnaire was dropped and feedback was given to the surveyor to ensure quality control. Once the data collection was completed, the data were processed into the computer by team of four individuals including the author herself. Data consistency was checked at all three stages including collecting, processing, and analyzing.

Table 3.3 presents the characteristic of respondents; most of them are married women with age between 41 and above 50 years old. In terms

Table 3.3 Characteristic of respondents. *Source* Survey, 2014

Characteristic	Proportion (%)
Marital status	a. Married=91.67
	b. Widowed=8.33
Education	a. Elementary school=49.30
	b. Junior high school=25.35
	c. Senior high school=25.35
Age	a. 21–30 years old=2.78
	b. 31–40 years old=27.78
	c. 41–50 years old=34.72
	d. >50 years old=34.72
Income	a. <US$ 100/month=21.13
	b. >US$ 100—US$ 200=36.62
	c. >US$ 200—US$ 300=29.57
	d. >US$ 300—US$ 1000=12.68

of the highest education level, the proportion of all respondents is less educated, more than 70% of respondent has graduated from elementary and junior high schools. Their average monthly earning is only less than US$300.

Table 3.4 summarizes the entire exogenous and endogenous variable used in the o-probit and bi-probit regressions. Table 3.4 provides summary statistic for the preference-related indicator of empowerment. Table 3.5 summarizes the autonomy-based indicators of empowerment.

Most of the variables are self-explanatory; few need further explanation. In Table 3.4, the two exogenous variables—'working female before loan' and 'first utilization by respondent'—need some clarification. Working female before loan is a dummy variable constructed by assigning '1' to all the women who had a working status; before taking the loan will not be influenced by intervention, this variable serves as an exogenous proxy for initial endowment of empowerment. The choice of this proxy is motivated from economic theory, where one of the routes identified for empowerment earlier is through access to independent income.[7] As a natural extension, we argued that by controlling the women who were working prior to taking a loan, we can capture most of the unobserved heterogeneity between the incoming borrowers and those who took the loan at an earlier date. Likewise, the dummy for the 'first loan utilized by the respondents' captures whether they were already empowered at the time of taking the loan and acts as another exogenous proxy for controlling the levels of initial empowerment.

There is significant drop in the number of observations available for each indicator both in the treatment and in the control group (Table 3.5). Observations on widowed women who are household heads are dropped from the analysis (it is about 30 respondents). Also, some of the questions were inapplicable to those women who have not yet been required to make such a decision. For instance, women having young children did not know whether their preferences would be reflected in their children marriages. In such cases, the observation is dropped. Nevertheless, for most of the variables, there are enough observations in the control and treatment groups to allow for a meaningful estimation, except for the decision regarding children marriages.

Table 3.4 Summary statistic: Explanatory variable from household data set. *Source* Survey, 2014

Variable name	Definition	Treatment group mean and SD	Control group mean and SD
Endogenous variable			
Treatment dummy	0–1 Dummy variable: =1 if the client registered with MFI before December 2013; =0 for clients registering in/after January 2014	0.554 (0.498)	
Exogenous variables			
Age of respondent	Reported age of respondent confirmed by observation	46.395 (10.916)	43.550 (9.535)
Schooling of respondent	Number of years of schooling completed by the respondent	8.058 (2.536)	7.594 (2.528)
Children	Number of total children of the respondent	2.081 (1.356)	2.086 (1.094)
Age difference	Difference between the reported ages of husband and wife	3.965 (3.63)	4.449 (4.009)
Number of family	Number of people who live in the same house at the time of observation	4.860 (1.915)	4.839 (1.560)
Joint family	0–1 Dummy Variable, =1 if the respondent lives with the parents of her husband; = 0 otherwise	0.337 (0.475)	0.304 (0.463)
First utilization by respondent	0–1 Dummy Variable, =1 if the first loan taken from MFI was utilized by respondent herself; = 0 otherwise	0.581 (0.496)	0.376 (0.488)
Working female before loan	0–1 Dummy Variable, =1 if the respondent was a working womenwomen prior to taking loan; = 0 otherwise	0.627 (0.486)	0.333 (0.474)
Interaction term			
Institution[a]treatment	0–1 Dummy Variable, =1 if the respondent is a member of DPU-DT; = 0 if the respondent is a member of BAZ	0.860 (0.340)	0.681 (0.469)
Number of observation		144	96

Note [a]standard deviations are reported in the parenthesis

Hence, the question regarding children marriage is dropped from the final analysis.

Moreover, it is important to note that the difference in unconditional mean across control and treatment group comes out to be negative for some variable such as family planning, purchase household, and social mobility decision as reported in Table 3.5 and Table 3.6. The differences, however, are positive and significant for financial decision and child-related schooling decision.

The pattern in the data gives some credence to our earlier conjecture that power distribution is difference across various domains of household decision. In other word, the basic statistics suggest that microcredit might be important to reduce or increase the level of power coefficient in the household decision making.

3.4.5 Estimation Results

This section uses nine ordinal dependent variables as summarized in Table 3.4 to test whether participation in the microcredit program has increased the extent to which women's preference is taken into consideration in various domains of household decision. The ordinal dependent variables take a value on an increasing scale of 1–5 where the lower end of scale indicates virtually no 'say' in decision making while higher end values indicate full recognition of her 'voice' in household decisions. The dependent variables span five broad categories of household decisions regarding children, economic, health, social mobility, and resources allocation sufficient to indicate the extent of women's centrality within the household.

3.4.5.1 Hypotheses 1: Preference-Based Indicators of Empowerment

The results from ordered probit regression are reported in Table 3.7, 3.8, 3.9 and 3.10. The results are grouped on five different dimensions

Table 3.5 Summary statistic: Outcome indicators—'Say' in HH decision making: Ordinal development variable (1–5). *Source* Authors' own calculation

Dependent variable	Treatment group mean and SD	N	Control group mean and SD	N	t-stat for difference in means
Boy's schooling decision	4.9531 (0.2122)	128	4.5432 (1.0845)	81	3.05[a]
Girl's schooling decision	4.9457 (0.2595)	129	4.4074 (1.1914)	81	4.24[b]
Children marriage decision	4.3178 (1.4306)	129	3.9506 (1.5483)	81	−0.17
Respondent medical care	4.9302 (0.3350)	129	4.7407 (0.6078)	81	1.60
Children medical care n	4.9457 (0.2274)	129	4.7530 (0.5369)	81	2.55[a]
Family planning decision	4.8449 (0.5652)	129	4.7625 (0.6212)	80	−0.95
Social visits to women's women families	4.8372 (0.5122)	129	4.7283 (0.5480)	81	0.93
Social visit in husband's families	4.7984 (0.5502)	129	4.7283 (0.5703)	81	−1.91[a]
Work for earned income	4.7441 (0.7733)	129	4.5555 (0.9354)	81	−0.13
Borrow money from MFI	4.8682 (0.5913)	129	4.6049 (0.8467)	81	2.79[b]
Purchase of HH assets	4.7751 (0.6026)	129	4.7530 (0.5369)	81	−2.92[b]
Decision about house repair	4.6434 (0.8996)	129	4.6419 (0.7954)	81	−0.25
Sale/purchase house	4.7054 (0.8043)	129	4.4444 (1.1832)	81	0.72
Social visit in neighborhood	4.7829 (0.7066)	129	4.4074 (1.2427)	81	−0.65

[a]All the dependent ordinal variables measure the extent to which women's womenpreferences are reflected in decision-making process; 1 indicates that her preferences are never reflected in these decisions, while 5 indicates that her preferences are always taken into account
[b]Standard deviations are reported in the parenthesis

of empowerment: children-related decision; health decision; economic decision[8]; social mobility decision; and major household purchases.

The preferred regression is regression (1) in Table 3.7, 3.8, 3.9 and 3.10. It uses proxies including a dummy for 'working women before taking a loan' and a dummy for self-utilization of first loan by

Table 3.6 Summary statistic: Outcome indicators—'Autonomy' in HH decision making: Dichotomous dependent variable (0/1). *Source* Authors' own calculation

Dependent variable	Treatment group mean and SD	N	Control group mean and SD	N	t-stat for difference in means
Purchasing ice cream for children	0.9922 (0.8804)	129	0.9753 (0.1561)	81	0.29
Purchasing grocery/fruits	0.9689 (0.1740)	129	0.9135 (0.2827)	81	−1.24
Purchasing medicine for herself	0.9844 (0.1240)	129	0.8271 (0.3804)	81	2.47
Purchasing clothes/cosmetics for herself	0.9534 (0.2114)	129	0.7037 (0.4594)	81	1.04
Purchasing books/uniform for children	0.8837 (0.3218)	129	0.6666 (0.4748)	81	2.01
Taking a child to a doctor	0.7209 (0.4502	129	0.5432 (.4993)	81	–0.50
Purchasing furniture	0.3255 (0.4704)	129	0.2469 (0.4339)	81	–0.41
Purchasing refrigerator/TV	0.3798 (0.4872)	129	0.2345 (0.4263)	81	1.29
Sale/purchase of personal assets (jewelry)	0.2248 (0.4190)	129	0.1604 (0.3693)	81	0.27

Note *all the dependent binary variables measure whether the women women-requires someone's permission in making the decision. '0' indicates that she does require someone's permission in the HH, while '1' indicates complete autonomyautonomy in decision making. ** standard deviations are reported in the parenthesis

respondent. Both these proxies seek to control for potential endogeneity stemming from initial differences between control and treatment group. The first regression is preferred since it assumed that all types of microcredit from any institution will influence women empowerment. Regression (2) adds an interaction term of institution dummy interacted with treatment dummy to control for any unobserved institutional differences between the treated units of participating institution.[9]

The estimated effect of treatment on indicators of empowerment based on first specification shows that all three dimensions relating child decision are statistically significant at 95% confidence level. On the contrary, the treatment effect has no impact on child-relating decision as indicated by second specification. Moreover, variable interaction term is significant for 'girl's schooling' dimensions as shown in

Table 3.7 Ordered probit estimates of women's empowerment 'Say' in child-related decision
Women's opinion taken into consideration in household decisions on. *Source* Authors' own calculation

Independent variables	Boy's schooling oprobit coefficients		Girl's schooling oprobit coefficients		Child's medical care oprobit coefficients	
	1	2	1	2	1	2
Treatment dummy	0.9631***	0.4694	1.203***	0.5903	0.8545***	0.3662
	(0.2728)	(0.4580)	(0.2635)	(0.4465)	(0.2700)	(0.4605)
Age difference with husband	0.0256	0.0208	−0.0102	−0.0161	0.0010	0.0002
	(0.0256)	(0.0314)	(0.0277)	(0.0282)	(0.0295)	(0.0296)
Age of respondent	0.0079	0.0039	0.0054	0.0006	0.0112	0.0077
	(0.0120)	(0.0125)	(0.0118)	(0.0123)	(0.0124)	(0.0128)
Education	0.0110	0.0130(0.0532)	0.0194	0.0182	0.0028	0.0065
	(0.0521)		(0.05058)	(0.0517)	(0.0525)	(0.0535)
Number of children	−0.0106	−0.0320	−0.1601	−0.1939	−0.2352	−0.2673
	(0.1520)	(0.1569)	(0.1500)	(0.1561)	(0.1696)	(0.1774)
Number of HH member	0.0795	0.0990	0.1201	0.1432	0.2341*	0.2598*
	(0.1319)	(0.1386)	(0.1311)	(0.1377)	(0.1501)	(0.1597)
Joint family	0.0984	0.0966	0.0878	0.0836	−0.3917	−0.3787
	(0.3138)	(0.3168)	(0.2994)	(0.3032)	(0.2944)	(0.2981)
Working female before loan	−0.1015	−0.1322	−0.2081	−0.2588	−0.0722	−0.1064
	(0.2635)	(0.2689)	(0.2471	(0.2538)	(0.2611)	(0.2656)
First utilization by respondent	0.0797	0.0679	−0.1219	−0.1137	0.1306	0.1014
	(0.3277)	(0.3284)	(0.3136)	(0.3127)	(0.3121)	(0.3149)
Interaction term		0.6372		0.7893*		0.6126
		(0.4968)		(0.4900)		(0.4891)
Number of observation	209	209	210	210	210	210
Pseudo R–squared	0.0966	0.1048	0.1269	0.1376	0.1002	0.1091
Chi–square statistic	18.25	19.81	28.68	31.10	16.62	18.09
Log likelihood	−85.377	−84.601	−98.679	−97.470	−74.591	−73.858

Note Standard deviations are reported in the parenthesis
$*p < 0.1$, $**p < 0.05$, $***p < 0.01$

Table 3.8 Ordered probit estimates of women's empowerment 'Say' in health and economic decision Women's opinion taken into consideration in household decisions on. *Source* Authors' own calculation

Independent variables	Medical checkup oprobit coefficients		Family planning oprobit coefficients		Working for earned income oprobit coefficients		Borrowing money from MFI oprobit coefficients	
	1	2	1	2	1	2	1	2
Treatment dummy	0.7122***	0.2161	0.1331	−0.4669	0.4727**	0.3554	0.6802**	0.2462
	(0.2679)	(0.4700)	(0.2418)	(0.3882)	(0.2131)	(0.4261)	(0.2326)	(0.4396)
Age difference with husband	0.0000	−0.0023	0.0314	0.0257	−0.0078	−0.0081	−0.0223	−0.0233
	(0.0292)	(0.0294)	(0.0289)	(0.0293)	(0.0245)	(0.0245)	(0.0265)	(0.0266)
Age of respondent	0.0086	0.0054	0.0246**	0.0199*	0.0068	0.0060	0.0002	−0.0014
	(0.0131)	(0.0134)	(0.0120)	(0.0123)	(0.0100)	(0.0103)	(0.0109)	(0.0110)
Education	0.0710	0.0715	0.1093**	0.1103**	0.0271	0.0278	0.0869*	0.0897*
	(0.0582)	(0.0592)	(0.0538)	(0.0547)	(0.0448)	(0.0450)	(0.0517)	(0.0522)
Number of children	−0.5992**	−0.6068**	−0.4647***	−0.4552***	−0.1953	−0.2000	−0.0368	−0.0295
	(0.2434)	(0.2447)	(0.1762)	(0.1746)	(0.1404)	(0.1418)	(0.1384)	(0.1388)
Number of HH member	0.4873**	0.5022**	0.2673*	0.2627	0.2563**	0.2604**	0.0525	0.0512
	(0.2128)	(0.2158)	(0.1446)	(0.1455)	(0.1268)	(0.1283)	(0.1111)	(0.1120)
Joint family	−0.5961**	−0.6131**	−0.4806*	−0.5177	−0.1954	−0.1921	−0.0951	−0.0925
	(0.2891)	(0.2921)	(0.2791)	(0.2829)	(0.2444)	(0.2448)	(0.2794)	(0.2817)
Working female before loan	0.2627	0.2198	0.2557	0.2430	−0.0421	−0.0467	0.3367	0.3382
	(0.2718)	(0.2756)	(0.2403)	(0.2429)	(0.2104)	(0.2110)	(0.2342)	(0.2356)
First utilization by respondent	−0.0670	−0.1167	0.2775	0.2103	−0.2355	−0.2446	0.0688	0.0405
	(0.3482)	(0.3542)	(0.2982)	(0.3049)	(0.2870)	(0.2887)	(0.2946)	(0.2969)
Interaction term		0.6287		0.7695**		0.1364		0.5194
		(0.5065)		(0.3971)		(0.4315)		(0.4589)
Number of observation	210	210	209	209	210	210	210	210
Pseudo R^2	0.1341	0.1425	0.0993	0.1177	0.0423	0.0427	0.0950	0.1004
Chi-square statistic	22.91	24.35	19.63	23.26	11.85	11.95	20.90	22.10
Log likelihood	−73.98	−73.25	−89.00	−87.19	−134.05	−134.00	−99.58	−98.97

Note Standard deviations are reported in the parenthesis
$^{*}p < 0.1$, $^{**}p < 0.05$, $^{***}p < 0.01$

Table 3.9 Ordered probit estimates of women's empowerment; 'Say' in HER social mobility decision Women's opinion taken into consideration in household decisions on. *Source* Authors' own calculation

Independent variables	Social visits to women's family oprobit coefficients		Social visits to man's family oprobit coefficients		Social visits in neighborhoods oprobit coefficients	
	1	2	1	2	1	2
Treatment dummy	0.4133** (0.2196)	−0.1391 (0.4031)	0.2918 (0.2155)	−0.3488 (0.3810)	0.5318*** (0.2128)	0.4706 (0.4481)
Age difference with husband	−0.0112 (0.0255)	−0.0144 (0.0257)	−0.0190 (0.0251)	−0.0243 (0.0254)	−0.0080 (0.0254)	−0.0083 (0.0255)
Age of respondent	−0.0061 (0.0105)	−0.0091 (0.0107)	−0.0095 (0.0102)	−0.0145 (0.0106)	0.0037 (0.0100)	0.0032 (0.0104)
Education	0.0504 (0.0471)	0.0496 (0.0476)	0.0070 (0.0445)	0.0048 (0.0453)	0.0446 (0.0464)	0.0451 (0.0465)
Number of children	−0.2375* (0.1280)	−0.2438** (0.1284)	−0.1517 (0.1199)	−0.1735 (0.1223)	0.0046 (0.1218)	0.0033 (0.1221)
Number of HH members	0.1523 (0.1014)	0.1597 (0.1029)	0.0942 (0.0969)	0.1075 (0.0997)	0.0370 (0.0976)	0.0377 (0.0979)
Joint family	−0.2159 (0.2479)	−0.2310 (0.2494)	−0.0045 (0.2483)	0.0041 (0.2507)	0.0079 (0.2602)	0.0085 (0.2602)
Working female before loan	−0.0359 (0.2177)	−0.0611 (0.2195)	−0.1333 (0.2124)	−0.1710 (0.2155)	0.0918 (0.2138)	0.0898 (0.2142)
First utilization by respondent	−0.2130 (0.3080)	−0.2570 (0.3120)	−0.2296 (0.3003)	−0.2780 (0.3047)	−0.4124 (0.3136)	−0.4138 (0.3136)
Interaction term		0.6566* (0.4101)		0.7702** (0.3852)		0.0706 (0.4562)
Number of Observation	210	210	210	210	210	210
Pseudo R-squared	0.0459	0.0566	0.0225	0.0382	0.0389	0.0390
Chi-square statistic	10.37	12.80	5.52	9.35	10.54	10.56
Log likelihood	−107.80	−106.59	−119.62	−117.70	−130.24	−130.23

Note Standard deviations are reported in the parenthesis
$^{*}p < 0.1$, $^{**}p < 0.05$, $^{***}p < 0.01$

Table 3.10 Ordered probit estimates of women's empowerment: 'Say' in sale/purchase of HH assets decision Women's opinion taken into consideration in household decisions on. *Source* Authors' own calculation

Independent variables	Purchase HH assets oprobit coefficients		House repair oprobit coefficients		Sale/purchase house oprobit coefficients	
	1	2	1	2	1	2
Treatment dummy	0.0597 (0.2145)	0.0566 (0.4181)	0.0542 (0.2061)	0.1317 (0.4108)	0.3316* (0.2040)	0.4836 (0.4431)
Age difference with husband	−0.0176 (0.0246)	−0.0176 (0.0247)	0.0299 (0.0262)	0.0308 (0.02663)	0.0152 (0.0247)	0.0169 (0.0252)
Age of respondent	0.0124 (0.0099)	0.0124 (0.0102)	0.0077 (0.0099)	0.0084 (0.0103)	−0.0017 (0.0098)	−0.0008 (0.0101)
Education	0.0539 (0.0451)	0.0539 (0.0452)	0.0410 (0.0422)	0.0409 (0.0421)	0.0400 (0.0426)	0.0407 (0.0426)
Number of children	0.0133 (0.1127	0.0133 (0.1128)	−0.1720 (0.1137)	−0.1710 (0.1138)	−0.1550 (0.1147)	−0.1546 (0.1148)
Number of HH members	−0.0262 (0.0900)	−0.0262 (0.0900)	0.0632 (0.0922)	0.0630 (0.0921)	0.0998 (0.0915)	0.0994 (0.0914)
Joint family	−0.1154 (0.2517)	−0.1153 (0.2522)	−0.1750 (0.2405)	−0.1754 (0.2405)	0.0143 (0.2430)	0.0178 (0.2434)
Working female before loan	0.1461 (0.2125)	0.1459 (0.2130)	0.1047 (0.2040)	0.1076 (0.2046)	−0.0045 (0.2021)	−0.0007 (0.2024)
First utilization by respondent	−0.2065 (0.2980)	−0.2067 (0.2993)	−0.3491 (0.2970)	−0.3474 (0.2973)	−0.2428 (0.2854)	−0.2323 (0.2864)
Interaction term		0.0035 (0.4157)		−0.0891 (0.4075)		−0.1734 (0.4465)
Number of observation	210	210	210	210	210	210
Pseudo R-squared	0.0227	0.0227	0.0251	0.0253	0.0236	0.0242
Chi-square statistic	5.46	5.46	7.49	7.54	6.97	7.12
Log likelihood	−117.74	−117.74	−145.46	−145.44	−144.01	−143.93

Note Standard deviations are reported in the parenthesis
$*p < 0.1$, $**p < 0.05$, $***p < 0.01$

the second regression. It can be explained that by joining microfinance institution, member can propose scholarship for their children particularly for their daughter; thus, it can be said that *Misykat* program has significant impact to persuade women to be more empower in 'girl schooling' decision. In contrast, although decision of boy's schooling is affected by treatment effect, there are no other variables which have affected significantly to support this decision as indicated by first and second specification.

Number of household families together with treatment variable had significant effect on women to decide children medical care for both specifications. It might say that in the big family, women have more support from other family member to make this decision. Therefore, it can be concluded that the preference empowerment related to child decision between the mature and new client is affected by their participation into the such microfinance.

Turning to health and economic decision, in Table 3.8, we find strong positive and significant effect of treatment for all variable for first specification, except for 'family planning decision,' but it is insignificant for the second specification. Other dependent variables, such as number of children, number of household member, and type of join family, also had significant effect to women decision on their medical checkup. The more number of their children, the less power of women to decide their own medical checkup. It is because they tend to give priority for their children health. However, for the women who live in bigger family, they tend to care on their own health. Similarly, for the women who live with other family (they still depend on other family assistances), their power to decide on medical checkup is reduced significantly.

In the second specification, interaction term variable for 'family planning decision' has significant impact at 95% confidence level. It seems that the more active the member, the more they understand to decide whether they take family planning program or not. The *Misykat* program, which has regular meeting for their clients, tends to educate them about 'family planning' in the perspective of Islam.[10] Meanwhile, BAZNAS does not have such program. Therefore, it has implication on the influence of the number of children in the family planning decisions. According to both specifications, it can be said that the lesser the number of children, the more powerful women in making decision on their family planning. Other variables such as education and age of respondent have positive sign and significantly influence women decision on family planning. It means the more educated and mature women, the higher level of empowerment they have. Thus, it can be concluded that microfinance has good treatment to their client (specific program for empowerment) and could influence their client's perception on family planning, particularly for educated and mature age clients. It is supported by significant level of dependent variables such as education of respondent and the age of respondent.

Women also have preference decision for work to earn money in condition that the number of household members is increasing. This variable is significant for both specifications. The education level of women is significant to influence women in borrowing money from microfinance institution. The higher their education level, the more preference they borrow money from MFI. Therefore, it can be concluded that women participation in microcredit from such Islamic microfinance institution has significant effect on their empowerment in health and economic decision.

The effect of participation in microfinance is significant for 'say' her mobility decision (Table 3.11) for first specification, except for 'social visit man family' decision. The number of children has significant effect on 'social visit women family' decision. The lesser the number of children, the higher the power of women empowerment makes this decision. However, there is no significant for other dependent variables to support 'social visit man and neighborhoods' decision except treatment variable and interaction term. Thus, it can be concluded that participation in microcredit has effect on women mobility decision.

On the contrary, for major household decisions such as purchase household asset, households repairs, and sale or purchase of house, the treatment effect is only significant for sale or purchase of houses, but not for others variables. Therefore, participation in microcredit has no effect on major household decision. Although urban area of Bandung city consists of multicultural people, most of the dweller is Sundanese who hold patriarchy system. Thus, big decision regarding purchase household asset and households repair becomes the authority of men rather than women. However, if the couple wants to buy or sale house, they should do it together as most of them usually take a loan that needs spouse's agreement. In this context, women's voice will be important to comply with the law.

Consider then the second test for robustness of our coefficients for treatment in the above regression: the propensity score matching (PSM) as outlined in methodology section. As a common knowledge, in the evaluation problems particularly for non-randomized observational studies like our study, there is a problem of bias estimation. Rosenbaum and Rubin (1983) proposed propensity score matching as a method to reduce bias in the estimation of treatment effects with observational data sets. Grilli and Rampichini (2011) argued that there are some reasons why matching could be better than OLS:

1. The additional common support condition focuses on comparison of comparable subjects.
2. Matching is a nonparametric technique:
   - It avoids potential misspecification of E (Y(0) I X)
   - It allows for arbitrary heterogeneity in causal effects E(Y(1)−Y(0) I X)
3. If OLS is correctly specified, it is more efficient and make OLS less parametric adding interactions.

The choice of variables used for participation regression is motivated by the potential determinants influencing the timing of participation. Table 3.11 reports the result of the first-stage probit regression. We found that participation in Islamic microfinance is influenced by age of respondent (at time of taking loan), education of respondent, and working women before taking loan from Islamic microfinance. Other variables such as, age difference with husband, number of children, number of household member, first loan utilization by respondent, and join family are not significant at 95% level of confidence. It shows the importance of the education of the respondent in influencing the timing of participation in the program. Based on our interview with some clients and it is supported by questionnaire data, we found

Table 3.11 Participation in Islamic microfinance program probit regression Dependent variable treatment (0/1). *Source* Authors' own calculation

Independent Variables	Probit coefficients	P-value
Age of respondent (at time of taking loan-TTL)	−0.1245	0.040**
Age of respondent—TTL-squared	0.0016	0.022**
Education of respondent	0.4923	0.003**
Education of respondent square	−0.0208	0.004**
Age difference with husband	0.0125	0.476
Number of children	0.1227	0.279
Number of HH members	−0.0530	0.545
Working women	0.6807	0.001***
First loan utilized by respondent	0.1927	0.702
Join family	0.3102	0.220
Number of observations	210	
Pseudo R-squared	0.2959	
Chi-square statistic	27.97	
Log likelihood	−29.2948	

Note $^{*}p < 0.1$, $^{**}p < 0.05$, $^{***}p < 0.01$

that clients with higher education (9–12 year of schooling) tend to be longer as clients of microfinance, especially for DPU-DT case, which gave an opportunity for potential clients to be mentor and future mentor. This mentor can arrange their own group without any influences from DPU-DT Board. The model has been over parameterized, using squared terms of observable covariates to improve predicted probability of assignment to the treated group (Godtland et al. 2004) and (Rubin and Thomas, 1996).

The key assumption in estimating average treatment effect (ATE)[11] requires that the propensity score satisfies the common support condition. The idea for testing this assumption is to inspect the multivariate covariate distribution of propensity scores for both control and treatment group. We assessed the common support condition by plotting the propensity scores estimated for both the treatment and control group. If there is considerable overlap in the covariate distribution, then both the groups are similar in terms of observed characteristics.

We tested systematic differences between treatment and comparison groups constructed by propensity score matching. We used the balancing test developed by Smith and Todd (2005) for this purpose. The 'balancing test' reveals whether the comparison group constructed with PSM sufficiently resemble the treatment group, by testing whether the means of observable variables are significantly different (Smith and Todd 2005). Within each block of treated and control matches constructed by PSM, a t-test of equality of means is conducted for each variable included in the probit for participation equation.

A non-rejection of the null implies that there are no significant differences between treated and comparison units in their observed characteristics. This predicted probability of participation in the program or propensity score then used it to match treated units with observationally similar control units. A number of different matching algorithms can be used to match the treated and control units based on propensity scores. All these methods include nearest neighbor, kernel, radius and stratification matching yield similar results asymptotically. Typically, one treatment case is matched to several control cases, but one-to-one matching is also common and may be preferred (Glazerman et al. 2003). Moreover, Smith and Todd (2005) demonstrated that estimates are highly sensitive to matching methods in case of small samples.

Table 3.12 reports the result for the balancing test on difference in means of observables covariate. The balancing property is satisfied with statistically insignificant difference in means between all the observed covariates of propensity scores. The results with bootstrapped standard errors for all five categories of dependent variables are reported in

Table 3.12 Balancing test T-stat for equality of means for observed variables in the treated and control groups. *Source* Authors' own calculation

Independent variables	t-stat
Age of respondent	−0.9867
Age difference with husband	0.0106
Education	−1.6045
Number of children	0.4270
Number of HH member	−0.0827
Join family	−1.1244
First utilization by respondent	−2.2477
Working female before loan	−3.5907
Number of Observation	
Controls	81
Treated	129

Table 3.13. For three specifications, we find different result to the ones reported for ordered probit regressions. The decision relating to child decision only for schooling Kernel and radius matching but nearest neighbor matching yield tends to reduce the power of empowerment.[12] Negative sign indicates significant reduction of power coefficient of empowerment indicator; meanwhile, positive sign indicates

Table 3.13 Treatment effect estimates of women's empowerment propensity score matching method Women's opinion taken into consideration in decision regarding. *Source* Authors' own calculation

Independent variables	ATT (Nearest neighbor matching) (1)	ATT (Kernel) (2)	ATT (Radius) (3)	NT	NC
Boy's schooling decisions	−0.124	0.036*	−0.001	125	69
Girl's schooling decisions	0.062*	0.098*	0.044*	129	58
Children medical care	−0.039	−0.002	0.037*	129	58
Family planning decision	0.085*	0.094*	0.181*	129	69
Respondent's medical care	0.047*	0.054*	0.046*	129	69
Social visit to women's family	0.016*	0.067*	0.137*	129	81
Social visits to husband's family	0.031*	0.087*	0.159*	125	69
Social visits in neighborhood	0.093*	0.077*	0.399*	129	69
Work for earned income	0.047*	0.056*	0.112*	129	69
Borrow money from MFI	0.000	0.035*	0.094*	129	58
Purchase of HH assets	0.016*	0.084*	0.105*	129	58
Decision about house repair	0.062*	0.140*	0.197*	129	69
Sale/purchase of house	0.000	0.037*	0.124*	129	58

Note Standard deviations are reported in the parenthesis
*$p < 0.1$, **$p < 0.05$, ***$p < 0.01$

improvement in the power of empowerment coefficient. Girls schooling decisions for instance the empowerment of women engaged in microfinance increase significantly for all matching methods. This result is similar to that of both ordered regression specifications. This shows that PSM results confirm OLS result where all treated clients have positive ATT value, except for boys schooling decision and child medical care decisions.

The validity of our estimates both for the simple ordered probit regressions and propensity score matching relies critically on the conditional mean independence assumption or selection on observables. Even after controlling for initial levels of empowerment through proxies and making the control units resemble treated units as closely as possible, through propensity score matching, we still fear for endogeneity or selection on un-observables. So that why, for future studies, we need some test such as (1) instrumental variable techniques (IV regression); (2) Bounding. The drawback is they often give (if we are not willing to impose strong assumptions) quite wide uninformative bounds; and (3) sensitivity analysis: to assess the bias of causal effect estimates when the uncounfoundedness assumption is assumed to fail in some specific and meaningful ways.

3.4.5.2 Hypotheses 2: Autonomy-Based Indicators of Empowerment

In this section, we use another set of empowerment indicators. We asked respondents whether they require someone's permission to make decisions related to household's purchases and children. We generate dummy variable to capture their independence in decision making whenever they do not require someone's permission to make such decisions.

We divided our indicators into three group categories: 'small' purchases like grocery, medicine, and clothes/cosmetic for herself. Second category includes children-related decisions like buying sweets/ice cream, book/uniforms and taking child to the doctors. We dropped variable 'purchase ice cream for a children' because this variable is perfectly success predicted and has multicollinearity with variable 'first utilization' and treatment. The multicollinearity happened since all respondents say perfectly 'empowered' (1) for 'purchase ice cream for children.' To all women who have earned their income and treated as mature clients of MFI (which is indicated with '1'), this variable is small decision that needs someone's permissions. Third category includes purchasing household assets, sale/purchase of personal assets like jewelry, and purchase/sale of house.

The results are presented in Tables 3.14, 3.15 and 3.16 for the same specification used to test the earlier hypothesis. The estimated coefficient of treatment dummy is statistically significant across both categories at 95% of level of confidence. We introduce institutional level fixed effects in the second specification; the significance of the coefficient on this particular question is also significant for 'purchasing refrigerator' only. One possible explanation for the strong fixed effect could be their participation in microfinance programs which capacitated them to run a small business (i.e., particularly for those who had a loan with DPU-DT where clients are given education). Thus, for working respondent, they are more independence to decide any purchase of major household that could support their business. Nevertheless, most of the findings presented in this section are consistent with our earlier results. It is obvious that if there are first-order changes in the extent to which women's preference is reflected in decision-making process, then there will be higher order changes in the 'autonomy' or independence in decision making for the female partner.

In Table 3.17, we present results for the propensity score matching. The covariate used for propensity score matching is identical to the ones used earlier. The table reports result for kernel matching which has positive sign for all empowerment indicators by participating in microfinance. To all decisions regarding major households such as purchase and sale houses, the power of empowerment increases significantly. This finding is similar to previous PSM test for ordered regressions. However, for marginal significant of 'purchase clothes/cosmetics' and 'purchase uniform or book for children' have negative effect for all matching estimates. The role of MFI on treated clients (mature) in DPU-DT tends

Table 3.14 Probit estimates of 'Autonomy' in HH decisions Women do not require someone's permission to purchase. *Source* Authors' own calculation

Independent variables	Grocery/fruits probit coefficients		Medicine for herself probit coefficients		Personal clothes/ cosmetics probit coefficients	
	1	2	1	2	1	2
Treatment dummy	2.1726***	2.1861***	3.2055***	3.0371***	2.0551***	1.9984***
	(0.6229)	(0.6858)	(0.8620)	(0.8980)	(0.3750)	(0.3860)
Age difference with husband	0.0327	0.0330	0.0298	0.0254	−0.0315	−0.0303
	(0.0740)	(0.0741)	(0.0775)	(0.0759)	(0.0438)	(0.0439)
Age of respondent	0.0159	0.0169	−0.0112	−0.0156	0.0134	0.0101
	(0.0278)	(0.0344)	(0.0328)	(0.0335)	(0.0204)	(0.0208)
Education	0.2102	0.2088*	0.1401	0.1486	0.0726	0.0817
	(0.1384)	(0.1411)	(0.1158)	(0.1170)	(0.0783)	(0.0804)
Number of children	1.3649***	1.3632***	0.6545**	0.6377**	0.0283	0.0440
	(0.4359)	(0.4366)	(0.3310)	(0.3352)	(0.1916)	(0.1943)
Total number of family	−0.0097	−0.0091	0.2680	0.2773	0.0859	0.0814
	(0.1910)	(0.1911)	(0.3374)	(0.3405)	(0.1375)	(0.1395)
Joint family	1.9905**	2.0054**	–	–	−0.1985	−0.2137
	(1.0712)	(1.1174)			(0.4920)	(0.4964)
First utilization by respondent	0.0909	0.0967	−1.2696	−1.3295*	0.06017	−0.0162
	(0.6533)	(0.6643)	(1.017601)	(1.0239)	(0.4397)	(0.4512)
Working female before loan	–	–	1.2213	1.1396*	0.9163**	0.9043**
			(0.7345)	(0.7361)	(0.4551)	(0.4636)
Institution*Treatment	–	−.0409		0.3738		0.3614
		(.8513935)		(0.7749)		(0.3957)
Number of observation	**108**	**108**	**138**	**138**	**210**	**210**
Pseudo R-squared	0.5606	0.5606	0.6004	0.6030	0.4278	0.4344
Chi-square statistic	39.85	39.86	51.72	51.96	56.51	57.38
Log likelihood	−15.61	−15.61	−17.21	−17.09	−37.78	−37.35

Note Standard deviations are reported in the parenthesis
*$p < 0.1$, **$p < 0.05$, ***$p < 0.01$

to be more understood how they utilize their money, as they got some guidance to utilize their loan and income by their mentor in the regular meeting. Thus, it can be concluded that participation on microcredit program has significant effect to improve women empowerment and their position in their family. It is also obvious that if there are changes in ordered decision-making process, it is likely that there will be higher order changes in the autonomy decision making for the female partner.

Table 3.15 Probit estimates of 'Autonomy' in HH decisions Women do not require someone's permission to purchase. *Source* Authors' own calculation

Independent variables	Buy book/uniform for children probit coefficients		Take a child to the doctor probit coefficients	
	1	2	1	2
Treatment dummy	2.7077***	2.6104***	3.1054***	3.0506***
	(0.3390)	(0.3445)	(0.4932)	(0.4970)
Age difference with husband	0.0054	0.0027	0.0645**	0.0616***
	(0.0407)	(0.0412)	(0.0305)	(0.0307)
Age of respondent	−0.0224	−0.0271*	−0.0226**	−0.0246***
	(0.0189)	(0.0197)	(0.0117)	(0.0122)
Education	0.1147*	0.1171*	−0.0039	−0.0073
	(0.0721)	(0.0740)	(0.0478)	(0.0482)
Number of children	−0.3599**	−0.3450**	−0.2043*	−0.2054*
	(0.1589)	(0.1602)	(0.1206)	(0.1207)
Total number of family	0.0123	−0.0012	0.1632**	0.1620**
	(0.1188)	(0.1192)	(0.08554)	(0.0855)
Joint family	−0.2902	−0.2763	−0.6581**	−0.6552**
	(0.4231)	(0.4269)	(0.2890)	(0.2889)
Working female before loan	0.4069	0.3414	−0.1273	−0.1579
	(0.3380)	(0.3488)	(0.2293)	(0.2348)
First utilization by respondent	0.3236	0.2759	0.3202	0.2867
	(0.4426)	(0.4506)	(0.2945)	(0.2994)
Institution * Treatment		0.4209		0.1523
		(0.3372)		(0.2441)
Number of observation	210	210	210	210
Pseudo R-squared	0.5640	0.5718	0.3694	0.3708
Chi-square statistic	113.69	115.27	100.22	100.61
Log likelihood	−43.94	−43.15	−85.54	−85.34

Note Standard deviations are reported in the parenthesis
$*p < 0.1$, $**p < 0.05$, $***p < 0.01$

3.4.6 Summary of Empirical Results

The empirical result presented in the last section can be concluded for our testable hypotheses as follows:

Hypothesis 1:
Impact of participation in microcredit program on preference-based indicators of women's empowerment:

Table 3.16 Probit estimates of 'Autonomy' in HH decisions Women do not require someone's permission to purchase. *Source* Authors' own calculation

Independent variables	Purchasing furniture Probit coefficients		Purchasing refrigerator Probit coefficients		Sale/purchase of house Probit coefficients	
	1	2	1	2	1	2
Treatment dummy	1.2760***	1.2626***	1.4683***	1.2922***	1.2731***	1.2540**
	(0.3728)	(0.3805)	(0.3694)	(0.3729)	(0.4959	(0.5039)
Age difference with husband	0.0159	0.0154	0.0394*	0.0345**	0.0617**	0.0611**
	(0.0245)	(0.0246)	(0.0245)	(0.0247)	(0.0266)	(0.0268)
Age of respondent	−0.0241**	−0.0245**	−0.0145*	−0.0204**	−0.0312***	−0.0317
	(0.0101)	(0.0104)	(0.0098)	(0.0102)	(0.0113)	(0.0116)
Education	−0.0717*	−0.0729*	−0.0440	−0.0565	−0.0409	−0.0428
	(0.0430)	(0.0436)	(0.0416)	(0.0429)	(0.0475)	(0.0484)
Number of children	−0.0409	−0.0414	−0.1186	−0.1287	0.0395	0.0385
	(0.1044)	(0.1045)	(0.1063)	(0.1085)	(0.1253)	(0.1254)
Total number of family	0.0601	0.0603	0.0421	0.0410	−0.0212	−0.0208
	(0.0738)	(0.0738)	(0.0739)	(0.0742)	(0.0911)	(0.0911)
Joint family	−0.5045**	−0.5059**	−0.4861**	−0.5000*	−0.2315	−0.2331
	(0.2663)	(0.2667)	(0.2664)	(0.2724)	(0.3118)	(0.3121)
Working female before loan	0.2888*	0.2830*	−0.1495	−0.2460	0.5453**	0.5344
	(0.203)	(0.2059)	(0.1994)	(0.2067)	(0.2344)	(0.2401)
First utilization by respondent	0.2511	0.2411	0.1480	0.0040	−0.3757**	−0.3896
	(0.2812)	(0.2867)	(0.2673)	(0.2718)	(0.2834)	(0.2911)
Institution*Treatment		0.0373		0.5467***		0.0512
		(0.2166)		(0.2176)		(0.2486)
Number of observation	210	210	210	210	210	210
Pseudo R-squared	0.1212	0.1213	0.1134	0.1377	0.1780	0.1782
Chi-square statistic	30.89	30.92	30.00	36.43	37.41	37.46
Log likelihood	−111.9	−111.9	−117.2	−114.0	−86.3	−86.3

Note Standard deviations are reported in the parenthesis
$^{*}p < 0.1$, $^{**}p < 0.05$, $^{***}p < 0.01$

1.1: Upon 'say' in child-related decisions: Reject the null hypothesis: Microcredit has no effect on power coefficient 'θ_1'

1.2: Upon 'say' in health-related decisions: Reject the null hypothesis: Microcredit has no effect on power coefficient 'θ_1'

1.3: Upon 'say' in economic decisions: Reject the null hypothesis: Microcredit has no effect on power coefficient 'θ_1'

1.4: Upon 'say' in social mobility decisions: Reject the null hypothesis: Microcredit has no effect on power coefficient 'θ_1'

1.5: Upon 'say' in sale or purchase of major household items decisions: Do not reject the null hypothesis: Microcredit has no effect on power coefficient 'θ_1'

Table 3.17 Treatment effect estimates of women's empowerment propensity score matching method Women's opinion taken into consideration in decision regarding. *Source* Authors' own calculation

Independent Variables	ATT (Nearest matching) (1)	ATT (Kernel) (2)	ATT (Radius) (3)	NT	NC
Purchase grocery/fruits	−0.023	0.003*	−0.003	129	62
Purchase medicine for herself	−0.008	0.002*	−0.012	129	77
Purchase personal clothes/cosmetics	−0.008	−0.009	−0.035	129	62
Purchase book/uniform for children	0.000	−0.000	−0.045	129	77
Take a child to the doctor	0.000	0.022*	0.022*	129	77
Purchasing furniture	0.008*	0.058*	0.079*	129	77
Purchasing refrigerator	−0.008	0.088*	0.113*	129	77
Sale/purchase of house	0.023*	0.050*	0.089*	129	77

Note Standard deviations are reported in the parenthesis $*p < 0.1$, $**p < 0.05$, $***p < 0.01$

Hypothesis 2:
Impact of participation in microcredit program on 'autonomy'-based indicators of women's empowerment:

2.1: Upon 'independence' in small personal purchase: Do not reject the null hypothesis: Microcredit has effect on power coefficient 'θ_1'

2.2: Upon 'independence' in child-related decisions: Do not reject the null hypothesis: Microcredit has effect on power coefficient 'θ_1'

2.3: Upon 'independence' in purchasing household assets: Do not reject the null hypothesis: Microcredit has effect on power coefficient 'θ_1'

3.4.7 Discussion of Results

Our empirical findings suggest that microcredit intervention in the urban area of the Bandung city in Indonesia has impact on child-related, health, economics, and social mobility decisions, except for 'purchase/sale major households' decision. The results using proxy controls and matching methods clearly demonstrated the robustness of our findings for these five dimensions of empowerment. However, we are unable to find convincing evidence for the set of indicators relating to child-related decisions. It seems that women have more power related to their daughter rather than their son, particularly to decide about child schooling and medical care.

The results under maintained assumptions of selections on observables are well aligned with the dynamics on the ground. The results suggest that women are gaining more 'say' when it comes to lesser order decisions regarding purchase/sale of household assets, while both control and treated enjoy the same level of participation in decisions relating to children, health, social mobility, and paid work.

Within the framework of patriarchy, we believe that this is the best that women can score on these outcomes and hence an intervention like microcredit will have marginal effects if any for these indicators. In the framework of the 'perpetual dependency,' hypothesis means that women have reached level of maturity in their relationship with their spouses. They have been given the bargaining power in these decisions commensurate with the prescribed gender norms of the society.

When it comes to decisions relating to major household decisions like purchase of assets, house repairs, and sale/purchase of house, women do not have much 'say.' The unconditional mean values for those decisions have a value of about 2 on scale of 5 suggesting that female preferences are rarely or never considered for these household decisions. It seems reasonable that once women have gotten more involved in economic and financial matters by borrowing money from MFI, they enjoy greater confidence of their husbands, and hence, we see their participation increasing in decisions making which initially fell under the prescribed domain of 'male only' decisions. The result from our ordered probit and matching estimators reinforced this finding that microcredit intervention empowers women by giving her more 'say' in decisions where she had limited or no participation before this intervention.

Our results are consistent with autonomy-based indicators reported in Table 3.14. These results also serve as an informal check for the patriarchy framework proposed in this chapter. Critics might be argued that if microcredit is not increasing women's 'say' in the decisions-making process beyond a societal threshold level, it is still possible that they may have greater independence in making decisions. Our results suggest that on average women in the treatment group are more independent or autonomous than the control units, even when it comes to decisions relating to small household purchases. This further reinforces our earlier findings that women have reached a certain threshold level of independence within the structural norms of the society and microcredit has marginal effect on all such indicators.

3.5 Conclusion

Empirically, this chapter has sought to contribute the first econometric impact assessment of Islamic microfinance on women's empowerment in Indonesia. First, our results suggest that microcredit program proposed by Islamic microfinance institution has effect on the bargaining power of women within the household for a broad range of decisions including child related, health and economic, and social mobility decisions, except on 'purchase/sale major households' decision. Second, our results suggest that Islamic microcredit intervention is empowering women in the domains of household decisions where they are the least empowered to begin with. These include decisions relating to purchase of TV/refrigerator and house repair and 'sale/purchase of house.' The decisions generally fall within the domain of 'man-only' decisions in patriarchal societies.

Our results show that all testable estimators using ordered probit regression, simple probit regression, and propensity score matching are robust. We also have shown that most of the concern raised in the literature regarding biased estimates of impact can be controlled through careful design and better understanding of ground dynamics and this methodology is proved and supported the previous methodological framework that is designed by Asim (2008). Therefore, this methodology can be applied to other setting for further research.

The findings of this chapter have implications for policy makers and future research. First, we confidence that model of microcredit program that proposed by Islamic microfinance with close assistance and well design program for empowering women economically have significant effect on different aspect of intra-households decisions. All estimators are robust across all econometric specification. Therefore, we can pursue recommendation to policy maker to set up any regulation that supports *Zakat*, *Infaq*, and *Sadaqa* utilization as resources fund for microcredit program under special specification and indicators.

One very important finding is that official *Zakat* management organization under government institution tends to be careful to utilize *Zakat* fund for economic empowerment. They tend to distribute this fund only for charity program without the impact to empowering the poor to be more independent in economic aspect. Educating clients through regular training will improve their performance and increase their independent to make their own decision. The *Misykat* program has good experience to set up some educating program, not only to run their own businesses but also to support their clients with beneficial information for the entire life regarding women and their family. In this case, we also found that the more educated women who joined microfinance, the longer they affiliate with the institution. Thus, formal as well as informal education should be considered by Microfinance Board to design their program, so it can work more properly to improve women empowerment and eliminate poverty.

In addition, this chapter provides gender-specific approach for microcredit services, which may be over-rated in the context of urban people in Bandung. Future research with richer data sets could compare the results from this quasi-experimental framework with randomized intervention. Research in this direction will provide a good comparative analysis for the robustness of the estimates reported in this study.

Notes

1. BAZNAS is Amil *Zakat* National Agency, the agency that manage, collect and distribute *Zakat* nationally.

2. *Zakat* collection can be direct or indirect. Direct collection is where *muzaki* (one who is obliged to pay *zakat*) come to an operational unit of BAZ or LAZ, whereas indirect collection is where the *muzaki* pay their *zakat* at a post office, by bank transfer, or salary deduction. Although, the *Zakat* law has led to an increase in *Zakat* institutions, it has been challenging to improve coordination, consultation and information dissemination among institutions.
3. *Zakat* is defined as 'a determined portion taken from wealth and allocated to those deserving it, by a Qur'anic injunction'.
4. FGD with mentor of Myskat program in Bandung, 24 April 2014. It was attended by 13 mentor, 7 women and 6 men mentors.
5. Wallet Caring Ummah (DPU-DT) is a community-owned non-profit organization engaged in raising (fundraising) and utilization of *Zakat* (*Zakat*, Infaq, and Charity) and other funds from the lawful and legal individual, group, company or institution. It is founded on June 16, 1999 by KH. Abdullah Gymnastiar (Aa Gym) as part of the Foundation Daarut-Tauhid with LAZ determination be trustful, professional and accountable. DPU-DT effectively carrying out its activities on June 16, 2000, on the basis of a database, where each donor has the number and membership card so caring and donor commitment can be measured. From the formal legal aspects, DPU-DT confirmed as *Zakat* Institution by the Governor of West Java, dated August 19, 2002. By Decree No.: 451.12/Kep. 846 - YANSOS/2002. DPU-DT foundation also got the attention of the central government, in a short amount of time since the days of standing DPU-DT, and became LAZDA, has managed to become the National Institute of Amil *Zakat,* LAZNAS, in accordance with the Decree of the Minister of Religious Affairs No. 410 of 2004 on October 13, 2004. After becoming LAZNAS, DPU-DT develop a network of up to eight cities, namely Jakarta, Bogor, Tasikmalaya, Garut, Semarang, Yogyakarta, Lampung and Palembang. Besides, it has hundreds of network utilization program from Sabang to Papua.
6. *Zakat* revenue can be spent for raising the productivity of the poor. Such as financing various development projects in education, health care, safe water and other social welfare activities, designed exclusively for the benefit of the poor. It is expected that this program can create multiplier effect for the poor welfare. However, it is intuitively plausible that an increase in income from *Zakat* investment is expected to have

a multiplier larger in size than an increase in income from *non-Zakat* funds investment. It is due to the fact that in addition to the leakage into saving, some portion of income at the successive rounds of income and spending would be siphoned off by other leakages such as taxes, and imports, mostly in case of the income of the rich (Mannan, 2000).

7. To some extent, it is presumed that if working women (with or without her husband permission) would like to spend her income, her husband will not forbid or intervene it. However, they tend to inform their husband on how they spent their income.
8. Household and economic decisions are both reported in Table 8 for spatial convenience.
9. Note that the experiment design constrained by dynamics on the ground as outlined in the sampling framework precludes the use of simple institutional dummy to capture fixed effect.
10. Indonesia is known for its successful family planning program, which has roughly halved the total fertility rate for the country since the 1970s and increased the contraceptive prevalence to almost 60%. Part of this success has been due to the development of strategic partnerships with Muslim leaders, who have supported uptake of the program among their communities (UNFPA 2014).
11. The ATE=E [Y(1)–Y(0)] is useful to evaluate what is the expected effect on the outcome if individuals in the population were randomly assigned to treatment. However, Heckman (1997) notes that ATE might not be relevance to policy makers because it includes the effect on persons whom the program was never intended.
12. Nearest Neighbor match treated and control units taking each treated unit and searching for the control unit with the closest propensity score. Although it is not necessary, the method is usually applied with replacement, in the sense that a control unit can be a best match for more than one-treated units and the outcome of the matched control units is computed. The ATT (Average Treatment Effect on the Treated) of interest is then obtained by averaging these differences. Thus, according to Grilli and Rampichini (2011) it is better to use other matching methods that have better result for ATT.

References

Ahmad, Z. (2000). Comment. In I. A. Imtiazi, M. A. Mannan, M. A. Niaz & A. H. Deria (Eds.), *Management of Zakah in modern Muslim society* (2nd ed.). Jeddah: Saudi Arabia.

Ahmed, H. (2004). The role of *zakah* and *awqaf* in poverty alleviation. *Islamic Research and Training Institute. Occasional Paper No.8.* Jeddah: Saudi Arabia.

Ashe, J., & Parrott, L. (2001). *Impact evaluation of PACT's women's empowerment program in Nepal.* Cambridge, Massachusetts: Freedom From Hunger USAID.

Asian Development Bank. (2007). *Effect of microfinance operations on poor rural households and the status of women.* Asian Development Bank Evaluation Document. (May 15, 2014).

Asim, S. (2008). Evaluating the impact of microcredit on women's empowerment in Pakistan. http://www.microfinancegateway.org/gm/document1.9.40843/Evaluating%20The%20Impact.pdf (June 30, 2013).

BAZNAS, West Java Province. (2013). Zakah disbursement and distribution report, unpublished report.

Chapra, M. U. (1980). The Islamic welfare state and its role in the economy. *Economic Studies, 9*(1), 1–16.

Charon, J. M. (1979). *Symbolic interactionism: An introduction, an interpretation, an integration.* Englewood Cliffs, NJ: Prentice-Hall.

Chavez, R. A., & Gonzales-Vega, C. (1996). The design of successful rural financial intermediaries: Evidence from Indonesia. *World Development, 24*(1), 65–78.

Citi Foundation. (2009). Microfinance industry report: Indonesia. *The Banking with the Poor Network in collaboration with the SEEP Network.*

Dompet Peduli Ummat–Daarut Tauhid. (2014). A guidance for member of Misykat program, unpublished document.

Glazerman, S., Levy, D., & Myers, D. (2003). Nonexperimental versus experimental estimates of earnings impacts. *The Annals of the American Academy of Political and Social Sciences, 589*(1), 63–93.

Godtland, E. M., Sadoulet, E., Janvry, A. D., Murgai, R., & Ortiz, O. (2004). The impact of farmer field schools on knowledge and productivity: A study of Potato Farmers in the Peruvian Andes. *Journal Economic Development and Cultural Change, 53*(1), 63–92.

Grilli, L., & Rampichini, C. (2011). Propensity scores for the estimation of average treatment effects in observational studies. *Training sessions on causal Inference* (pp. 28–29). Bristol.

Kaleem, A. (2007). Application of Islamic banking instrument (Bay Salam) for agriculture financing in Pakistan. *Inclusive Financial Services for Micro and Medium Sized Entreprises*. Brunei Darussalam: Islamic Research and Training Institute, The National Sciences Foundation.

Khan, S., Sajid, M. R., & Rehman, H. (2011). Women's empowerment through microcredit: A case study of district Gujarat Pakistan. *Academic Research International, 1*(2), 332–343.

Kholis, N. (2008). Murabahah mode of financing for micro and medium sized enterprises: A case study of Baitul Mal Wattamwil (BMT), Yogyakarta Indonesia. *Inclusive Financial Services for Micro and Medium Sized Entreprises*. Brunei Darussalam: Islamic Research and Training Institute.

Landes, A. Q. (2013). *Secular is not always better: A closer look at some woman-empowering features of Islamic law*. Washington, DC: Institute for Social Policy and Understanding.

Mannan, M. A. (2000). Effects of *Zakah* assessment and collection on the redistribution of income in contemporary Muslim countries. In I. A. Imtiazi, M. A. Mannan, M. A. Niaz & A. H. Deria (Eds.), *Management of Zakah in modern Muslim society* (2nd ed.). *Zakah* Jeddah: Saudi Arabia.

Martowijoyo, S. (2007). Indonesian microfinance at the crossroads: Caught between popular and populist policies. *Essays on Regulation and Supervision* (p. 23). Maryland: IRIS Center, University of Maryland, Department of Economics.

Mohieldin, M., Iqbal, Z., Rostom, A., & Fu, X. (2011). The role of Islamic finance in enhancing financial inclusion in Organization of Islamic Cooperation (OIC) Countries. *Policy Research Working Paper*. New York: The World Bank Islamic Economics and Finance Working Group 5920.

Obaidullah, M., & Latiff, H. S. H. A. (2007). *Islamic finance for micro and medium enterprises: Inclusive financial services for micro and medium sized enterprises*. Brunei Darussalam: Islamic Research and Training Institute.

Purwakananta, M. A., & Abilawa, M. S. (2010). *Peta kemiskinan, data Mustahik, Muzzaki dan potensi pemberdayaan Indonesia (Poverty map, data of Zakah recipients and Zakah contributor and empowerment potential in Indonesia)*. Jakarta: Dompet Dhuafa.

Robinson, M. S. (2002). *The microfinance revolution: Volume 2, lessons from Indonesia*. Washington, DC: World Bank.

Rosenbaum, P. R., & Rubin D. B. (1983). The central role of the propensity score in observational studies for causal effects. *Biometrika, 70*, 41–55.

Rubin, D. B. & Thomas, N. (1996). Matching using estimated propensity scores: Relating theory to practice. *Biometrics, 52*(1), 249–264.

Sanrego, Y. D., & Antonio, M. S. (2013). The effect of social capital on loan repayment behavior of the poor: A study on Group Lending Model (GLM) application in Islamic Microfinance Institution. *Journal of Indonesian Economy & Business, May 2013, 28*(2), 188–210.

Smith, J., & Todd, P. (2005). Does matching overcome Lalonde's critique of nonexperimental estimators. *Journal of econometrics, 125*(91–2), 305–353.

Sumardjo. (1999). *Transformasi model penyuluhan pertanian menuju pengembangan kemandirian petani: kasus di provinsi Jawa Barat, Doctoral Dissertation*. Bogor Agricultural University.

UNFPA. (2014). *Annual report: A year of renewal.* WWW.UNFPA.ORG,https://www.unfpa.org/sites/default/files/pubpdf/UNFPA_annual_report_2014_en.pdf (November, 2015).

Wee, V., & Shaheed, F. (2008). Women empowering themselves: A framework that interrogates and transforms. Pakistan: University of Hong Kong.

World Bank. (2012). *The little data book on financial inclusion*. Washington, DC, USA: The International Bank of Reconstruction and Development/The World Bank.

Yaumidin, U. K. (2010). Economic growth, unemployment and employment opportunities. In L. Adams (Ed.), *Economic growth, employment and poverty rbook*. Jakarta.

Yaumidin, U. K. (2011). Assessing the role of *Zakah* for poverty alleviation in Indonesia. *Journal of Review of Indonesian Economic and Business Studies, 2*(1), 89–112.

Yaumidin, U. K., & Dharmawan, D. A. (2013). *The dynamics of income inequality, poverty and welfare in the Indonesian economic corridors*. Paper presented at the 23rd Pacific Conference of The Regional Science Association International, July 2–4, 2013, Bandung, Indonesia.

4

Financial Inclusion and Poverty Alleviation in Muslim-majority Countries: The Role of Islamic Finance and Qard Hassan

Amin Mohseni-Cheraghlou

Abstract Global Findex database reports that 75% or about one billion adults among self-identified Muslims do not have an account in a formal financial institutions. The first part of this chapter suggests that overall access to Islamic financial products is positively correlated with levels of financial inclusion in Muslim majority countries. One such product is Qard Hassan and the second part of this chapter highlights its theoretical potentials in reducing poverty and increasing shared prosperity. This theoretical treatment is then complemented with the third part of the chapter where a case study of Akhuwat Foundation, a Pakistani Islamic microfinance organization operating on a Qard Hassan model is presented in some detail and its relative success in breaking the cycle of poverty through Qard Hassan is highlighted.

JEL classification C83 · D03 · E22 · G30 · O16

A. Mohseni-Cheraghlou (✉)
Faculty of Economics, University of Tehran, Tehran, Iran
e-mail: amohseni@ut.ac.ir

© The Author(s) 2017

M. Zulkhibri and A. G. Ismail (eds.), *Financial Inclusion and Poverty Alleviation*, Palgrave Studies in Islamic Banking, Finance, and Economics,
https://doi.org/10.1007/978-3-319-69799-4_4

Keywords Financing constraints · Financial intermediation
Investment models · Islamic countries

4.1 Introduction

The growing volume of theoretical and empirical findings over the past decade shows that access to diverse forms of financial services has positive impacts on economic development and growth, and if done in an equitable and responsible manner, it can also reduce poverty and inequality and boost shared prosperity (Beck et al. 2004; Beck and Demirguç-Kunt 2008; Levine 2005; World Bank 2007).

It is estimated that more than 50% of world's adult population or 2.5 billion adults do not have access to formal financial institutions and majority of them reside in emerging market and developing economies (EMDEs) (Demirguc-Kunt and Klapper 2012). The picture is substantially grimmer for member countries of Organization of Islamic Conference (OIC). According to Global Findex Database, 40 out of the 48 OIC member countries represented in this database have formal account penetration rates[1] that were less than the world average of 50%. The median account penetration rate among the OIC member countries was only about 20%, a figure that is significantly less than the global average. Also, in comparison with other regions, Middle East and North Africa (MENA) region had the lowest penetration rate of 18% (Fig. 4.1).

Furthermore, according to Global Findex, 75% or about 1 billion adults among self-identified Muslims do not have an account in a formal financial institution. In other words, about two in every five adults without a formal account around the world are Muslims. This may be one reason as to why efforts for reducing poverty or enhancing shared prosperity in many of the MENA and other Muslim-majority countries are not as successful as one would have desired them to be.[2]

Islamic teachings pay particular attention to (a) eliminating absolute poverty; (b) reducing inequality, relative poverty, and marginalization of the poor; and (c) enhancing inclusive growth, social solidarity and shared prosperity. Islamic financial institutions (IFIs) play a central

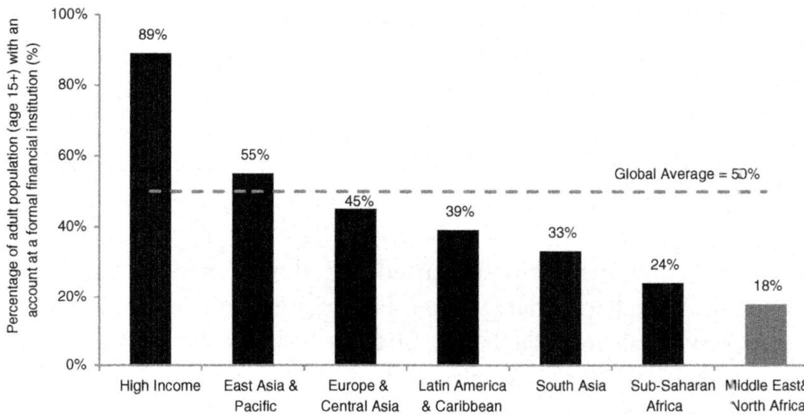

Fig. 4.1 Account penetration rates by regions, 2011. *Source* Global Financial Inclusion (Global Findex) Database

role in materializing these objectives through providing a diverse set of *Shari'ah*-compliant financial instruments that are designed to address the heterogeneous needs of their clients including those of the vulnerable and the poor. One such instrument is *Qard Hassan*. Often overlooked and not appropriately practiced by formal IFIs in most of the Muslim-majority countries, *Qard Hassan* (*QH*) is an interest-free loan (or *Qard*) that is also characterized by elements of goodwill, benevolence, and generosity (or *Ihsan*). This work suggests that if implemented appropriately, *QH* can potentially provide an effective mechanism to pave the path for the financially prudent and deserving poor who are unbanked or financially excluded to eventually become bankable and gain access to various forms of financial services and the many benefits associated with them. Additionally, *QH* could:

1. Distribute the limited financial resources designated for the poor (such as *Zakat* and *Sadaqa*) in a more productive and efficient manner.
2. Target the heterogeneous needs of the poor more effectively.
3. Encourage financial responsibility, creativity, and austerity among the receivers of *QH* (i.e., the vulnerable and the poor) as well as among the donors of *QH* (i.e., the non-poor).

4. Facilitate the transfer of knowledge and skills from the donors to the receivers of *QH*.
5. Increase the human capital, pride, and self-confidence of the receivers of *QH*.
6. Promote social solidarity and harmony between donors and receivers of *QH*.

The rest of the chapter is organized as follows. Through an empirical analysis based on data from Findex, BankScope, and World Development Indicator databases, first part of this work suggests that access to Islamic financial services is positively correlated with levels of financial inclusion in Muslim-majority countries. Therefore, the first part of the chapter provides support for the hypothesis that Islamic financial instruments can help reduce poverty and increase shared prosperity through enhancing financial inclusion among Muslim communities. The second part of the chapter will focus on the specific case of *Qard Hassan* (*QH*). First, a theoretical discussion around *QH* is presented, and its position vis-à-vis *Qard*, *Zakat*, and *Sadaqa* is analyzed in some detail. This theoretical discussion is important, as it will have significant practical implications for the sustainable operation of *QH* funds, an issue that is discussed next in this part of the essay. The third part of this essay will present a detailed case study of *Akhuwat*. *Akhuwat* is an Islamic microfinance institution in Pakistan that has been operating successfully based on a genuine *QH* model since 2002 and has been able to assist more than 900,000 poor families in various parts of Pakistan. A short conclusion ends this essay.

4.2 Islamic Finance and Financial Inclusion

Before analyzing the relationship between Islamic finance and financial inclusion, it must be mentioned that financial inclusion, if promoted responsibly, can result in significant benefits in terms of inclusive and equitable growth and poverty reduction. A 2013 World Bank report entitled *Financial Inclusion*[3] provides a rich and comprehensive synthesis of the existing literature as well as World Bank's own detailed research on this topic. The report concludes that:

- There is a notable level of inequality in access to financial services. "The poor, women, youth, and rural residents tend to face greater barriers to access financial services. Among firms, the younger and smaller ones are confronted by more binding constraints. For instance, in developing economies, 35% of small firms report that access to finance is a major obstacle to their operations, compared with 25% of large firms in developing economies and 8% of large firms in developed economies."[4]
- Financial inclusion is important for equitable growth and poverty reduction. "Considerable evidence indicates that the poor benefit enormously from basic payments, savings, and insurance services. For firms, particularly the small and young ones that are subject to greater constraints, access to finance is associated with innovation, job creation, and growth."[5]
- Financial inclusion must be done responsibly to benefit the targeted population. This does not mean finance for all at all costs. "Some individuals and firms have no material demand or business need for financial services. Efforts to subsidize these services are counterproductive and, in the case of credit, can lead to over-indebtedness and financial instability."[6]

Therefore, it should not come as a surprise that access to financial services is strongly correlated with productivity and income.

4.2.1 Reasons for Financial Exclusion

The reasons for financial exclusion, defined here as not having an account at a formal financial institution or being unbanked, are rooted in a complex set of economic, legal, social, political, cultural, and personal factors but can be classified into two main categories: voluntary and involuntary reasons. As shown in Fig. 4.2, some adults are financially excluded and voluntarily so because of religious considerations.

A 2011 survey, the Global Findex Database,[7] is the first international database that makes it possible to get a first glimpse at the various aspects of financial exclusion at the individual level. In addition to many other questions, this survey asks the unbanked respondents (i.e., adults

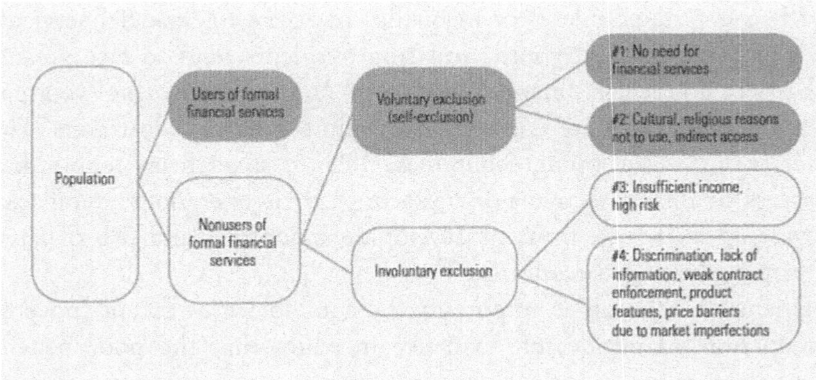

Fig. 4.2 Financial exclusion. *Source* Global Financial Development Report 2014

lacking a formal account) about the reason(s) as to why they do not have an account at a bank, credit union or other formal financial institution. The respondents could choose one or more of the following reasons:

a. They are too far away.
b. They are too expensive.
c. You do not have the necessary documentation (ID, wage slip).
d. You do not trust them.
e. You do not have enough money to use them.
f. Because of religious reasons.
g. Because someone else in the family already has an account.

Two notes are in order here. First, one can think of many more reasons for an individual not to have an account that are not part of the above seven reasons. For example, one can think of concerns with government taxes and identification of wealth, no need, preferences in using informal financial services, being illiterate and not knowing how to open an account as some other valid reasons for not having an account. Second, while allowing to select multiple reasons provides a more complete picture of the reasons behind an individual's lack of an account, it makes it impossible to identify the ultimate binding constraint facing the unbanked individuals who have provided more than one reason. For example, if a person has pointed to distance and costs

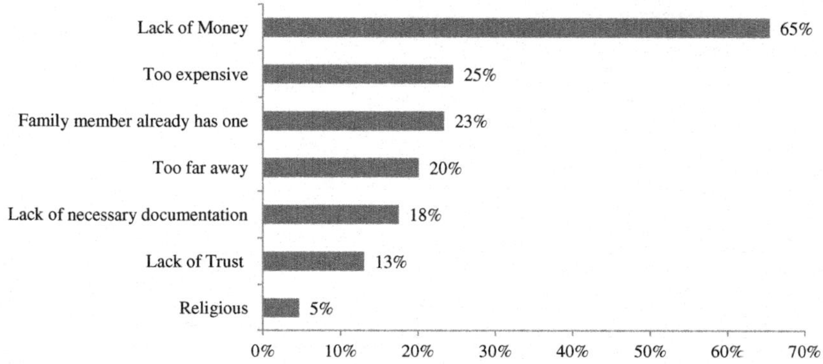

Fig. 4.3 Reasons for financial exclusion, 2011. *Source* Global Financial Inclusion (Global Findex) Database; author's own calculation. *Note* Respondents could choose more than one reason

(options a and b above) as her reasons for being unbanked, then one would have no way of knowing if the responder will remain unbanked if one of the obstacles (either distance or cost) is removed, presenting policymakers with a certain level of uncertainty.

Acknowledging these two caveats, this question nevertheless provides a valuable entry point for analyzing the reasons for which 2.5 billion adults around the globe have remained unbanked. According to this question, not having enough money is the most cited reason for being unbanked, followed by cost, another family member having an account, and distance (Fig. 4.3) with exclusion for religious reasons is the least cited reason.

Reasons of financial exclusion vary across regions (Fig. 4.4). While lack of sufficient funds was by far the most frequently cited reason for not having an account for the unbanked adults in all regions, there was no other common pattern in reasons of exclusion across all regions. For example, lack of trust was second most frequently cited reason for being unbanked in Europe and Central Asia (ECA), while being too expensive was the second reason in Latin America and the Caribbean (LAC), Middle East and North Africa (MENA), and Sub-Saharan Africa (SSA). Also, while religious factor was the third highest cited reason for not having an account in MENA (12%), it was the least frequently cited reason for the unbanked adults in other regions.

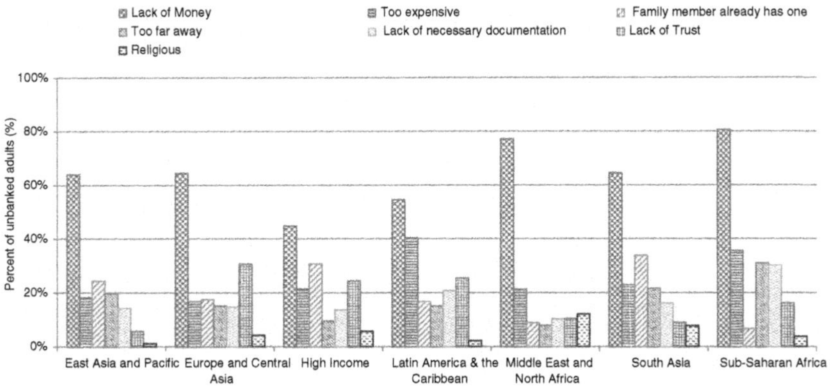

Fig. 4.4 Reasons for financial exclusion by regions, 2011. *Source* Global Financial Inclusion (Global Findex) Database; author's own calculation

The complex combination of social, economic, political, demographic, historical, security, and legal factors in countries would make reasons of financial exclusion also vary widely across countries. A look at Table 4.1 highlights the stark differences between different countries even when they are in the same income group or region. For example, one can point to Afghanistan and Bangladesh, two South Asian low-income economies that have widely different account penetration rates and differ widely on reasons of financial exclusion. Namely, 32% of unbanked adults in Afghanistan reported religious reasons for not having an account, while this figure is only at 4% in Bangladesh. This is despite the fact that both countries have comparable ratios of Muslim population (98% and 90% in Afghanistan and Bangladesh, respectively) and religiosity levels[8] (97% and 99% in Afghanistan and Bangladesh, respectively).

4.2.2 Financially Excluded for Religious Reasons: Who and Where?

About five percent (or 125 million) of the unbanked adults around the world reported religious reasons for not having an account. But who are these adults, which religion they adhere to, and in which region and countries they reside in? A review of Table 4.1 shows

Table 4.1 Reasons of financial exclusion by country in 2011. *Source* Global Financial Inclusion (Global Findex) Database; author's own calculation. OIC countries are in bold

Country	Adults with no account (% age 15 +)	Too far away (% unbanked adults)	Too expensive (% unbanked adults)	Lack of necessary documentation (% unbanked adults)	Lack of Trust (% unbanked adults)	Lack of Money (% unbanked adults)	Religious (% unbanked adults)	Family member already has one (% unbanked adults)
Afghanistan	**91**	**39**	**37**	**37**	**37**	**40**	**32**	**13**
Albania	**72**	**11**	**14**	**14**	**12**	**49**	**7**	**17**
Angola	60	18	30	37	21	48	11	15
Argentina	67	5	36	20	27	62	1	13
Armenia	83	8	23	17	24	74	0	5
Australia	1	0	0	0	0	34	0	24
Austria	1	0	4	1	3	20	0	8
Azerbaijan	**85**	**5**	**16**	**22**	**20**	**68**	**5**	**6**
Bangladesh	**60**	**13**	**30**	**10**	**9**	**71**	**4**	**23**
Belarus	41	20	14	13	28	65	3	24
Belgium	2	0	3	5	1	0	0	34
Benin	**90**	**23**	**26**	**37**	**24**	**91**	**2**	**5**
Bolivia	72	35	41	15	34	52	2	14
Bosnia and Herzegovina	**43**	**14**	**14**	**13**	**19**	**53**	**1**	**36**
Botswana	70	36	35	46	19	89	5	9
Brazil	44	15	42	25	19	62	1	29
Bulgaria	47	10	12	11	25	83	0	20
Burkina Faso	**87**	**30**	**28**	**21**	**9**	**90**	**1**	**2**
Burundi	93	15	39	9	7	87	2	1
Cambodia	96	15	10	10	15	87	4	2
Cameroon	**85**	**24**	**27**	**11**	**29**	**79**	**1**	**1**

(continued)

Table 4.1 (continued)

Country	Adults with no account (% age 15 +)	Too far away (% unbanked adults)	Too expensive (% unbanked adults)	Lack of necessary documentation (% unbanked adults)	Lack of Trust (% unbanked adults)	Lack of Money (% unbanked adults)	Religious (% unbanked adults)	Family member already has one (% unbanked adults)
Canada	4	20	30	1	11	16	0	44
Chad	**91**	**40**	**37**	**42**	**23**	**60**	**9**	**13**
Chile	58	10	45	23	37	65	2	11
China	36	13	8	7	3	57	0	31
Colombia	70	10	47	17	30	61	2	15
Comoros	**78**	**9**	**15**	**22**	**10**	**82**	**6**	**6**
Congo, Dem. Rep.	96	34	26	22	23	71	2	1
Congo, Rep.	91	11	13	26	9	81	0	2
Costa Rica	50	9	19	16	20	33	2	21
Croatia	11	10	11	20	13	53	0	36
Cyprus	**15**	**3**	**7**	**1**	**8**	**34**	**1**	**29**
Czech Republic	19	11	45	10	41	69	3	46
Denmark	0	0	0	30	0	30	0	30
Djibouti	**87**	**20**	**31**	**24**	**18**	**69**	**22**	**13**
Dominican Republic	62	4	15	14	11	73	1	6
Ecuador	63	18	38	21	29	53	4	14
Egypt, Arab Rep.	**90**	**1**	**13**	**5**	**2**	**95**	**3**	**2**
El Salvador	86	16	29	24	19	38	3	7
Estonia	3	16	14	6	8	36	2	40
Finland	0	9	9	0	0	0	0	9

(continued)

Table 4.1 (continued)

Country	Adults with no account (% age 15 +)	Too far away (% unbanked adults)	Too expensive (% unbanked adults)	Lack of necessary documentation (% unbanked adults)	Lack of Trust (% unbanked adults)	Lack of Money (% unbanked adults)	Religious (% unbanked adults)	Family member already has one (% unbanked adults)
France	2	17	3	21	0	21	5	51
Gabon	**81**	**20**	**32**	**30**	**15**	**84**	**1**	**2**
Georgia	67	7	18	17	12	80	1	9
Germany	1	4	4	20	16	17	0	28
Ghana	71	28	21	22	17	83	2	5
Greece	22	7	10	4	21	73	2	44
Guatemala	78	18	31	28	24	61	5	14
Guinea	**96**	**22**	**22**	**26**	**7**	**89**	**5**	**2**
Haiti	78	25	35	34	31	67	9	8
Honduras	79	20	24	19	21	52	4	13
Hong Kong SAR, China	11	31	37	46	27	77	14	57
Hungary	27	10	39	6	29	70	0	27
India	65	23	24	17	8	63	8	41
Indonesia	**80**	**37**	**43**	**27**	**9**	**83**	**1**	**9**
Iraq	**89**	**15**	**17**	**13**	**32**	**66**	**24**	**10**
Ireland	6	16	31	10	9	35	4	53
Israel	9	6	26	28	21	60	3	37
Italy	25	0	19	5	9	32	0	29
Jamaica	27	3	12	20	12	51	3	9
Japan	2	6	0	26	0	7	0	39
Jordan	**75**	**3**	**23**	**4**	**1**	**70**	**10**	**27**
Kazakhstan	**57**	**12**	**13**	**16**	**20**	**58**	**2**	**22**

(continued)

Table 4.1 (continued)

Country	Adults with no account (% age 15 +)	Too far away (% unbanked adults)	Too expensive (% unbanked adults)	Lack of necessary documentation (% unbanked adults)	Lack of Trust (% unbanked adults)	Lack of Money (% unbanked adults)	Religious (% unbanked adults)	Family member already has one (% unbanked adults)
Kenya	58	35	43	25	12	88	4	5
Korea, Rep.	7	13	9	14	7	30	0	45
Kosovo	55	12	17	12	12	40	10	33
Kuwait	**13**	**2**	**15**	**32**	**3**	**32**	**2**	**81**
Kyrgyz Republic	**96**	**32**	**18**	**11**	**21**	**73**	**7**	**3**
Lao PDR	73	21	13	8	7	85	1	8
Latvia	10	11	4	4	13	64	0	38
Lebanon	**63**	**2**	**27**	**1**	**7**	**82**	**7**	**19**
Lesotho	82	49	51	33	14	84	3	11
Liberia	81	36	29	43	30	71	6	12
Lithuania	26	6	12	11	28	71	0	40
Luxembourg	4	2	5	4	5	32	2	59
Macedonia, FYR	26	15	19	25	22	58	7	43
Malawi	83	13	25	17	10	89	1	2
Malaysia	**33**	**27**	**16**	**35**	**3**	**56**	**0**	**26**
Mali	**92**	**35**	**21**	**23**	**8**	**87**	**3**	**2**
Malta	5	1	5	2	9	38	0	32
Mauritania	**83**	**31**	**29**	**23**	**24**	**66**	**16**	**13**
Mauritius	20	7	8	19	8	66	2	31
Mexico	71	19	47	21	29	35	2	12
Moldova	82	12	29	12	28	87	2	7
Mongolia	22	18	5	8	7	61	0	49

(continued)

Table 4.1 (continued)

Country	Adults with no account (% age 15 +)	Too far away (% unbanked adults)	Too expensive (% unbanked adults)	Lack of necessary documentation (% unbanked adults)	Lack of Trust (% unbanked adults)	Lack of Money (% unbanked adults)	Religious (% unbanked adults)	Family member already has one (% unbanked adults)
Montenegro	49	5	13	18	19	65	5	32
Morocco	**61**	**18**	**49**	**36**	**22**	**60**	**25**	**32**
Mozambique	**60**	**13**	**18**	**27**	**10**	**78**	**2**	**10**
Nepal	74	25	25	9	6	71	1	18
Netherlands	0	0	8	0	0	8	0	26
New Zealand	0	13	0	0	75	13	0	75
Nicaragua	86	17	25	27	18	36	10	11
Niger	**98**	**68**	**54**	**59**	**37**	**92**	**23**	**4**
Nigeria	**70**	**30**	**37**	**40**	**13**	**83**	**3**	**8**
Oman	**26**	**13**	**17**	**21**	**19**	**56**	**15**	**54**
Pakistan	**89**	**14**	**13**	**14**	**8**	**71**	**7**	**9**
Panama	75	20	28	40	34	33	10	22
Paraguay	78	9	11	8	20	72	5	14
Peru	79	24	55	16	37	54	2	11
Philippines	73	34	51	42	14	78	7	26
Poland	29	11	24	15	24	68	1	27
Portugal	15	1	9	2	10	23	1	11
Romania	55	11	19	12	23	69	0	13
Russian Federation	51	12	15	13	38	69	4	22
Rwanda	67	24	38	19	6	88	1	7
Saudi Arabia	**53**	**5**	**12**	**13**	**10**	**45**	**23**	**51**
Senegal	**94**	**28**	**37**	**34**	**13**	**84**	**6**	**5**

(continued)

Table 4.1 (continued)

Country	Adults with no account (% age 15 +)	Too far away (% unbanked adults)	Too expensive (% unbanked adults)	Lack of necessary documentation (% unbanked adults)	Lack of Trust (% unbanked adults)	Lack of Money (% unbanked adults)	Religious (% unbanked adults)	Family member already has one (% unbanked adults)
Serbia	37	10	18	22	17	58	1	35
Sierra Leone	**85**	**37**	**44**	**42**	**20**	**82**	**9**	**7**
Singapore	2	0	16	0	6	71	0	28
Slovak Republic	20	15	44	11	29	75	0	41
Slovenia	3	5	24	21	6	63	0	66
South Africa	46	34	40	23	18	73	3	12
Spain	7	19	30	19	32	52	9	42
Sri Lanka	31	26	17	13	12	67	2	27
Sudan	**93**	**23**	**45**	**27**	**13**	**82**	**4**	**15**
Swaziland	71	30	34	38	13	72	6	10
Sweden	1	0	19	39	10	10	0	0
Syrian Arab Republic	**77**	**9**	**33**	**0**	**4**	**27**	**15**	**2**
Taiwan, China	12	7	9	10	7	43	6	44
Tajikistan	**97**	**28**	**18**	**22**	**21**	**78**	**8**	**4**
Tanzania	83	48	46	35	13	78	4	8
Thailand	27	13	9	4	3	57	1	47
Togo	**90**	**27**	**20**	**32**	**17**	**91**	**1**	**2**
Trinidad and Tobago	21	4	35	38	13	67	1	10
Tunisia	**68**	**15**	**25**	**17**	**18**	**73**	**26**	**20**
Turkey	**42**	**13**	**26**	**21**	**26**	**48**	**7**	**20**
Turkmenistan	**100**	**36**	**12**	**21**	**10**	**52**	**10**	**3**

(continued)

Table 4.1 (continued)

Country	Adults with no account (% age 15 +)	Too far away (% unbanked adults)	Too expensive (% unbanked adults)	Lack of necessary documentation (% unbanked adults)	Lack of Trust (% unbanked adults)	Lack of Money (% unbanked adults)	Religious (% unbanked adults)	Family member already has one (% unbanked adults)
Uganda	**80**	**42**	**54**	**38**	**23**	**85**	**3**	**7**
Ukraine	59	24	19	11	55	67	4	18
United Kingdom	2	20	29	10	32	21	6	13
United States	11	14	28	17	46	49	7	19
Uruguay	76	7	26	8	19	70	0	5
Uzbekistan	**77**	**19**	**7**	**16**	**15**	**60**	**6**	**9**
Venezuela, RB	55	8	16	3	16	75	0	15
Vietnam	78	13	8	13	9	50	1	12
West Bank and Gaza	**81**	**3**	**23**	**5**	**12**	**67**	**24**	**18**
Yemen, Rep.	**96**	**13**	**17**	**9**	**8**	**86**	**9**	**3**
Zambia	79	21	50	32	9	85	1	6
Zimbabwe	60	14	39	27	20	82	1	8

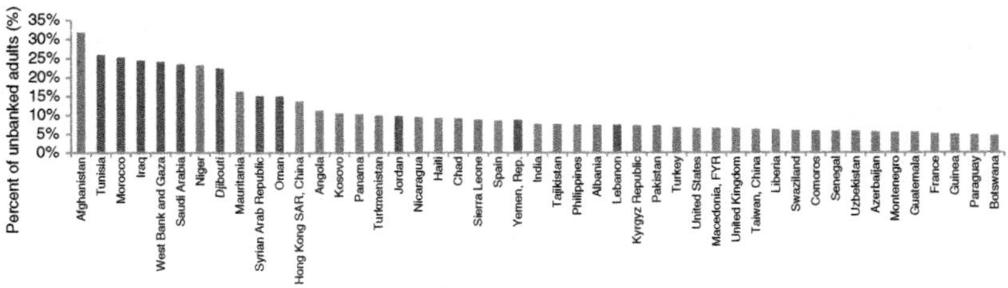

Fig. 4.5 Financially excluded due to religious reasons, 2011. *Source* Global Financial Inclusion (Global Findex) Database; author's own calculation. *Note* Green and red bars refer to countries where followers of Islam constitute at least 60% or more of the population. Red bars refer to countries in the MENA region

that compared to other countries, the unbanked adults in Muslim-majority countries tend to have higher likelihood of citing religious reasons for not having an account. This information is summarized in Fig. 4.5. As evident from this figure, 28 out of 47 countries where religious reasons were cited by at least 4% of the unbanked adults are countries where Muslims constitute majority of the total population (highlighted in green and red bars). From these 28 countries, 11 are located in the MENA region (highlighted in red bars). It is important here to realize that while about 5% of adults worldwide cited religious reasons for not having an account, financial exclusion rates because of religious reasons are above 20% for eight OIC countries, six of which are located in the MENA region. Furthermore, 13 OIC countries (which include eight MENA countries) have financial exclusion rates because of religious reasons at 10% or more. Overall, based on Global Findex, about 12% of unbanked individuals in the Arab MENA (or 17 million) and 7% of the unbanked in OIC member countries (or 47 million) reported not having an account because of religious reasons.[9]

Figure 4.6 also confirms that self-identified Muslims are about twice less likely to have an account in comparison with their non-Muslim counterparts (24% vs. 44%), and this gap is about 13% points in the MENA region.

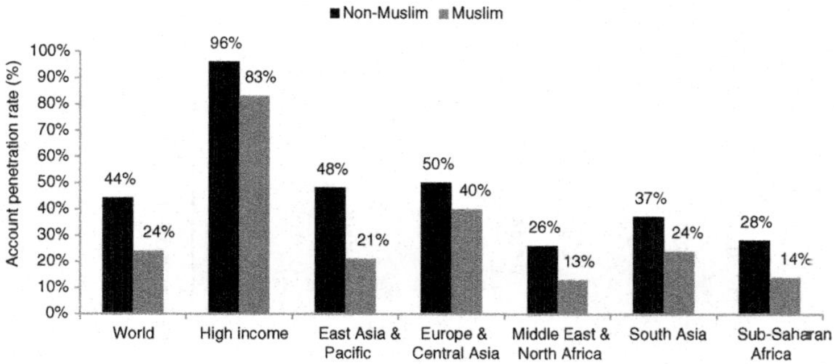

Fig. 4.6 Differences in financial inclusion between Muslims and non-Muslims, 2011. *Source* Demirguc-Kunt, Klaper, and Randall (2013). *Note* The difference between Muslims and non-Muslim is statistically significant at 1% level. Analysis is based on 64 countries. Countries with less than 1% and more than 99% Muslim population are excluded from the analysis

Cross-country regressions also support the idea presented in tables and figures above. Regression results in Table 4.2[10] and a close look at changes in R-squared values between different models and the size and significance of coefficients suggest that being in the MENA region followed by share of Muslim population in a given country is the most important determining factor for being financially excluded because of religious reasons.

Overall, the available data, albeit limited in scope, suggest that financial exclusion due to religious reasons is a phenomenon that is predominantly characteristic of Muslim-majority countries and especially those in the MENA region. In other words, in comparison with other religious and non-religious communities around the world, the followers of Islam are more likely to avoid formal financial institutions altogether because of religious reasons as the operations of vast majority of those institutions are primarily interest oriented.

4.2.3 Islamic Finance and Financial Inclusion

Based on the evidence presented thus far, it could be argued that enhancing the size of and access to *Shari'ah*-compliant financial

Table 4.2 Determinant of financial exclusion due to religious reasons

	Model 1	Model 2	Model 3	Model 4	Model 5	Model 6	Model 7	Model 8	Model 9
GDP (2005 Billion $)	0.000061	0.000255	0.000091	0.00028*	0.00034*	0.00158	0.00032*	0.00054***	0.00036*
GDP per Capita, PPP (2005 international thousand $)	−0.0694*	−0.0110	0.0152	0.0236	−0.0416	−0.0892	−0.0256	−0.123	−0.0666
Muslim Population (% total population)		**0.0927*** **		**0.0914*** **	**0.0762*** **	**0.0512*** **	**0.0755*** **	**0.0624*** **	**0.0626*** **
Religiosity (% adults)			0.0745***	0.0258	−0.0160	−0.00866	−0.0172	−0.0209	−0.0190
East Asia and Pacific dummy					−1.480	−1.907	−1.953	−1.674	−1.802
Europe and Central Asia dummy					−1.476	−0.233	−2.071	−1.487	−1.695
Latin America & the Caribbean dummy					1.291	0.499	0.978	0.915	0.646
Middle East and North Africa dummy					**6.493***	**7.997** **	**5.906***	**9.447** **	**8.926** **
South Asia dummy					3.018	−3.642	2.044	2.789	2.982
Sub-Saharan Africa dummy					−0.224	−2.991	−2.382	−1.318	−1.322
Literacy rate (% people 15+)						−0.0964			
Life expectancy at birth							−0.116		
Commercial bank Branches per 100,000 adults								−0.00142	
Commercial bank branches per 1000 km^2									−0.00791***
Observations	133	133	102	102	102	83	102	86	86
R-Squared	0.024	0.361	0.071	0.364	0.455	0.536	0.459	0.500	0.546

Note OLS regressions with robust standard errors. * $p<0.10$, ** $p<0.05$, *** $p<0.01$. Dependent variable is the percentage of adults reporting religious reasons for not having an account, which is taken from Global Findex Database. GDP and GDP per capita are included in all models as proxies for the quality of institutions

Table 4.3 Density of *Shari'ah*-compliant assets and financial exclusion due to religious reasons

	Model 1	Model 2
GDP (2005 Billion $)	0.000527***	0.000420***
GDP per Capita, PPP (2005 international thousand $)	–0.0791*	–0.0405
Religiosity (% adults)	0.00559	0.0102
Muslim population (% total)	0.0718***	0.0623**
Middle East and North Africa dummy	11.97***	11.31***
Commercial bank branches per 1000 km2	–0.00748**	–0.00636*
Ratio of *Shari'ah*-compliant assets to total assets (%)	**–0.296*** **	
***Shari'ah*-compliant assets per adult (1000s $)**		**–0.553*** **
Observations	85	86
R-Squared	0.588	0.557

Note OLS regression with robust standard errors. * $p<0.10$, ** $p<0.05$, *** $p<0.01$. Dependent variable is the percentage of adults reporting religious reason for not having an account, which is taken from the Global Findex Database. Only those variables that were significant in at least one of the models in Table 4.2 were included in these regressions. *Shari'ah*-compliant (Islamic) assets and total assets are from BankScope

products can reduce voluntary financial exclusion because of religious reasons. In other words, if the earlier findings are true, one should expect to see a negative relationship between the density of *Shari'ah*-compliant financial services and the percentage of adults that are unbanked due to religious reasons. Table 4.3 provides some evidence supporting this hypothesis. The negative and statistically significant coefficients for two different measures of density of *Shari'ah*-compliant assets show that after controlling for other relevant factors, the percentages of people who report religious reasons for not having an account in formal financial institutions are lower in countries where Islamic finance has stronger presence in the formal banking sector. Put differently, one could expect that as the density of *Shari'ah*-compliant assets increases, the share of unbanked people because of religious reasons decreases.

This suggests that increasing the presence of formal *Shari'ah*-compliant financial services in countries with considerable Muslim population could reduce the level of voluntary exclusion from formal financial institutions because of religious considerations. At the very minimum, this is certainly true for at least 13 million adults who, according to Global Findex Database, cited only and only religious reasons for not having an account, more than 11 million of which reside in OIC member countries.

Table 4.4 provides some anecdotal evidence that increasing the share of *Shari'ah*-compliant assets vis-à-vis total banking assets in a country can help reduce the percentage of small firms who cite access to finance as a major obstacle for their operations. This is in line with the fact that small firms are often managed and operated by members of a family, where religious considerations are more likely to surface in their financing decisions when compared to medium and large firms, which are often operated by professional executives who might also be from non-Islamic backgrounds and thus have lesser or no care toward *Shari'ah*-compliant financing.

4.2.4 Islamic Finance and Financial Inclusion in Other Studies and Reports

In addition to the empirical results above, several recent case studies have also highlighted the potential role of Islamic finance in reducing voluntary financial exclusion among the Muslim population in both Muslim-majority and Muslim-minority countries. For example, Adeyemi et al. (2012) show that Islamic microfinance can in fact provide financial services to a considerable segment of Nigerian society whom for religious reasons avoid dealings with conventional financial institutions. Also, according to the 2006 Sachar Committee Report on the status of minorities in India, the share of Muslims in amount outstanding is about 4.6% while that of other minorities is about 6.5%, which is disproportionate to their share in India's population (13.4% for Muslims and 5.6% for other minorities). In a joint report prepared by Infinity Consultants and Ethica Institute of Islamic Finance, it is proposed that only through increasing the presence of Islamic Finance in India's financial fabric, the Indian government can increase the use of financial services by its largest minority group, the 180 million Muslims

Table 4.4 Density of *Shari'ah*-compliant assets and financial obstacles of firms

	All firms	Small firms	Medium firms	Large firms
GDP (2005 Billion $)	0.00527	0.00256	0.00437	0.0117
GDP per Capita, PPP (2005 international thousand $)	–0.648*	–0.670**	–0.466	–0.578
Religiosity (% adults)	0.0449	0.0903	–0.0282	0.0311
Muslim population (% total)	–0.0107	–0.0219	0.00266	0.00703
East Asia and Pacific dummy	–7.151	–4.761	–0.674	–14.36
Europe and Central Asia dummy	6.191	8.228	6.648	4.250
Latin America & the Caribbean dummy	2.243	3.251	5.120	–6.898
Middle East and North Africa dummy	14.63	21.39***	22.01	38.76
South Asia dummy	–2.692	–1.287	3.233	–7.182
Sub-Saharan Africa dummy	17.36*	20.30**	19.21*	0.186
Commercial bank branches per 1000 km^2	–0.0419	–0.169	–0.0225	–0.214
Ratio of *Shari'ah*-compliant assets to total assets (%)	**–0.0723**	**–0.157*** **	**–0.389**	**–0.744**
Observations	68	68	68	68
R-Squared	0.475	0.482	0.375	0.384

Note OLS regression with robust standard errors. * $p<0.10$, ** $p<0.05$, *** $p<0.01$. Dependent variable is the percentage of firms reporting access to finance as a major obstacle in their operations, which is from World Bank Enterprise Survey. Only those variables that were significant in at least one of the models in Table 4.2 were included in these regressions. Shari'ah-compliant (Islamic) assets and total assets are from BankScope.

residing in India.[11] This will add to the economic growth of India while at the same time increasing the well-being of and reducing poverty among its poverty-ridden Muslim population.

Over the past few years, an increasing number of Muslim and non-Muslim policymakers, central bank governors, and politicians have also shown growing interest for a more pronounced presence of Islamic finance in the global financial architecture because of its potentially important role in enhancing financial inclusion. In her Islamic Development Bank (IDB) Prize Lecture On November 2013, Governor Zeti Akhtar Aziz, Governor of the Central Bank of Malaysia (Bank Negara Malaysia), referred to the potential role of Islamic financing modes in enhancing financial inclusion.[12] Again, in November 2013, the governor of Central Bank of Nigeria, Mr. Lamido Sanusi, identified Islamic finance as having the capacity of increasing financial inclusion among a large segment of population in Nigeria. In September 2013, Mr. Nestor Espenilla, deputy governor of the Bangko Sentral Pilipinas (BSP), Philippines' central bank, laid out one of the most ambitious efforts in the world in introducing Islamic finance in a Muslim-minority country, in an effort to enhance financial inclusion among the Muslim population of Philippines.[13] Finally, on December 2013, IMF's Director of Middle East and Central Asia Department, Mr. Masood Ahmed, highlighted the fact that if properly regulated, faster expansion of Islamic finance in MENA can lead to higher levels of financial inclusion among religiously minded population.[14]

4.2.5 Concluding Remarks

Based on the above, it is safe to suggest that Islamic finance can play an important role in enhancing financial inclusion among the unbanked adults in OIC member countries. For example, risk-sharing contracts such as *Murabahah*, *Musharakah*, and *Mudarabah* as well as wealth redistribution instruments in the Islamic financial system such as *Zakat*, *Sadaqa*, and *Qard Hassan* are a few of the main mechanisms through which Islamic finance could promote financial inclusion, boost shared prosperity, and reduce poverty and inequality.

Shari'ah-compliant risk-sharing contracts can provide access to finance and insurance (*Takaful*) for micro, small, and medium enterprises (MSMEs). This is crucial because as pointed by World Bank's Enterprise Survey somewhere between 30 and 40% of all small- and medium-sized firms in the MENA region identify access to finance as a major constraint in their operations. Furthermore, built in the Islamic law and code of ethics is mandatory and voluntary almsgiving known as *Zakat* and *Sadaqa*, respectively, with *Qard Hassan* falling between the two (as discussed below). Through analyzing the available data for nine MENA countries, Mohieldin et al. (2012) find that if implemented effectively, *Zakat* funds in all these countries are more than sufficient to eliminate the extreme poverty (measured as having an income of less US$1.25 a day).[15]

It must be pointed out that while increasing the availability of Islamic finance is a necessary ingredient for increasing access to finance and insurance for the poor households and MSMEs, other supporting factors such as adequate physical, legal, financial, regulatory, and educational infrastructure must also be in place for Islamic finance to operate effectively and efficiently. It is a reality that most OIC member countries lack many of these necessary prerequisites, creating extra hurdles for growth and efficient operation of *Shari'ah*-compliant financial institutions in OIC member countries. As a result, community-based local financing schemes seem to be the most appropriate venue for boosting financial inclusion among the estimated 700 million poor residing in OIC member countries. *Murabahah* (cost plus markup sale contract) and *Qard Hassan* (benevolent interest-free loan) are examples of such locally oriented Islamic financing programs, which are also the most popular forms of Islamic microfinance schemes in the MENA region and other Muslim-majority countries such as Indonesia, Pakistan, and Bangladesh (Fig. 4.7). These schemes are practically risk-free financial instruments suitable for the vulnerable and the poor who would otherwise have no other opportunity of access to financial services. This would in turn increase the chance of the poor to move themselves out of poverty by potentially providing them with a temporary financial breathing space, increasing financial literacy and capability, and building credit history.

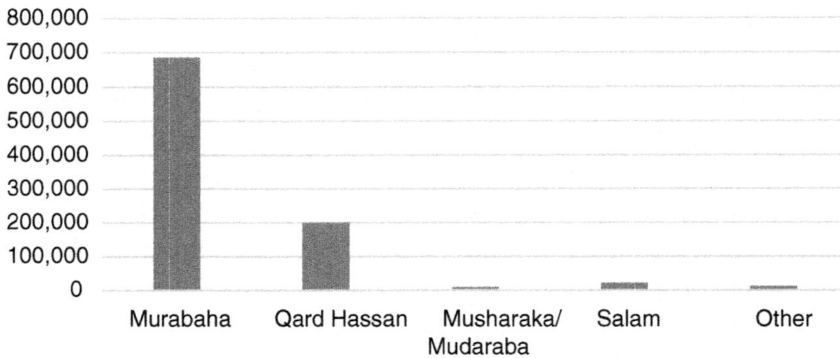

Fig. 4.7 Islamic microfinance schemes, number of active clients, by product type. *Source* El-Zoghbi and Tarazi (2013). *Note* Countries included are Afghanistan, Bangladesh, Burkina Faso, Cambodia, Cameroon, Côte d'Ivoire, Egypt, Iraq, Indonesia, Jordan, Kosovo, Lebanon Pakistan Palestine (West bank and Gaza), Saudi Arabia, Sri Lanka, Sudan, Syria, and Yemen

4.3 Qard Hassan

In order to gain a better understanding of *Qard Hassan* (*QH*), it is necessary to juxtapose this financial instrument with some of the other main Islamic financial instruments. Therefore, a brief list and explanation of each of the main Islamic financial instruments is provided below:

- *Mudarabah* (Profit-Sharing). Supplier of capital contracts with a working partner on the basis of sharing the resulting profits. Losses, if any, are considered loss of capital and borne by the owner of capital. The working partner, in that case, goes unrewarded for its efforts. This is the "loss" borne by the working partner, a feature of *Mudarabah* which has made some to characterize it as profit and loss sharing (PLS). The sharing contract when applied to farming is called *Muzara'ah* or sharecropping.
- *Shirkah* or *Musharakah* (Partnership). In partnership, two or more parties supply capital as well as work/effort. They share the resulting profits according to agreed proportions, but losses are to be borne in proportion to respective capitals.
- *Murabahah*. A sale agreement under which the seller purchases goods desired by a buyer and sells it to him/her at an agreed marked up

price, payment being deferred. It is also referred to as *Bay' Mu'ajjal* or *Bay' bi Thaman Ajil*. It is a modern adaptation of an earlier contract in which deferment was not necessarily involved. The higher price paid would leave a margin for the seller in order to reward him/her for expertise in bargaining and better knowledge of market conditions.

- *Wakala* (Agency). An agent appointed by the principal-owner manages business. Agent's compensation may take different forms.
- *Ju'ala*. Reward that is given on successful completion of a specified job. There is no compensation in case of failure.
- *Ijara*. It refers to the leasing of a property, capital good, or any other good.
- *Salam* (Future Contract). Payment is extended now for agricultural products to be delivered at a specified time in future with the price agreed upon now.
- *Istisna'*. *Salam* applied to manufactured goods, with the possibility of payment in installments as the goods are delivered.
- *Urboon*. Depositing a small fraction of price in a deal to be concluded in future. It binds the seller to wait but allows the buyer to back out of the deal, with the seller keeping the deposit.
- *Qard* (Interest-free Loan). The only acceptable loans in Islamic financial institutions (IFIs) which are interest-free loan.
- *Qard Hassan* (The Benevolent Loan). It is a charitable loan which, in addition to being a *Qard* (interest-free loan), also contains elements of goodwill, benevolence, and generosity.
- *Zakat* (Mandatory). Money or any form of capital donated to the poor on a mandatory basis, the rates and conditions of which are stipulated by the *Shari'ah*.
- *Sadaqa* (Voluntary Alms). In-kind or monetary donations to the poor on a voluntary basis.

From the above list, the instruments of *Qard*, *Qard Hassan*, *Zakat*, and *Sadaqa* are particularly fit to address the financial needs of the vulnerable[16] and the poor. This is because the poor are often highly risk averse and are therefore unwilling to participate in risk-sharing business contracts such as *Mudarabah* and *Musharakah*. Furthermore, the poor usually lack the necessary physical and human capital as well as basic financial literacy and capability to establish and maintain successful business and financial partnerships. As a result, *Qard*, *Qard Hassan* (*QH*), *Zakat*, and *Sadaqa* are the most appropriate financial instruments to address the financing needs of the vulnerable and the poor.

4.3.1 Qard Hassan: Qard and Ihsan

QH is composed of two elements that are clearly laid out in its name: *Qard* (interest-free loan) and *Ihsan* (goodwill, benevolence, and generosity). Mirakhor and Iqbal (2007) provide a detailed discussion of *QH* terminology and the relevant *Quranic* verses referring it. Below, some of the main *Shari'ah* guidelines of *QH* as it pertains to its elements of *Qard* and *Ihsan* are highlighted separately. First, let's highlight the main *Shari'ah* requirement for the *Qard* component of *QH*:

1. A contract is completed in accordance with Islamic guidelines.
2. The lender may ask the borrower for collateral or guarantee.
3. While the borrower has to repay the principle, he/she is not obligated to make any form of interest payments for the loan.
4. The lender cannot request a payment from the borrower prior to the agreed date stipulated on the contact.
5. If the borrower manages to make positive profits, the lender cannot expect to receive any portion of it.
6. The borrower may only use the loan for the agreed activity(s) stated in the contract. If the borrower fails to do so, the contract is voided, and the lender can request for an immediate repayment of the principle.
7. In the case of borrower's default, the lender may not take possession of the borrower's basic living needs (shelter, cloth, food, and the capital by which the borrower makes a living for himself and his dependents).

Now, some of the features associated with the *Ihsan* element of *QH* are highlighted. All of these features are rooted in the Islamic code of conduct (*Akhlaq*) that is driven from many *Quranic* verses and traditions of the Prophet Muhammad (i.e., *hadith*) and are only voluntary in nature:

1. The lender is willing to extend a *QH* loan without requesting a collateral and/or guarantor.
2. If the borrower, due to factors beyond his control, fails to adhere to the terms of contract, the lender is willing to be benevolent and flexible toward the borrower. Furthermore, if the borrower, because of unexpected events and factors beyond his control, defaults on the loan, the lender is willing to forgive or restructure the debt. This would essentially convert a *QH* into *Sadaqa*.
3. The lender is expected to reserve the usage of social[17] and legal enforcement mechanisms only for scenarios where the borrower is using the *QH* funds in an irresponsible and wasteful manner and in ways that are contrary to the original *QH* contract.
4. In cases of default or latency in the payment, if the lender does not forgive the debt, the borrower is expected to abide by the terms of the contract as soon as he is able to do so. An intentional failure in this regard by the borrower is considered to be a sinful (*Haram*) act and must be avoided.

From the above, one can safely argue that *QH* is an Islamic financial instrument that stands somewhere between *Qard* and *Sadaqa*. In other words, when *Ihsan* (or goodwill, benevolence, and generosity) is applied to a *Qard* contract, it will convert *Qard* into a *QH*. Furthermore, in case of unexpected and genuine financial hardships of the part of the borrower, through forgiving some or all of the *QH* loans, a *QH* can in turn be turned into *Sadaqa*; in such a scenario, *Ihsan* is clearly applied at its maximum level of forgiving the debt.

It must be emphasized that *Ihsan* elements of *QH* must not and in fact cannot be explicitly written in a *QH* contract and are practiced on purely volunteer basis by the lender. Therefore, a *QH* contract starts as regular interest-free loan (*Qard*) agreement, and only when the lender relaxes some or all of the terms of the *Qard* contract and acts in a charitable manner toward the borrower, the original interest-free loan *(Qard)* would be converted to *QH* and possibly *Sadaqa* (Fig. 4.8).

It becomes clear that there is a common misunderstanding in the literature where *Qard* is often seen and treated as synonymous to *QH*. While every *QH*, because of being an interest-free debt, is a *Qard*, the

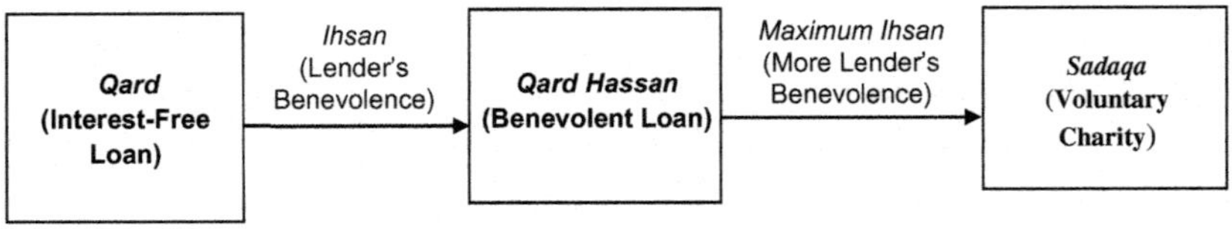

Fig. 4.8 Relationship between *Qard, Qard Hassan*, and *Sadaqa*. *Source* Author's own illustration

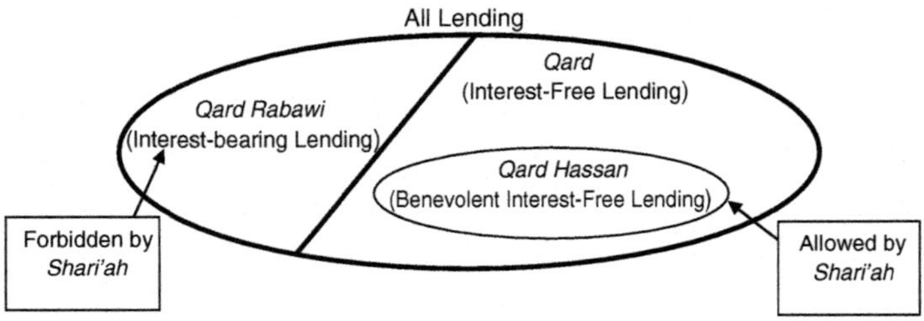

Fig. 4.9 Venn diagram of all lending: *Qard Rabawi, Qard,* and *Qard Hassan*. *Source* Author's own illustration

reverse is not true. Farooq (2010) discusses this issue in length and emphasizes the fact that an interest-free loan is simply a *Qard* and not a *QH* because *Shari'ah* requires every loan or *Qard* to be interest-free in the first place. In other words, *Shari'ah* does not recognize interest-bearing lending as *Qard*. Such lending is termed as *Qard Rabawi* highlighting the fact that the term *Qard* in *Shari'ah* is referring to interest-free lending, making *QH* to be something beyond interest-free lending (Fig. 4.9). So, in a nutshell:

- *Qard Rabawi*: is an interest-bearing loan that is considered as a grave sin by *Shari'ah* and thus forbidden.
- *Qard*: is an interest-free loan that is recognized as lawful by *Shari'ah*.
- *Qard Hassan*: is an interest-free loan (*Qard*) that has elements of *Ihsan* or benevolence added to the *Qard*.

Therefore, the majority of the so-called formal *QH* funds and institutions in Muslim countries actually operate on *Qard* principles as the elements of *Ihsan* are widely missing through the application of different kinds of fees including late repayment fees and the requirement of collateral.

4.3.2 Financial Needs of the Poor: Qard Hassan vs. Qard and *Zakat/Sadaqa*

The poor are heterogeneous in the factors leading to their poverty. Therefore, their financial needs are also diverse.[18] While in comparison with other Islamic financial instruments, *Qard, Qard Hassan, and Zakat/Sadaqa* are more appropriate mechanisms to address the needs of the poor and vulnerable, any of these instruments are more suitable in a given context.

4.3.3 Qard Hassan vs. *Zakat/Sadaqa*

Besides the many legal and contractual differences between *Zakat/Sadaqa* and *QH*, there are many differences between these two instruments in as far as their applicability and efficiency are concerned. First is related to the heterogeneous nature of poverty and characteristics of the poor. Given that *QH* funds are often much larger in size and less frequent than *Zakat/Sadaqa*, they are suitable to finance human capital investment and entrepreneurial activities of the poor and the vulnerable. As a result, *QH* is, and *Zakat/Sadaqa* is not, a suitable financing mechanism for those poor and vulnerable that are financially savvy and have financial and entrepreneurship capabilities but lack the necessary capital. Furthermore, in cases where one's poverty is a direct result of sudden adverse shocks,[19] *QH* is again a better form of financing, because in such cases the borrower has a higher likelihood to move out of poverty in the near future and thus repay the debt.

QH can and again *Zakat/Sadaqa* cannot be used to prevent potential poverty in the future among those people who are not currently poor but have high likelihoods of slipping into poverty if not financially assisted now. This is because, in the Islamic legal system, *Zakat/Sadaqa* funds are not to be allocated to those who are not currently poor. Students with little or no financial support are one clear example. If not supported throughout their schooling years, many borderline poor students would have to drop out of school and join the labor force, jeopardizing their future income trajectory and economic well-being, the negative impacts of which may also impact their future generations.

Zakat/Sadaqa are appropriate forms of financing for those poor who have little or no outlook, at least in the near future, to become economically productive and overcome poverty. Such people include the elderly, the children, the refugees, and the permanently ill and the mentally or physically challenged.

Second, while *QH* and *Zakat/Sadaqa* both depend on the benevolence and goodwill of the lenders and donors, when compared to *Zakat/Sadaqa*, *QH* is associated with a number of advantages as it motivates a more responsible set of decisions and behaviors on the part of the borrowers as well as the lenders. In comparison with *Zakat/Sadaqa*, *QH* is more likely to encourage financial responsibility, productivity, and hard work on the part of the borrower while there are no such mechanisms in *Zakat/Sadaqa*. The recipients of the *QH*, in order not to jeopardize their image and reputation in the local community and their creditworthiness for future financial contracts, would be more motivated to abide by the terms in a *QH* contract to the best of their ability. As a result, they will be more inclined to exert more effort and to be more cautious and prudent in their expenditures, investments, and other economic activities. On the other hand, such motivations are less or altogether missing for *Zakat/Sadaqa* recipients, as they have no financial and contractual obligations toward the donors, leaving them with no external pressures and monitoring. Therefore, while, in the long run, *QH* increases financial responsibility, prudence, and independence among its recipients, *Zakat/Sadaqa* may perpetuate financial dependence and recklessness.

QH may also encourage the benevolently minded donors or lenders to act in a more responsible manner. The expectation of getting repaid motivates the *QH* lender to be cautious in his benevolent lending practices and is more likely to extend *QH* loans to only those individuals who seem to be financially dependable and responsible and have a high probability of repaying the principle and abiding by the terms of the contract. As a result, a *QH* lender will be motivated to acquire as much information about a borrower as possible, his particular economic conditions and needs, and the ways in which he is envisioning to use the

QH funds. In the case of *Zakat*/*Sadaqa*, however, because the donors do not expect any repayments, they take little to no care on who the recipients are and how the *Zakat*/*Sadaqa* funds are to going to be utilized.

As a result of this lower level of care and prudence on the part of the recipients and donors, *Zakat*/*Sadaqa* donations, which are often much smaller in size but more frequently distributed than *QH*, have higher probability of being distributed inefficiently or even end up in the hands of those who are not truly deserving of alms. This fact is highlighted in a *Hadith* from the Prophet *Muhammad* (peace be upon him and his progeny) where he considers *Qard* (and by extension *QH*) as more preferable to *Zakat*/*Sadaqa*. In this *Hadith* reported by *Imam Ja'far Ibn Muhammad as-Sadiq* as well as by *Ibn Hisham* and *Ibn Majah*, the Prophet (peace be upon him) is reported to have said:

> It is written on the gate of the paradise: The reward for Sadaqa is tenfold and the reward for Qard is eighteen times; and Qard has become superior to Sadaqa because a borrower will not borrow except because of need, while a person who does not need Sadaqa may ask for it.

Third, compared to *Zakat*/*Sadaqa*, *QH* develops stronger sense of solidarity between the lenders and the borrowers. This is because *QH* lenders, in an effort to increase the probability of full repayment, are more motivated to get to know the borrowers at personal levels and to keep an open communication channel with the borrowers throughout the duration of the contract. Overcoming the communication and cooperation gap that often exists between the "haves" and "have-nots" will inevitably lead to the development of stronger solidarity between these two groups and transfer of knowledge, skills, and expertise. In turn, this would reduce the social barriers that have often perpetuated poverty and inequality in a community.

Fourth, *QH* can be more conducive for economic development and poverty reduction than *Zakat*/*Sadaqa*. This is because *QH* recipients are more likely to be financially deserving, prudent, and responsible than *Zakat*/*Sadaqa* recipients. Therefore, one could expect for *QH* to result into better allocation of scarce financial resources than *Zakat*/*Sadaqa*.

Moreover, the repayment element of *QH* makes it possible for these funds to be recycled and circulated among several individuals or families in need. Finally, being larger in size, the recipients of *QH* could benefit from the economies of scale. As a result, *QH* is more suitable for the purposes of human capital development as well as financing of small business ventures while *Zakat*/*Sadaqa* are often used for immediate consumption needs.

Final, and probably most important of all, is the issue of protecting the honor and dignity of the poor. There is little disagreement on the importance of protecting the honor and pride of the poor and in fact, many *hadith* refer to one's honor as the most important ingredient of human capital. Contrary to *Zakat*/*Sadaqa*, *QH* has the advantage of protecting the honor and dignity of its recipients, as they consider themselves borrowing on favorable terms and not receiving alms and charity.

Overall, *QH* is a more effective financial instrument to address the needs of the vulnerable or those poor who have a higher likelihood of moving out of poverty if financial helped now. On the other hand, *Zakat*/*Sadaqa* funds should mainly be channeled to those poor who have little or no likelihood of moving out of poverty or have pressing needs (such as food, medical care, and shelter) that must be immediately addressed.

4.3.4 Qard Hassan vs. Qard

As mentioned earlier, *Qard* refers to an interest-free loan contract that may also include other mutually agreed conditions such as the necessity of collateral and guarantor and penalties for late payments. Therefore, the element of *Ihsan* in *QH* makes this instrument more attractive to the poor than a pure *Qard* contract because in cases of unpredictable financial hardships, the poor can probably receive a benevolent treatment from a *QH* lender whereas such treatments are absent in a purely *Qard* contract. As a result, some of the poor who shy away from *Qard* or other financial contracts may in fact welcome *QH*. *Qard* is most suitable for the non-poor who are financially more stable and need extra sources of financing to cover unexpected expenditures or undertake a planned economic activity such as purchasing a real estate or starting or expanding a business. Also, many of the poor lack adequate collateral or guarantor, making it harder for them to access *Qard* contracts.

To sum, for the vulnerable and poor, *QH* has many economic, social, and psychological advantages over *Zakat*/*Sadaqa* and *Qard*. Keeping in mind the heterogeneous nature of poverty and economic vulnerability, *QH* and *Zakat*/*Sadaqa* are complements rather than substitutes. Each of these instruments is effective and efficient in addressing certain financial needs of specific groups of the poor and those who are socially and financially marginalized. While *QH* is associated with many economic, social, and psychological advantages, it is not implemented as a wide-scale potential mechanism for reducing or preventing poverty in Muslim-majority countries. What is being widely implemented in the name of *QH* is *Qard* where various elements of *Ihsan* are altogether missing making such financing schemes inaccessible to the poor and the vulnerable. In turn, *Zakat* and *Sadaqa* have been the dominant channels of assisting the poor and the vulnerable regardless of heterogeneous causes of their poverty and differences in the level of their human capital and capabilities, leading to serious misallocations of scarce resources that are set aside for the poor.

It can be concluded that *QH*, through the various reasons highlighted above, has the potential of paving the path for the unbanked population to eventually become bankable. In other words, while *QH* can increase financial inclusion among the poor and the vulnerable, *Zakat*/*Sadaqa* do not have such mechanisms built into them. This is because *QH* has the potential to increase human and physical capital of the less privileged and reduce their social and economic marginalization, making them better positioned to engage in *Qard* and other financial contracts in the future.

4.3.5 Qard Hassan and the Question of Its Sustainability in the Long Run

Serious practical challenges have hindered *QH* to be offered through formal financial institutions. The first main obstacle relates to the above-discussed misunderstandings surrounding *QH* and its widespread confusion with *Qard*. As a result, when extending "*Qard Hassan*," majority of formal IFIs in reality are offering *Qard* and therefore often collect processing fees and require collaterals and guarantors. Not only are these policies in clear contradiction with the element of *Ihsan* (benevolence and generosity) highlighted above, but they also discourage or make it difficult for the vulnerable and the poor to enter a *QH* contract, therefore increasing their dependence on *Zakat* and *Sadaqa* and reducing their chances of ever becoming financially included and independent. To address this issue, IFIs and Islamic finance training centers need to engage in concerted training and information disseminating campaigns to clearly and more accurately present *QH* to policymakers, financial institutions, and the general public and highlight its various features and potentials for the vulnerable and the poor while also explicitly distinguishing it from *Qard*.

The second challenge relates to the distinguishing element of *QH* from *Qard*: *Ihsan*. As discussed earlier, in genuine *QH* contracts, the lenders are willing to act benevolently and generously toward the receivers of the *QH* funds who face financial hardships beyond their control. This will clearly undermine the long-run sustainability and operation of *QH* funds as the sums lent out may not get fully recovered in timely manner, posing liquidity challenges for *QH* funds. One cannot ignore the effect of inflation on sustainability and effectiveness of *QH* lending, where the purchasing power of the sum lent out as *QH* is reduced in inflationary environments, which is characteristic of many Muslim-populated countries. The following few paragraphs will address some of these issues.

First, the novel definition of *QH* presented above, will permit *Zakat* and *Sadaqa* funds to also be employed for *QH* lending to the poor who have the potential of moving out of poverty if provided with adequate financial assistance to boost their human capital or jump-start their entrepreneurial activities. It is important here to emphasize here that *QH* lending using *Zakat* and *Sadaqa* funds would only applicable to the poor and not the non-poor who run the risk of moving into poverty. *QH* lending to the non-poor facing risks of poverty needs to be funded through other source of charitable lending.

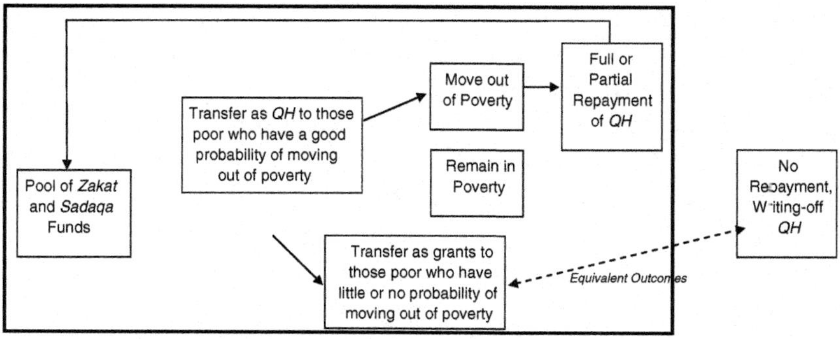

Fig. 4.10 Transfer of *Zakat* and *Sadaqa* through Grant and *QH* lending. *Source* Author's own illustration

Donors of *Zakat* and *Sadaqa* do not expect to get paid back, and their intention is to assist the poor through financial transfers. However, as discussed earlier, a group of poor, if financially assisted, have the potential of moving out of poverty and returning the financial assistance they have received. Considering this fact, *Zakat* and *Sadaqa* funds could be transferred to this group of poor in form of *QH*. Thereafter, the portion of *QH* loans that are recovered can again be transferred to other poor families in form of *QH* loans, and the portions that are not recovered are simply forgiven and translated into *Zakat* and *Sadaqa* from operational and *Shari'ah* perspective (Fig. 4.10). Through such *QH* lending process, a portion of *Zakat* and *Sadaqa* funds can reach more than one poor individual or family, not only increasing the coverage of the limited *Zakat* and *Sadaqa* funds, but also increasing their effectiveness in boosting human and physical capital through the channels highlighted earlier. Thus, the usage of *Zakat* and *Sadaqa* to fund *QH* lending to the poor will enhance the sustainability of *QH* lending to poor families in the long run.

Second, in an effort to protect the purchasing power of *QH* funds against inflation and therefore increasing the sustainability of these funds in the long run, these loans could be delivered in kind. The recipients of *QH* loans could then be requested to make repayments in kind or in the monetary equivalent of the goods they received as *QH*. Although this may seem equivalent to charging nominal interest rates equivalent to the rate of inflation, it is perfectly permissible under the *Shari'ah*. Furthermore, some *Shari'ah* scholars have permitted the charging of nominal interest rates up to the rate of inflation, arguing that money is not a commodity and is simply a medium of exchange, and it would be unjust for the donor of *Qard* or *QH* to experience loss of purchasing power due to inflation. Not only these measures would protect the *QH* funds against inflation, it will also encourage the borrowers to start repayment as soon as they are able to do so, therefore increasing the rate of recovery of *QH* funds.

Third, considering the multifaceted benefits of *QH* and its advantageous position over *Zakat* and *Sadaqa* to prevent and reduce poverty, local and central governments should establish publically funded but locally operated *QH* institutions. In this scenario, some of the funds allocated to public welfare programs can be channeled through *QH* lending to the poor and the vulnerable who are already qualified to receive public welfare assistances.

Fourth, efforts should be undertaken to change public's behavior and perception toward *Sadaqa*, *Qard*, and *QH*. Namely, the public should be actively informed of two facts:

a. In as far as Islamic teachings are concerned, *Qard* and *QH* are superior to *Sadaqa* and carry more rewards with Allah (SWT).
b. *QH* is a more effective form of financial assistance to the poor and vulnerable, and it has more potential to reduce and/or prevent poverty in a more sustainable manner.

Indisputably, religious scholars play a crucial role in this front. A shift of public perception in favor of *QH* over *Sadaqa* will channel some of the *Sadaqa* donations toward *QH* funds, increasing its funding base and therefore its sustainability.

Fifth, borrowers of *QH* are usually non-banked and do not have access to formal financial services for various reasons including lack of credit history. In such a scenario, if *QH* loans are considered and recorded as part of one's credit history, it can be employed as a gateway to access other formal financial services. Therefore, in an effort to protect their social as well as financial reputation and creditworthiness, borrowers of *QH* are motivated to abide the terms of the contract and try to limit the feature of *Ihsan* in a *QH* contract as much as possible. The establishment of agencies that keep track of borrowers' credit and financial history would be an additional source of motivation for borrowers to keep their credit history clear from any contract britches, therefore increasing the recovery rate of *QH* loans.

Sixth, *Waqf* funds dedicated for social welfare programs could be utilized to fund *QH* institutions and fill the funding gaps arising from default or late payments. For example, if a *Waqf* is to finance the education of the poor, a portion of that *Waqf* could be transferred in form of educational *QH* to those poor and vulnerable that have a high likelihood of repaying the loan.

Many of the suggested solutions above to increase the sustainability of *QH* funds are being successfully implemented in at least one Islamic microfinance institution, *Akhuwat*. *Akhuwat* has been offering *QH* loans to more than 900,000 families over the past 15 years. The next part provides a brief case study of *Akhuwat*, which is headquartered in Pakistan.

4.4 *Qard Hassan* Islamic Microfinance: A Case Study of Pakistan's *Akhuwat*

4.4.1 Background: Microfinance and Islamic Microfinance in Pakistan

Similar to the ratio of Islamic finance to conventional finance, globally Islamic microfinance constitutes less than 1% of the overall microfinance sector and so it is in its embryonic stages.[20] By the end of 2014, Pakistan's microfinance industry had assets above US$983 million and getting close to the milestone of 3 million active borrowers. The active borrowers have increased from 1.6 to 2.8 million with more than half of the borrowers being women. Operating Self-Sufficiency (OSS) and Financial Self-Sufficiency (FSS) increased by 121% and 120%, respectively, whereas the Portfolio at Risk (PAR>30) ratio has fallen to 1.1%.[21]

In 1998, Pakistan Microfinance Network was set up to represent and regulate the emerging microfinance institutions. In 2000, Pakistan Poverty Alleviation Fund (PPAF) was established with the help of World Bank to provide wholesale refinancing to microfinance institutions. The first microfinance bank, *Khushali* bank, was established in 2000. Three different platforms are followed in Pakistan: Microfinance Banks, Microfinance Institutions, and Rural Support Programs.[22] With only 14 Islamic microfinance institutions operating in Pakistan, this industry is still in its infancy stages in Pakistan.[23]

However, in Pakistan, the microfinance industry charges interest. Because of *Shari'ah* requirements and also the fact that interest-free loans reduce the financial burden on the poor, such loans are more popular among Pakistani society. Programs such as Punjab Rural Support Program lose the spirit of helping the poor when it charges interest rate of up to 20%, making the repayment of the loan impossible by many of the needy borrowers.

On the other hand, for the institutions giving out interest-free loans, sustainability becomes a major issue. The extensive growth strategy adopted by the sector results in huge investments in physical infrastructure and rapid increases in recruitment. This has led to high costs per borrower and low-efficiency ratios, creating challenges for the sustainability of these institutions.[24]

4.4.2 Akhuwat: An Introduction

To fill in the gap, a few organizations have been established with the primary objective of serving the poor through offering interest-free loans. Microfinance institutions providing *Shari'ah*-compliant microfinance products in Pakistan are *Akhuwat*, Centre for Women Co-operative Development (CWCD) and *Wasil* Foundation. The sources of financing for these intuitions include *Waqf*, *Zakat*, and *Sadaqa*.

Akhuwat is an organization that came into existence in 2001 in Pakistan by a group of civil servants. Dr. Amjad Saqib, who was then working for a Government project named Punjab Rural Support Program, was extremely disappointed by the exorbitant interest rates that were being charged on loans extended to the poor. Therefore, he and a few of his close colleagues decided to extend interest-free loans to deserving poor and vulnerable population, through founding the *Akhuwat*. Improving the welfare of the poor through social philanthropy is *Akhuwat's* main objective, which is accomplished through the following channels:

- To provide interest-free microfinance services to poor families enabling them to become self-reliant.
- To promote *Akhuwat*'s interest-free loans as a viable model and a broad-based solution for poverty alleviation.
- To provide social guidance, capacity building, and entrepreneurial training.
- To institutionalize the spirit of brotherhood, compassion, and volunteerism.
- To transform *Akhuwat* borrowers into donors.
- To make *Akhuwat* a sustainable, growth-oriented, and replicable organization.

In 2003, the non-profit organization was formally registered with the name of *Akhuwat*. The name meant brotherhood that was practically seen in Islamic history when Prophet Muhammad (pbuh) migrated from *Mecca* to *Madinah*. During that time, *Madinah* locals shared their wealth and property with the immigrants to help them settle down. *Akhuwat* has the same underlying model in which the public is asked to help their poor brothers and sisters in which brotherhood and sisterhood become means to achieving the goal of reducing poverty.

Akhuwat started his operations in Lahore but to date, it has expanded to Rawalpindi and Faisalabad with the help of Chambers of Commerce and Industry and philanthropists willing to work with them. It has also opened branches like Multan, Gujrat, and Karachi and smaller towns like Sharaq pur, Dijkot, Samundri, Chiniot, Lodhran, ehanian, Duniyapur, Krore Pucca, and Khairpur. Few more branches are under process being established in Rahim Yar Khan, Sarghoda, and Farooqabad. It is also constantly looking for partner organizations to help them establish branches in other cities.[25]

A board of ten members, consisting of philanthropists, civil servants, and businessmen, governs the *Akhuwat* and mobilizes funds for the *Akhuwat*. Moreover, every branch consists of a steering committee that undertakes initiative at the branch level such as organizing fund-raising events especially so before the holy month of *Ramadan*. Awareness regarding *Akhuwat* services is created through campaigns in poor localities, marketplaces, previous borrowers, and local press. Marketing campaigns are delivered at local mosques and churches in between congregational prayers. Any poor household is eligible for completing an application for a loan regardless of his/her religion, gender, disability, and political bias. To keep the cost low and operations effective, the personnel are from local communities as they are better situated to identify the truly deserving poor in a more efficient and effective manner in their own communities.

First loan was given to a female, and it was approximately US$1000 that was donated by one of the fellow members of the group. This was successfully recovered after 6 months, after which the fund's pool expanded to approximately US$40,000 within two years. These sums were recycled into US$1,000,000 worth of loans extended to 900 men and women with no defaults at all. Initially, everyone worked for *Akhuwat* voluntarily, giving out his or her leisure time to the organization; but by 2003, due to its rapid growth and high demand for its services, it became impossible to manage the organization on voluntary basis.[26]

After formalizing the system, an administration fee of 5% of the loan was started being charged to cover the cost of operations. This is a fixed fee, irrespective of the repayment period. Grants received are not used to cover these costs and are only used to extend lending. This fee also provides access to other services provided through *Akhuwat*, such as medical camps and educational support to clients' offspring. Borrowers are also required to pay an obligatory one percent insurance fee, covering death or critical illness, whereby unsettled loans are dismissed. Their poor family members are then compensated an equivalent of three monthly payments along with a onetime cash payment of about US$50.

In Pakistan,, 80% of microloans are lent through group lending methodology. Initially, *Akhuwat* followed the same model, and loans were given to groups of approximately 10 people with a designated leader. However, it was soon realized that often times group leaders exploited their powers in selecting group members and extorted illicit payments from them. Hence, in 2006 as a policy, the group loans were discontinued and replaced with household loans, which were in the name of couples in a given household. Over time, it was observed that individual household loans had a 99.9% recovery rate which was substantially larger than the recovery of group loans, which had a lower recovery rate mainly because of frictions between members of a group.

In addition to being interest-free, four other elements make *Akhuwat* loans genuine *QH* loans. First, its sources of funding are from charitable donations. In other words, donors of *Akhuwat's* fund do not expect to get paid back. Second, in case of defaults that could have been avoided, there are no financial penalties apart from the awareness that privileges for future loans will be removed. Third, collateral is not required, and fourth in addition to financial lending, *Akhuwat* attempts to increase social and human capital of the borrowers and bridge the social and cultural gap between the poor and non-poor.

Donors are generally residents of Pakistan, but a handful of them are living abroad who are motivated to remit funds to make a difference in their local communities. One does not have to be wealthy to be a donor. In fact, so many of the poor, who have managed to move out of the vicious circle of poverty through *Akhuwat*'s financial assistance, have turned into donors themselves as they have a sense of identification with the institution. The board avoids taking donation from official foreign sources as they often come with "strings attached."[27]

Akhuwat not only provides monetary support but also helps training its clients with the required skills and updates them with the latest market information to make them more effective and successful in their business endeavors. Moreover, it organizes activities in collaboration with other NGOs and social welfare organizations. Two of the other successful projects *Akhuwat* are:

1. *Akhuwat* cloth bank: where used clothes are collected, repaired, washed, and packed to be distributed among the poor families.
2. *Akhuwat* health services: which aim at improving the health conditions among Pakistani poor by raising awareness, providing training, and focusing on preventive measures.

Akhuwat's lending procedure does not use collateral. Potential borrowers start by submitting an application form stating the amount of loan required and the potential business idea they want to invest in. Then *Akhuwat's* carefully screens them, making sure that their income is not greater than approximately US$10 per household member in a given month. The unit manager visits the applicant's house and interviews the family members, people in his/her neighborhood, and colleagues at workplace to have a better sense of the credibility, level of skills, and the reputation of the individual/household.

Next step is to ensure the borrower would be able to pay back the loan in timely manner. In this step, if the loan is to be used for micro or small business purpose, *Akhuwat* staff will study the feasibility and profitability of the business and provide expert consultation to the applicant. The loan is approved only after the mutual consent of the couple in a family, ensuring that both individuals are aware of the financial obligation the family is undertaking and agrees with it. Hence, both of the spouses are legal signatories. After the approval of the credit committee, the loan is disbursed in a mosque. It has been *Akhuwat's* experience that borrowers will be more in complaint with the terms of the loan when the contract is signed in a place of religious sanctity.

The disbursement of the loan has to be within 30 days from the day the application is submitted. Loans are disbursed twice a month in the local mosque where the applicant is accompanied by his/her guarantor(s).[28] Guarantors need not be wealthier. It would suffice for them to be respectable member of the community who are willing to stand behind the borrowers in case they have difficulty making repayments. Not requiring collateral as part of the loan application has made it possible for the poorest of the poor in Pakistan to gain access to the much needed *Akhuwat's* interest-free loans.

After the loan disbursement, the applicant and his business are monitored with regular visits by *Akhuwat* staff to keep a record of the progress being made. The payments are due on the 7th of every month, and if delayed beyond the 10th, the guarantor(s) is (are) contacted. The above procedures and setup, which mainly based the concept of social reputation, have made the loan recovery rate to be at 99.9% which is the highest in the industry. Three observations can be made here. First, maintaining social capital, reputation, and credibility creates a strong motivation for families to pay their installments in a timely manner. Second, awareness of the fact that future loans are possible but are contingent on the timely repayment of the current loan makes borrowers more likely to abide the terms of the contract and make timely payments. Finally, in comparison with interest-bearing loans, interest-free loans reduce the financial burden of the poor borrowers, therefore reducing the possibility of their default. All of these have increased the recovery rate of an *Akhuwat QH* loan.

In 2015, average loan size was about US$200. The loans are renewed only if the previous loan was used appropriately, and the borrowers have made repayments in a timely manner. The maximum amount of loan is US$250. Loan terms are flexible with maximum of 18 months, but on average, loans are paid within 11 months with an approximate payment of US$10 per month.

4.4.3 Akhuwat Loans and Operations: A Brief of Presentation of Available Data

Loans are taken out for various reasons: family business loans, education loans, emergency loans, health loans, housing loans, liberation loans, and marriage loans (Table 4.5). As seen from Table 4.5, between 2006 and 2015, family business loans comprise 97% of *Akhuwat*'s total lending portfolio and are mainly used to set up or expand the business. Liberation loans are extended when the applicant has taken interest-bearing loans from other sources and is forced to pay exorbitant interest amounts. In this case, *Akhuwat* pays off the loan on behalf of the applicant, and the applicant compensates *Akhuwat* in installments. Housing loans are given once a year of approximately US$400 – US$500 and need to be repaid in two years. These loans are used toward rent, purchase, or repair of applicants' house.

The *QH* loans given for education, health, emergency, and marriage (only for girls) are part of *Akhuwat*'s multidimensional efforts to reduce or prevent poverty. Another type of *QH* loan, called the silver loans, refers to loans given to increase the size of an existing business. *Akhuwat*

Table 4.5 Composition of *Akhuwat* loans (2006–2015). *Source Akhuwat*

	2006	2007	2008	2009	2010	2011	2012	2013	2014	2015	Total
Family business loans	6209	8470	11,103	13,036	19,219	31,425	64,786	153,486	228,296	329,489	865,519
Education loans	4	16	33	88	147	198	229	633	795	386	2529
Emergency loans	0	0	0	2	1	3	1	1	8	11	27
Health loans	9	23	24	58	142	235	243	459	497	292	1982
Housing loans	6	27	33	100	681	1193	870	1041	1350	780	6081
Liberation loans	20	81	100	366	519	627	748	2040	2353	970	7824
Marriage loans	16	57	95	171	364	513	806	1478	1584	900	5984
Total	**6264**	**8674**	**11,388**	**13,821**	**21,073**	**34,194**	**67,683**	**159,138**	**234,883**	**332,828**	**889,946**

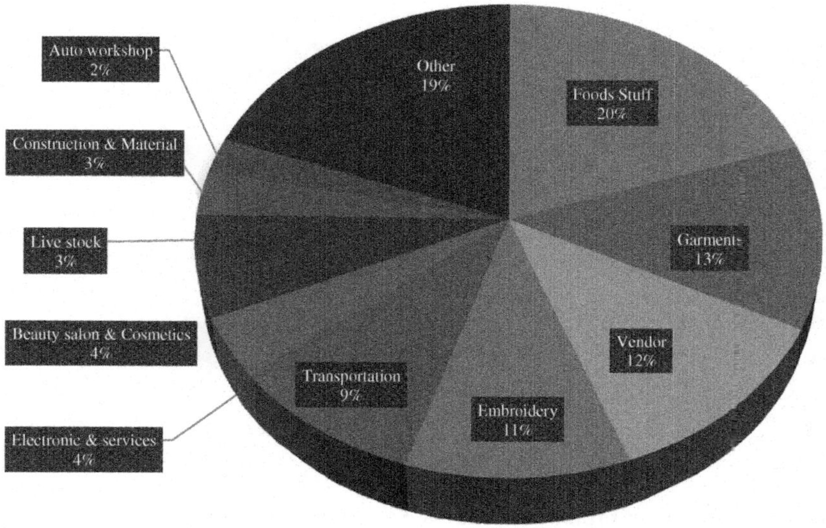

Fig. 4.11 Top ten industries that accounted for more than 80% of all akhuwat's family business loans. *Source* Author's own illustration

recently launched this new product. The average size of this loan is about US$500 and is given to those who have successfully completed three or more cycles of borrowing from *Akhuwat* and are interested to further expand their businesses.

Are there any industries in which the poor borrower is more likely to start a small business in using an *Akhuwat* loan? The answer is yes! Figure 4.11 identifies the top ten industries that accounted for more than 80% of all *Akhuwat's* family business loans. As evident from this figure, majority of these industries require little to no formal education and training which is in line with what is generally known about the education and skill levels of the poor in Pakistan.

Another important question relates to the gender of the borrower. Even though *Akhuwat* loans are "family-based" loans, and the loan contract must be signed by both spouses in a given family, nevertheless in as far as gender empowerment issues are concerned, it makes a substantial difference in which of the spouses is the primary applicant and borrower of the loan. This becomes more so important given

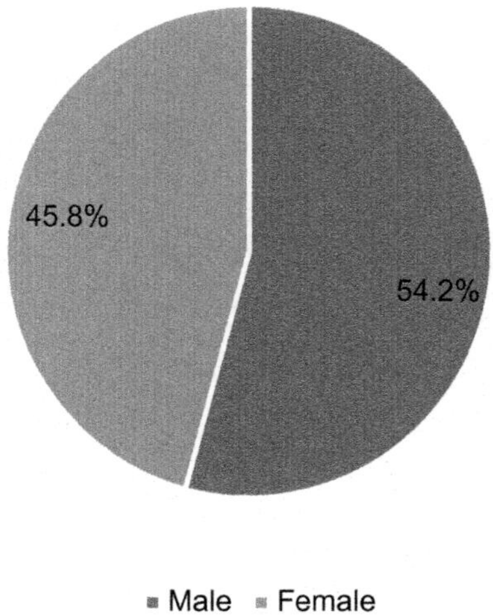

Fig. 4.12 Akhuwat's primary applicants. *Source* Author's own illustration

Table 4.6 T-test on means of average loans amount between female and male applicants (2003–2015). *Source* Akhuwat; author's calculation

Group	Mean	Std. Err.	Std. Dev.	[95% Conf. Interval]	
Female	19,040	30	7184	18,981	19,100
Male	18,272	34	8732	18,206	18,339
Combined	**18,624**	**23**	**8069**	**18,579**	**18,669**

Note The difference between Female and Male Groups is statistically significant at less than 0.0001% level

the inferior economic and social standing of women vis-à-vis men in Pakistani society, especially in the poorer segments of the population. As seen in Fig. 4.12, between 2003 and 2015, women accounted for more than 54% of *Akhuwat's* primary applicants. Furthermore, in comparison with male applicants, the loan amounts seem to have been 4.2% larger on average for the female applicants (Table 4.6). These findings point to *Akhuwat's* potentially important role in empowering poor women in Pakistan and in a way that is respectful to and cognizant of social norms and boundaries.

Not surprisingly, more than half of the female applicants used the *Akhuwat* loans to start micro-businesses in industries that were in

Table 4.7 Breakdown of industries in which female applicants started micro-businesses using Akhuwat loans (2002–2015). *Source* Akhuwat; author's calculation

Industry	Share of total female applicants (%)
Garments	18
Embroidery	16
Foods Stuff	16
Vendor	9
Transportation	9
Beauty salon & cosmetics	5
Livestock	4
Construction & materials	3
Electronic & services	3
Auto workshop	2
Dairy industry	2
Liberation loan	2
Decoration & gift	1
Furniture	1
Leather industry	1
Other	9
Total	**100**

line with their expected social roles in Pakistani society such as garments, embroidery, food, vendor, and cosmetics (Table 4.7). However, Table 4.7 points to another important point as it shows women applying for loans to start business in male-dominated industries such as construction, auto, electronics, and transportation. Given our understanding of the Pakistani society, clearly, such loans must have been channeled to other male members of the family. This again points to Akhuwat's potential role in increasing the bargaining power and socio-economic status of women in poorer population segment of Pakistan.

Table 4.8, the scale of *Akhuwat*'s operation and the number of families have been continuously and rapidly increasing over the past decade. This is one evidence pointing to the sustainability and effectiveness of its model. Below are some highlights of Table 4.8:

- As of May 2015, *Akhuwat* has 355 branches in more than 200 cities and towns in Pakistan.
- To date, about 900,000 families have benefited from *Akhuwat*'s *QH* loans with recovery rate of about 99.9%.[29]

Table 4.8 An overview of *Akhuwat* (2002–2015). *Source* Akhuwat

	2002	2003	2004	2005	2006	2007	2008	2009	2010	2011	2012	2013	2014	2015
Benefiting families	192	282	832	3124	6264	8674	11,388	13,821	21,073	34,194	67,683	1,59,138	2,34,883	3,32,828
Amount disbursed ('000s USD)	31.8	48.4	146.2	535.4	1097.20	1481.60	1738.80	2007.90	2956.20	4845.50	11,696.10	25,375.80	40,269.70	65,111.70
Average loan size (USD)	166	172	176	171	175	171	153	145	140	142	173	159	171	196
Cumulative due ('000s USD)	18.9	23.7	55.4	231.6	465.6	650.5	750.4	834.3	1211.60	2041.30	3867.90	10,116.40	15,811.10	18,725.40
Precentage recovery (%)	100	100	100	100	100	100	100	100	100	100	100	100	100	100
Active loans	154	271	802	2862	6156	8734	12,129	14,599	19,562	31,573	67,337	1,63,215	2,35,517	3,87,174
Outstanding loan porftfolio ('000s USD)	12.9	24.7	90.9	303.8	631.6	831.1	988	1173.10	1744.10	2801.90	7824.00	15,249.30	24,442.80	45,796.00
Number of branches	1	1	4	7	11	18	20	22	36	77	153	254	289	355
Number of cities and towns	NA	NA	NA	NA	NA	NA	NA	NA	NA	NA	NA	NA	200	210

- Every year *Akhuwat* has been able to reach more and more families. Just between 2013 and 2015, it has been able to reach twice more people, while its reach increased by a whopping 16-fold between 2010 and 2015.
- Since 2002, it has made US$160 million worth of *QH* loans, much of which was recycled from previous borrowers returning the sums they had borrowed.
- Number of branches increased by about tenfold between 2010 and 2015. Just between 2013 and 2015, the number of branches increased by 100 from 254 to 355, an increase of 40%.

Furthermore, more than 75% of *Akhuwat's* clients have been able to increase their monthly income by 30–40%, which is an important step in achieving its objective of moving the poor out of poverty.[30] One can highlight several factors (some of which already mentioned earlier) that have contributed to *Akhuwat's* thus far success, sustainability, and effectiveness.

One can highlight several factors (some of which already mentioned earlier) that have contributed to *Akhuwat*'s success, sustainability, and effectiveness thus far. First is keeping the operation cost as low as possible so that more and more of the donations are used toward extending loans to the poor. Cost to loan ratio is around 7%, one of the lowest observed in the industry. The 5% application fee helps cover 76% of the expenses, and the board of directors covers the remaining shortfall. While this may be a source of concern for the sustainability of *Akhuwat* in the long run, Harper (2008) thinks otherwise and argues "*Akhuwat* is sustainable in the sense of being able to survive and grow very fast.... It depends on the continuation of people's generosity rather than their greed. There is no reason to believe that generosity will wither away any more than greed will, we all share both sources of motivation" (132).

Infrastructural costs are kept low by operating at mosques, therefore avoiding utility bills and rents. Furniture is minimal, and sitting on the floor is encouraged. The institution owns no cars, and the staff are encouraged to use public transportation or motorbikes for visiting households and workplaces of the applicants. As for the cost of human resources, the senior management gets no remuneration, and the organizational setup has been kept simple. The staff hired are from the same community as the borrowers. Apart from that, the volunteer force working at *Akhuwat* is large, and a lot of students are trained as volunteers.[31] All of these combined with continuous generosity of donors have contributed to *Akhuwat's* low cost of operation and thus rapid growth rates in the past decade.

Second, "*Akhuwat* has managed to mobilize all members of the society to play their part in poverty alleviation in order to create a vibrant and economically strong society based on sharing resources" (Benedetto and Bengo 2014). One important example is that *Akhuwat* has been able to transform ex-borrowers to donors. In fact, it is the only microfinance model known in the world that encourages the borrower to become a donor and take part in uplifting the overall community. This is because *Akhuwat* goes beyond simply extending financial assistance. Rather, it engages with the borrowers throughout the life of the loan and establishes a trust-based relationship with them, similar to brotherhood, making the borrowers feel part of the *Akhuwat's* extended community.

Akhuwat's mandate extends beyond financial transactions as it makes every effort to guide, support, and empower the poor by providing social guidance, capacity building, and training to the poor. Therefore, when an ex-borrower moves out of poverty as a result of *Akhuwat's* financial, social, and technical assistances, he/she has the urge to support *Akhuwat's* cause in helping the other poor members of the community. Furthermore, in addition to financial donations, the better-off people in a community also volunteer their time, energy, and skills to advance the cause of *Akhuwat*.

All of the above bridges the existing gaps between the "haves" and "have-nots" of a community, therefore reducing marginalization of the poor and increasing social solidarity, all of which are in line with *Akhuwat*'s overall objective of alleviating poverty through the help of locals in a community.

Third, *Akhuwat* employs a "mosque-centric" model where all transactions including loan appraisals, disbursements, and collections take place at the local mosque and other religious centers. Hence, all activities revolve around the mosque and thus involve close interaction with the community. Moreover, faith-based activities increase social cohesion, solidarity, and inclusion. Furthermore, *Akhuwat* requires respectable community members to get involved in organization's activities as guarantors of loan applications. All of these elements increase the sanctity of the contract and raise the social and reputational stakes for the borrowers, therefore increasing the recovery rate.

Fourth, *Akhuwat* continuously seeks similarly minded local partners who support the objectives of *Akhuwat* and are willing to set up a local branch in their local community mosque or other religious centers. In such cases, *Akhuwat* provides training to the local staff and assists in setting up the branch. Leaving the operations to the partner organization, *Akhuwat* acts as a monitoring organization. A team from *Akhuwat's* head office regularly visits the branches for monitoring and training purposes. As a result of this inclusive and flexible view, it has been able to expand its branches by tenfold in the past five years from 36 in 2010 to 355 in 2015.

Fifth and as we saw from Table 4.5 above, 97% of *Akhuwat's* QH loans are extended for the purpose of setting up a micro or small family business. Considering that a comprehensive analysis of the business plan is part of *Akhuwat's* pre-lending procedure and that providing technical assistance, client referral, and marketing services are part of the *Akhuwat's* post-lending strategy, almost all of the businesses that are established through *Akhuwat's* lending end up being successful enterprises. This makes it possible for the borrowers to repay the loan in a timely manner. This strategy has also lead to an ever-growing network of *Akhuwat*-assisted businesses that support each other, be it through marketing, client referral, using each other's services, or through information dissemination.

Although *Akhuwat* has shown strong signs of success over the past decade in meeting its objective of improving the welfare of the poor in the communities it is serving, one cannot assume that the future will be as promising for *Akhuwat* as the past has been. The success of *Akhuwat* in future decades will depend on its ability to make its growing operations and demand sustainable in the long run. In this sense, *Akhuwat* needs to tap into new sources of funding and offer new financial products to cater to the diverse needs of the households it is serving. The implementation of products such as micro-*Mudarabah*, micro-*Musharakah*, micro-*Murabahah*, and micro-*Takaful* may prove to increase *Akhuwat's* funding sources while also helping the plight of the poor and vulnerable. Nevertheless, the successful case of *Akhuwat* to this date demonstrates the fact that if *Qard Hassan* is genuinely and appropriately practiced, it can achieve much of the theoretical results highlighted earlier in this study: reducing poverty, promoting shared prosperity, increasing social solidarity, and in a nutshell improving the overall well-being of individuals and societies.

4.5 Conclusion

According to the 2011 Global Findex Database, more than 125 million adults around the world avoid interactions with formal financial institutions for religious reasons. The first part of this chapter and Demirguc-Kunt et al. (2013) show that Muslims and especially those residing in the MENA region are more likely to be financially excluded for religious reasons. The results show that percentage of unbanked adults due to religious reasons is positively correlated with being situated in the Arab MENA countries and with the share of Muslim population in a given country and negatively correlated with the density of *Shari'ah*-compliant financial assets in an economy. These findings point to the potential role of Islamic finance in enhancing financial inclusion, thus leading to its many benefits for reducing poverty and inequality among Muslim communities around the world and especially in some of the OIC countries, where financial exclusion due to religious reasons is among the highest in the world.

The second part of this chapter suggests that *Qard Hassan*, which is more than simply being an interest-free loan (*Qard*), seems to be the most effective instrument in Islamic finance industry to address the financial needs of the poor and the vulnerable and pave the path for their inclusion in and access to formal financial services. However, as of now, genuine *Qard Hassan* is not being widely practiced by IFIs, and therefore, its potential benefits for reducing/preventing poverty are not fully being realized. Through presenting a novel definition and view of

Qard Hassan and its multifaceted benefits for the vulnerable and poor and the long-run health of an economy, this work hopes to start a theoretical and operational discussion around this widely misunderstood and misapplied lending instrument in Islamic finance industry.

The third part of this chapter presents the successful case of *Akhuwat*, which is a Pakistani microfinance institution operating on *Qard Hassan* principles highlighted in the second part of this essay. The case of *Akhuwat* confirms much of the theoretical discussions herein and shows that if implemented in ways that are in accordance with its spirit, *Qard Hassan* can achieve much in the way of reducing/preventing poverty and enhancing shared prosperity and social/financial inclusion.

Notes

1. Account penetration rate is measured as the percentage of adults age 15 and above with account(s) in formal financial institutions.
2. It is important to note here that while lacking an account at a formal financial institution is not always tantamount to lacking access to financial services, it is nevertheless a good proxy for measuring access to financial services. This is because most if not all forms of formal financial services are often linked to accounts in formal financial institutions. Therefore, individuals or firms without a formal account are often forced to address their financial needs through informal financial markets, which are often associated with higher costs and risks and little to no legal protection against frauds or breaches in the contract.
3. http://www.worldbank.org/financialdevelopment.
4. http://go.worldbank.org/GWESKFYMY0.
5. Ibid.
6. Ibid.
7. See http://go.worldbank.org/1F2V9ZK8C0. The 11 out of 18 MENA countries included in this survey are Algeria, Djibouti, Egypt, Iraq, Jordan, Lebanon, Morocco, Syria, Tunisia, West Bank and Gaza, and Yemen.
8. Religiosity level represents the percentage of adults in a given country who responded affirmatively to the question, "Is religion an important part of your daily life?" in a 2010 Gallup poll. See Crabtree (2010).

9. The 17 million estimate is on the conservative side as it does not include countries such as Algeria, Bahrain, Iran, Qatar, Somalia, and the United Arab Emirates, which are home to about 140 million Muslim (about 10% of the global Muslim population). These countries were not represented in the Global Findex Database.
10. All models include GDP and GDP per capita to control for different levels development in economic, legal, social, and governance fronts. This is based on the fact that legal, social, and political developments are often strongly correlated with levels of economic development and the size of an economy.
11. See Infinity Consultants and Ethica Institute (2013).
12. See Aziz (2013).
13. See Lema and Vizcaino (2013).
14. See Ahmed (2013).
15. These countries are Algeria, Djibouti, Egypt, Iran, Iraq, Jordan, Morocco, Syria, and Yemen.
16. The vulnerable are defined as individuals or households who are not currently poor but have a high likelihood of slipping into poverty if not assisted in a timely manner.
17. Such as shame and reputation.
18. Some factors that contribute to the heterogeneity of the poor are:
    Biological/Physiological
    The poor have different needs and capabilities based on their gender, age, health condition, and genetics.
    Geographical
    Geography imposes its own constraint on the available options to the poor and explains some of the causes of poverty.
    Cultural
    Poverty is defined, interpreted, and looked at differently across cultures. Furthermore, different cultures have different mechanism for fighting poverty. Therefore, cultural differences play major role in the heterogeneity of the poor population.
    Durational
    Protracted poverty leads to highly different needs than temporary and unexpected poverty. Therefore, the duration of poverty is yet another characteristic that adds to heterogeneity of the poor.
    Personal
    Each person's background, personal experiences, outlook on life, and future goals are different from others. Therefore, even if a group of poor

people were homogenous based on the above-mentioned factors, they are not homogenous at personal level.

19. Such as national/global economic shocks, unfavorable family circumstances, medical situations, natural disasters, accidents, loss of employment, theft, and simply a bad business decision.
20. See Ali (2013).
21. See Pakistan Microfinance Network (2014).
22. See Rauf and Mahmood (2009).
23. See GIFR (2012).
24. See Rauf and Mahmood (2009).
25. http://akhuwatonline.org/about_us_akhuwat-works.php.
26. http://www.akhuwat.org.pk/pdf/Akhuwat.pdf.
27. http://www.akhuwat.org.pk/akhuwatcaseStudy.asp.
28. http://akhuwatonline.org/about_us_akhuwat-works.php.
29. http://www.akhuwat.org.pk/progress_report.asp.
30. See Civil Services Pakistan & District Management Group (2007).
31. http://akhuwatonline.org/about_us_akhuwat-works.php.

References

Adewale, A. A., Pramanik, A. H., & Meera, A. K. M. (2012). A measurement model of the determinants of financial exclusion among Muslim micro-entrepreneurs in Ilorin, Nigeria. *Journal of Islamic Finance, 1*(1), 30–43.

Ahmed, M. (2013). *Keynote Speech: 5th Annual Arab policy forum on financial inclusion*. Washington, DC: International Monetary Fund.

Ali, K. (2013). *Islamic microfinance in Pakistan: The experience so far.* Washington, DC: Consultative Group to Assist the Poor.

Aziz, Z. A. (2013). Islamic finance—Financial stability, economic growth and development. Speech at the Islamic Development Bank (IDB) Prize Lecture on Islamic finance—Financial stability, economic growth and development, Jeddah, 27 November 2013.

Beck, T., & Demirguc-Kunt, A. (2008). Access to finance: An unfinished agenda. *World Bank Economic Review, 22*(3), 383–396.

Beck, T., Demirguc-Kunt, A., & Levine, R. (2004). *Finance, inequality, and poverty: Cross-country evidence* (Policy Research Working Paper Series 3338). Washington, DC: World Bank.

Benedetto, C. D., & Bengo, I. 2014. Microcredit system for building rehabilitation and strengthening arts and crafts. In Chap. 5 A. Del Bo & D. F. Bignami (Eds.), *Sustainable social, economic and environmental revitalization in Multan city*. London: Springer.

Crabtree, S. (2010). *Religiosity highest in world's poorest nations*. Washington, DC: Gallup.

Demirguc-Kunt, A., & Klapper, L. (2012). *Measuring financial inclusion: The Global Findex database* (Policy Research Working Paper 6025). Washington, DC: World Bank.

Demirguc-Kunt, A., Klapper, L., & Randall, D. (2013). *Islamic finance and financial inclusion: Measuring use of and demand for formal financial services among Muslim adults* (Policy Research Working Paper 6642). Washington, DC: World Bank.

El-Zoghbi, M., & Tarazi, T. (2013). Trends in Shari'a-compliant financial inclusion. *CGAP Focus Note 84*. Washington, DC: Consultative Group to Assist the Poor.

Farooq, M. O. (2010). Qard Hasan, Wadi'ah/Amanah and bank deposits: Application and misapplication of some concepts in Islamic banking. *Arab Law Quarterly, 25*(2), 115–146.

GIFR. (2012). *Global Islamic microfinance landscape*. Global Islamic Finance Report. http://www.gifr.net/gifr2012/ch_25.pdf, http://www.gifr.net/contact.html.

Harper, M. (2008). Akhuwat of Lahore. In Chap. 11 M. Harper, D. S. K. Rao, & A. K. Sahu (Eds.), *Development, divinity and dharma: The role of religion in development and microfinance institutions*. Washington, DC: Practical Action Publishing.

Infinity Consultants & Ethica Institute. (2013). Achieving financial inclusion for Muslims in India: How can Islamic finance help? https://www.ethicainstitute.com/webinar/Achieving-Financial-Inclusion-For-Indian-Muslims.pdf

Lema, K., & Vizcaino, B. (2013). Bangko Sentral's Islamic banking bid to boost financial inclusion of Muslims. September 27, 2013: Reuters.

Levine, R. (2005). Finance and growth: Theory and evidence. In Philippe Aghion & Steven Durlauf (Eds.), *Handbook of economic growth* (Vol. 1, pp. 865–934). Amsterdam: North-Holland Elsevier.

Mirakhor, A., & Iqbal, Z. (2007). Qard Hasan microfinance. *New Horizon,* (April–June), 164, 18–20.

Mohieldin, M., Iqbal, Z., Rostom, A., & Fu, X. (2012). *The role of Islamic finance in enhancing financial inclusion in organization of Islamic cooperation countries* (Policy Research Working Paper No. 4435). Washington, DC: World Bank.

Pakistan Microfinance Network. (2014). Pakistan microfinance review. Annual assessment of the microfinance industry.

Rauf, S. A., & Mahmood, T. (2009). Growth and performance of microfinance in Pakistan. *Pakistan Economics and Social Review, 47*(1), 99–122.

Sachar Committee Report. (2006). *Social, economic, and educational status of the Muslim community of India.* Prime Minister's High Level Committee, Cabinet Secretariat, Government of India, November 2006.

World Bank. (2007). *Finance for all? Policies and pitfalls in expanding access.* Washington, DC: World Bank.

World Bank. (2011). *The global findex database.* Washington, DC: World Bank.

World Bank. (2013). *Global financial development report 2014: Financial inclusion.* Washington, DC: World Bank.

Part II

Institutions and Instruments for Financial Inclusion and Inclusive Development in Muslim Countries

5

Application of *Zakat* to Food Security in the Context of Low-Income Rural Areas in Bangladesh: A Conceptual Model

Ishrat Hossain

Abstract Food security is at the forefront of worldwide policy debates. Food security is not only about production, but also includes accessibility, availability, and affordability of nutritious food. *Zakat* plays a central role in Islamic economic welfare system. The objective of this study is to outline a model to use *Zakat* as a tool to improve food security as well as fulfill the goal of taking care of the poor and needy of a rural locality. This faith-based novel approach to inclusive development would allow more flexibility to integrate moral and ethical codes in the process. The most vulnerable households among the eligible recipients of food as *Zakat* would receive food vouchers or ration cards, giving them easy access to the food bank on a weekly or monthly basis.

Keywords *Zakat* · Food security · *Salam* finance contract · Food bank

---

I. Hossain (✉)
Department of Finance and Economics, Qatar University, Doha, Qatar
e-mail: ishrat@qu.edu.qa

© The Author(s) 2017

M. Zulkhibri and A. G. Ismail (eds.), *Financial Inclusion and Poverty Alleviation*,
Palgrave Studies in Islamic Banking, Finance, and Economics,
https://doi.org/10.1007/978-3-319-69799-4_5

5.1 Introduction

Food is the most basic necessity for all human being. Thus, food security is an integral part of human rights and entitlements. Food price increases and volatility due to various supply and weather shocks have brought the issue of food security to the forefront of worldwide policy debates and actions. Most recently, 2007–2008 and 2010–2011 food price crises constitute prominent examples. Poverty and hunger in low-income countries were adversely affected by global food and financial crises. The number of food insecure people was estimated to increase by approximately 100 million during the period 2007–2009, reaching close to 1 billion people in the world in 2009 (USDA 2009). Furthermore, the 2010–2011 food price shock added approximately 44 million more people to the already existing 1.2 billion people who were living under the extreme poverty line of US$1.25 a day (World Bank 2011). The problem could be even worse in the Organisation of Islamic Cooperation (OIC) countries where it was estimated to have 31% of the total population living below the extreme poverty threshold, more than double the world average of 14% during the period of 2008–2010 (Savaş and Haneef 2015). Even during the relatively normal times, about 16% of the world's population remains chronically undernourished (Joshling 2011).

There is a general tendency to focus mainly on the supply side of the food equation in the food security concept. However, food security is not only about production, but its multifaceted nature also includes among other things availability, accessibility, and affordability of nutritious food. The 1996 World Food Summit agreed on a broad definition of food security which was refined in 2001: "Food security [is] a situation that exists when all people, at all times, have physical, social and economic access to sufficient, safe and nutritious food that meets their dietary needs and food preferences for an active and healthy life" (FAO 2002). Pinstrup-Anderson (2009) pointed out that "food preferences" concept is better interpreted as meaning foods that are socially and culturally acceptable and consistent with the religious and ethical values of the respective people.

Zakat is one of the five pillars of Islam. It is an obligatory religious act of paying charity depending on level and type of wealth of the eligible Muslim. Its importance can be gauged from the fact that *Zakat* is mentioned 30 times in Quran, out of which 27 times it is associated with Prayer, a fundamental practice of Islam, in the same verses (Qardawi 1999). One such verse is "Establish regular Prayer and give *Zakat*; and obey Allah and His Messenger" (33:33). The bond of *Zakat* with Prayer is also highlighted by Abu Bakr, the first leader of Muslims after the death of the Prophet (pbuh), when he declared war against people who refused to pay *Zakat*, by saying, "By Allah, I shall indeed fight those who separate Prayer from *Zakat*" (Qardawi 1999).

Zakat plays a central role in Islamic economic welfare system. By linking rich and poor, *Zakat* increases the sense of brotherhood, a key concept of Islam, in the society. It can be a significant tool to eradicate poverty and support the economically most vulnerable groups in the society. The contemporary Muslim societies have not borne the fruits of this noble system largely due to weak implementation of *Zakat*. Notwithstanding the importance of *Zakat*, it can be termed as one of the least understood pillars of Islam in terms of paying and distributing in innovative ways. Realizing the shortcomings so far, increasing efforts are made to diversify the utilization of *Zakat* funds to foster social empowerment and development instead of focusing on only the charity aspect, of course within the boundary of the Islamic law, the *Shariah* (Hassan and Khan 2007; Oran 2009; Nurzaman 2011). For the purpose, part of the huge amount of money collected as *Zakat* every year should be allocated to productive activities.

To solve development and welfare related issues, value-based Islamic instruments can be injected to the established development models to bring them closer to the cultural realities of indigenous people, especially in countries where Islam plays a strong role in the lives of destitute. The Islamic solutions to development and welfare allow more space for justice and equity. Reliance on secular ideals continues to dominate the development framework, however, increasing interest being placed to incorporate religion into development process such as the World Banks's World Faiths Development Dialogue initiative (Mesbahuddin 2010).

The objective of this chapter is to outline a model to use *Zakat* as a tool to improve food security as well as fulfill the goal of taking care of the poor and needy of a rural locality in Bangladesh. To the best of our knowledge, there has been only one conference paper which attempts to look at *Zakat*-based solutions to food security. Laila (2009) emphasizes centralized administration of *Zakat* fund mostly through government ministries by supporting small agro-producers in sourcing, training, market access, and storage. It is not clear whether some of their proposed activities fall within the permissible framework of *Zakat*. This chapter identifies a more complete and integrated framework by showing the connections between collection and distribution of *Zakat* with the food security issues making use of acceptable *Shariah* compliant methods. The approach in this paper is localized community administration with more academic rigor in contrast to the earlier paper.

5.2 The Context in Bangladesh

Bangladesh is a Muslim majority country with close to 90% of the population being Muslim (Banbeis 2017). Agriculture sector employs more than half of the total labor force and contributes to 20% of the Gross Domestic Product (Akter and Basher 2014). Approximately 75% of the country's 160 million population lives in rural areas, where the incidence of poverty is estimated at 35.2% compared to 21.3% in the urban area (BBS 2011). The widespread poverty in countries like Bangladesh makes them particularly vulnerable to food insecurity. FAO (2009) estimated close to half of the total population, 64 million, in Bangladesh to be food insecure in 2008. Per capita food consumption is low for the people of Bangladesh. Per capita intake of major food items, like rice, wheat, potato, meat, fish, and vegetables, was estimated to be approximately 416, 26, 71, 19, 49 and 166 grams per day, respectively, in 2010 (BBS 2011).

It is a well established fact that the poor are the most exposed to any food price shock as they spend a large share, somewhere between 35 and

65%, of their meager income on food (World Bank 2009). Banerjee and Duflo (2007) found looking at 13 developing countries that 56 to 78% of consumption was on food among rural households. Akter and Basher (2014) provided empirical evidence to conclude that the 2007–2009 food price hikes aggravated food insecurity disproportionately among the poorer and net-food-buyer households in the rural areas of Bangladesh. They found seasonal pattern of food insecurity incidences corresponding to the agricultural lean periods during the year when wage-earning opportunities in rural areas are limited.

A host of policies and programs are needed to insulate the poor people from food insecurity. Bangladesh government operates an array of safety net programs, such as Food for Work, Vulnerable Group Development, Test Relief, which give cash or in-kind support to directly or indirectly address food and nutrition insecurity of households. There are also special programs during the crisis periods like the Public Food Distribution System in 2008, which assisted 30 million vulnerable people throughout Bangladesh (Demeke et al. 2009). They would offer some short-term relief to the effect of food insecurity. However, their long-term viability is debatable due to well-known corruption problems and inefficiencies that come with poorly targeted and badly managed complex public subsidy schemes (World Bank 2012), in addition to placing heavy burden on already financially stressed government budget. Non-governmental Organizations (NGO), such as Bangladesh Rural Advancement Committee's (BRAC), Grameen Bank, are also actively involved with numerous programs. Mesbahuddin (2010) argues that Islamic solutions to welfare also has a prominent role to play in a country such as Muslim majority Bangladesh, where daily practices of rural villagers are shrouded by their Islamic beliefs. The powerful conventional NGO sector in the country heavily relies on secularized code of development practices such as the interest-based microfinance programs. Despite the success stories of NGOs, some of their other practices also have the potential to ignite cultural clashes due to underlying tones of anti-Islamism (Mesbahuddin 2010).

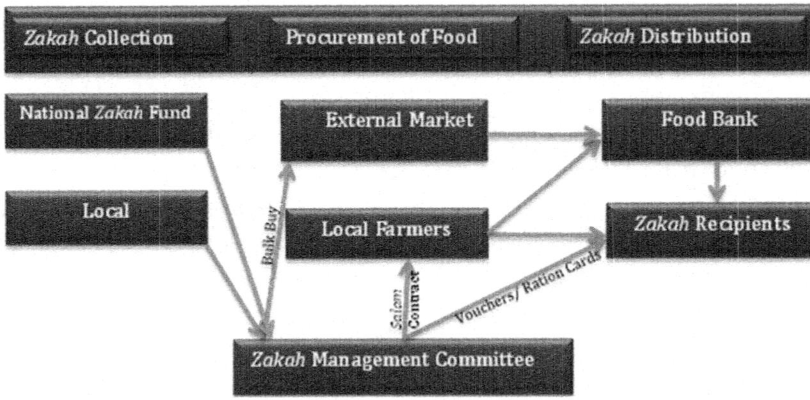

Fig. 5.1 Conceptual framework of the proposed model. *Source* Author's own illustration

5.3 Conceptual Framework

The proposed model is illustrated in Fig. 5.1. The focal point of the model would be a local *Zakat* Management Committee (ZMC). Setting up an effective and competent committee is vital to the success of the system. Local administrators may have better access to relevant information to effectively target the poor with social assistance programs (Alderman 2002). Local committee-based *Zakat* management models exist in some countries like Kuwait and Pakistan, where religious leaders or the committee members are expected to have superior understanding of the needs and priorities of the poor and the needy of the community (Kahf 1995; Ajeel 1995). Alatas et al. (2003) pointed out that localization would give the community members a voice in their affairs and encourage them to participate actively in the local activities. Using survey data from Malaysia, Wahid et al. (2012) found that localization of *Zakat* distribution would significantly improve the quality of life of *Zakat* recipients, not only economically but also mentally and spiritually.

It is possible that the committee and proposed *Zakat*-food security system suffer from the rampant institutional and human corruption factors prevailing in Bangladesh. However, religious obligation engrained in the system can be a strong motivational factor to set higher moral values and ethical codes that would ensure people have extra incentives to make it more efficient and corruption-free than the other comparable institutions.

ZMC's functions would include undertaking awareness campaign about *Zakat*, determining functional policies, managing the *Zakat* fund, setting up the food bank, choosing the *Zakat* recipients; in short coordinating the whole system. Their main activities can be categorized into three main parts: Collection of *Zakat*, Procurement of Food and Distribution of *Zakat*.

ZMC will carry out a household economic survey in the area to identify the two categories of families, namely the ones who are liable to pay *Zakat* and the ones who are eligible to receive it. The *Zakat* fund would include collections from the local community and an appropriate share from the national *Zakat* fund, if available. A food bank would be created, including some basic nutritious food items, which satisfy local customs, dietary needs, and local production practices. Special attention should be given to maintain dietary diversity to tackle micronutrient deficiencies and malnutrition. The committee would engage the local farmers with a "*Salam*," a *Shariah* compliant forward contract, which would make advance payment for future produce relevant for the food bank. Rest of the food items would be bought from external sources taking advantage of economies of scale in bulk buying to lower the purchase price. Eligible recipients of food as *Zakat* will be selected and updated yearly by the committee giving priority to the most vulnerable groups, such as widows, pregnant women, disables, orphans and old-aged people. They would receive food vouchers or ration cards, giving them access to the food bank on a weekly or monthly basis.

5.4 Discussion and Implications

This section explains how the proposed model mechanisms would work to improve food security. The main contribution will be in the production, availability and accessibility aspects of the food security.

5.4.1 Collection of *Zakat*

The implementation of *Zakat* has been one of the functions of the Muslim governments since the time of Prophet Muhamad (pbuh) until the fall of the Ottoman Empire (Kahf 2013). Kahf (2013) gave an account of the current role of the Muslim governments in collecting and distributing *Zakat*. Few of the countries, like Yemen, Saudi Arabia, Malaysia, Sudan, implement laws to make it obligatory to make *Zakat* payments to the government, whereas some other countries like Bangladesh, Egypt, Jordan, Qatar established government special institutions to collect *Zakat* on a voluntary basis. Most other countries with significant Muslim population have various mosques, NGOs and individuals taking the responsibility of collecting and distributing *Zakat*. The Islamic Foundation under the Ministry of Religious Affairs is in charge of accepting and distributing the collected *Zakat* funds in Bangladesh. Their effectiveness and activities are very limited due to their perceived inefficiency and people's general preference to manage *Zakat* affairs individually.

The model proposes mostly local collection of *Zakat* with a relevant share from the national *Zakat* fund. The allocation from the national fund should take into account the inter-regional heterogeneity in economic growth and poverty dynamics. The areas with lower economic opportunities and limited labor mobility should get priority in receiving larger share of the fund. On the other hand, by implementing a *Zakat* awareness campaign based on information, education, and motivation with positive social peer pressure, the local inhabitants can be encouraged to pool their contributions for the ZMC. Many Muslims do not comprehend the higher status of *Zakat* in Islam. Mosques, where community gathers at least once weekly for the Friday prayers, can be one of the powerful channels to raise the importance of *Zakat*. The pooling of *Zakat* funds would facilitate dealing with local farmers in a way that would have macro effects for the area in terms of improved food security at the same time directly meeting the needs of relevant people at the micro level.

5.4.2 Procurement of Food

The use of the *Zakat* fund to employ Salam contract to engage with the local producers has several benefits: reduce high interest-based borrowing common for the poor farmers, guarantees fair price by eliminating intermediaries, resulting in incentives for increased local production. Adding to the demand for local produce, it stimulates the local economy.

Salam is a *Shariah* compliant sale contract to finance production by providing advance payment at the time of contract to receive future delivery of fully specified goods in terms of types, quantity, quality, date, place, etc. It is particularly beneficial for small and marginal farmers, who constitute the majority of the agricultural workforce, by having the working capital during the production time to manage their expenses on various inputs. In fact, as mentioned by Kahf and Khan (1988), the *Salam* practice was common during the time of the Prophet (pbuh) in the agricultural sector of Madinah. They stated that lawfulness of the *Salam* contract, even with an apparent violation of the rule of prohibiting the sale of things not in possession of the seller at the time of contract, indicates an inclination to support business credit and loan. They also pointed out that some contemporary Muslim scholars suggested that institutional lending for such purposes might be made by the *Zakat* fund.

Rural households or individuals in the developing countries may borrow from formal lenders such as government banks and agencies, commercial banks and non-government microfinance institutions (MFIs), or from informal lenders such as relatives, friends, moneylenders, and shopkeepers. However, the poor farmers in many cases do not have access to formal credit markets due to lack of collateral. Furthermore, Hassan and Khan (2007) pointed out that credit servicing mechanisms with fixed interest rates can be a great impediment to reduce income inequality. According to the Institute of Microfinance (2011), farmers borrowed money with an average interest rate of 28.46% from MFIs. On the other hand, the annual interest rates charged by informal moneylenders vary considerably with a mean of 103.33% and standard deviation of 59.06 (Mallick 2012).

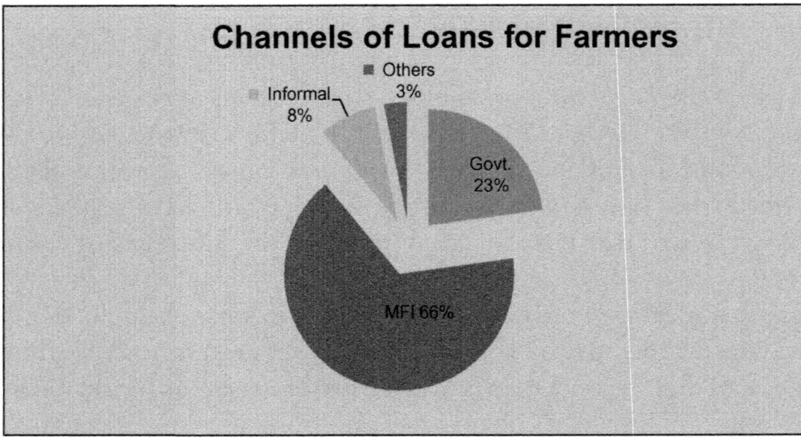

Fig. 5.2 Channels of loans for farmers. *Note* Author estimate the figure from Bangladesh's Household Income and Expenditure Survey conducted by Bangladesh Bureau of Statistics in 2010. The total sample size was 12,240 households where 7840 were from rural areas and 4400 from urban areas. This figure is considering the sources of loans only for the farmers out of all the respondents. *Source* Author's own compilation

The estimates from Bangladesh's Household Income and Expenditure Survey (HIES) in Fig. 5.2 show that MFIs are providing the highest percentage of loans for farmers, whereas the government institutions are in the second position followed by the informal lenders. With approximately 20.6 million active borrowers, Bangladesh actually has the largest microfinance program in the world (Mallick 2012). Though government institutions charge lower interest rates compared to other lenders, their (Govt.) bureaucratic process and corruption make it harder to borrow from those institutions. Despite the higher interest rates, MFIs are popular borrowing destination for the farmers due to their aggressive and comparatively easier lending policies. At the same time, the tight repayment schedule of MFI loans and lack of sufficient seasonal working capital for farming activities may force the borrowers to borrow from informal credit markets with excessively higher interest rates for additional funds. In fact, Mallick (2012) found that as the MFI coverage expands the moneylender interest rates increase due to increased demand for their funds. The evidence of borrowing from informal sources by rural households in Bangladesh is well documented (Zeller et al. 2001; McKernan et al. 2005). Further analysis from HIES shows that over two-thirds (69%) of the farmers who already borrowed money are not interested to borrow more money from their lenders, which highlights a general dissatisfaction about the borrowing. It is in line with other studies where the impact of commercial banks and microfinance on the borrowers' livelihood has been found to be limited (Mahmud 2010; Mesbahuddin 2010). Hence, it is fair to say that many rural farmers will have difficulty to be able to stabilize their income generation when they borrow from existing formal and informal lenders at higher interest rates. *Zakat*-based financing system can play a significant role in reducing poverty in Bangladesh (Raquib 2011). Introducing the *Zakat*-based financing would increase competition between the existing lenders, discipline the local interest rates, thus enabling farmers' improved access to funds at favorable conditions.

When funds to invest in farming become increasingly difficult to access, farmers resort to subsistence farming where many of the modern capital and high-yielding inputs such as irrigation, seed, fertilizer are not administered. The depressing investments along with other factors result in lower productivity in the farms (Mahmud et al. 2014), which is a serious setback for a country like Bangladesh where land is such a scarce resource. Farmers also very often fail to obtain fair price for their produce due to inadequate rural infrastructural facilities and lack of efficient rural markets, forcing them to sell their crops to the middlemen for a lower price compared to actual market price. Those intermediaries also exploit the situation by making syndicate in order to control the crops' prices. Moreover, farmers sometimes sell their crops at very low price in advance during production time when they cannot afford the rising prices of agricultural inputs.

Hence, many farmers have difficulty repaying their high interest-bearing loans, which may lead to selling their own precious land or other physical assets. They are likely to even migrate to urban areas in unfavorable conditions. In the worst scenarios, their frustration causes suicide, as Patel (2007) mentioned that more than 17,500 farmers killed themselves in India between 2002 and 2006.

Issues such as high interest rate borrowing, loss of productivity and intermediaries' exploitation contribute to vicious cycle of poverty for many small rural farmers. Making funds accessible through Salam forward contract, providing them instant capital during the production season at zero interest rate, give them a chance to come out of that cycle, in essence make farming attractive. This would have a positive impact on the local food security by tackling production or availability aspect of the food security. Availability of interest-free loans in contrast to interest-bearing ones will also help establish Islamic society that is more equitable. This mechanism is sustainable in the long term due to the nature of *Zakat* as a yearly affair.

5.4.3 Distribution of *Zakat*

Zakat can be spent on eight categories of people according to the following verse from the Quran: "*Zakat* expenditures are only for the poor and for the needy and for those employed to collect [*Zakat*] and for bringing hearts together [for Islam] and for freeing captives [or slaves] and for those in debt and for the cause of Allah and for the [stranded] traveler—an obligation [imposed] by Allah. And Allah is Knowing and Wise" (9:60).

Islam is unequivocal in the determination to take care of the poor. Qardawi (1999) argues that poor and needy, commonly referred to as the poor, are the most deserving groups to receive *Zakat*, which highlights fighting poverty as the primary aim of *Zakat*. The ZMC with superior knowledge about the local conditions of deserving recipients would prioritize to select the most vulnerable groups in the area. Expecting scarcity of the available *Zakat* fund and subsequent food bank, the selection process should take utmost care to have the greatest impact with the limited resources. Some groups deserve special mention.

High food prices are likely to disproportionately affect the net-food-buyer, landless, non-farming households in the rural communities (Akter and Basher 2014). High prevalence in South Asia of maternal undernourishment leading to underweight babies being born and children malnutrition have long-term negative consequences on health outcomes and labor productivity in the region (Bonnerjee and Kohler 2011). Sen (2010) explains how the unfair treatment of women in South Asia with respect to nutrition results in poor health of both men and women. Along with poorer households with young children, pregnant and lactating women, widows, disabled, orphans and old-aged people should get priority as recipients. As people may move in and out of the *Zakat* eligibility criteria, the list of people will be updated periodically.

The selected people would receive food vouchers or ration cards, giving them access to the food bank on a weekly or monthly basis. It is also possible to set up a system where some of the vouchers can be redeemable directly with the local contracted farmers at the harvest time making some part of the food bank virtual without any need for physical storage at the food bank facility. This virtual food bank system would reduce storage and transaction costs. Having a local food bank can alleviate the distance and long queue problems sometimes associated with accessing and buying food from government-operated subsidized outlets in the crisis times.

Akter and Basher (2014) find evidence that the risk of experiencing hunger by the rural households in Bangladesh was significant during the dry season agricultural lean periods, usually lasting for 3–4 months a year. The distribution of food can be prioritized around these lean periods to curb seasonal food insecurity. The food bank may also smooth consumption and reduce food price volatility in the respective areas.

While efforts to overcome food insecurity mostly focused on the production side, the success of such initiatives also hinges on how easily consumers can access food. The proposed model conveniently makes food available locally to the consumers who lack purchasing power, thus targeting the accessibility aspect of food security.

5.5 Conclusion

The scale of policy debates and innovations worldwide around food security issue, especially in the poor countries, is an acknowledgment of the importance of the particular issue and more generally of poverty and inclusive development. Poor households are more prone to food insecurity. There are a variety of pro-poor safety net programs available. Religion can play an increasing role in the development process as it brings a value-rationality based on equity and justice and adds stronger moral and ethical codes to institutions in developing countries like Bangladesh where states and markets are plagued by corruption. Food security is a common measure of household welfare, whereas *Zakat* system is also concerned about individual welfare. This chapter proposes a model that is connecting *Zakat*, an existing Islamic financing instrument, to the issue of food security in a novel way in the context of rural Bangladesh. Localized activities by a ZMC would ensure community participation and empowerment facilitating brotherhood in the society.

With the pooled local *Zakat* fund, the model tries to tackle some underlying structural problems to make farming more attractive. *Zakat*-based *Salam* forward contract could be an addition to traditional bank-centered modes of financing to provide farmers with much-needed working capital at zero interest rate and contribute to food security through increased food production. The vulnerable *Zakat* eligible households in the area will get easy access to food from a food bank created mostly with local produce from the contracted farmers. Giving priorities to eligible households with young children and pregnant women would also contribute to long-term productivity of the nation. Implementing the model in rural settings will have added benefit of making life attractive there, thus reducing harmful effects of rapid urbanization evident in many poorer countries.

The framework would be beneficial in the normal times, but it would also provide assistance in times of food price shocks. In case of food price shocks, landowners, self-employed farmers are likely to gain which may have a positive impact on *Zakat* collection in the rural communities. At the same time, the more of the likely losers in the area, the non-farming households, would be eligible for *Zakat*-based food bank. Hence, this safety net program would help balance the impact in the society.

Even though the preliminary proposal lacks empirical validation and comprehensive study of the institutional and administrative questions that have to be addressed, it nonetheless represents an initial but significant attempt to use an existing powerful Islamic instrument to tackle one of the very important issues, the food security. The idea at least deserves further exploration and therefore provides fertile ground for new and expanded research. Feasibility studies need to be undertaken to gauge the workability of the scheme. Details need to be considered with care, particularly the *Zakat* collection mechanisms, identification of vulnerable groups, choice of food items for the food bank, administration of the vouchers, monitoring of *Salam* contracts, etc. Accountability and competency of the management committee are of paramount importance and application of modern e-technology to improve transparency should be envisioned. Impacts of the proposed model's localized approach on the society and urbanization, and related macro effects also need to be investigated. Finally, the potential to generalize the model to other poor developing countries similar to Bangladesh should be studied.

Acknowledgements I am grateful to Munshi Masudul Haq for his excellent research assistance.

References

Ajeel, A. A. Q. D. (1995). Kuwait. In el-Ashker & Sirajul Haq (Eds.), *Institutional Framework of zakat: Dimensions and Implications* (pp. 259–295). Jeddah: Islamic Research and Training Institute, Islamic Development Bank.

Akter, S., & Basher, S. A. (2014). The impacts of food price and income shocks on household food security and economic well-being: Evidence from rural Bangladesh. *Global Environmental Change, 25,* 150–162.

Alatas, V., Pritchett, L., & Wetterberg, A. (2003). *Voice lessons: Local government organizations, social organizations, and the quality of local governance* (World Bank Policy Research Working Paper 2981). Washington, DC: World Bank.

Alderman, H. (2002). Do local officials know something we don't? Decentralization of targeted transfers in Albania. *Journal of Public Economics, 83*(3), 375–404.

Banbeis. (2017). *Bangladesh: Country profile*. Dhaka: Bangladesh Bureau of Educational Information and Statistics, Ministry of Education. Available at: https://web.archive.org/web/20110706132048/http://www.banbeis.gov.bd/bd_pro.htm.

Banerjee, A. V., & Duflo, E. (2007). The economic lives of the poor. *Journal of Economic Perspectives, 21*(1), 141–167.

BBS. (2011). *Report of the household income & expenditure survey 2010*. Dhaka: Bangladesh Bureau of Statistics, Planning Division of Ministry of Planning.

Bonnerjee, A., & Köhler, G. (2011). *The challenge of food and nutrition insecurity and policy innovations from the South*. Rethinking Development in an Age of Scarcity and Uncertainty, University of York, York.

Demeke, M., Pangrazio, G., & Maetz, M. (2009). Country responses to the food security crisis: Nature and preliminary implications of the policies pursued. *Agricultural Policy Support Service*. Rome: Food and Agriculture Organization.

FAO. (2002). *The State of Food Insecurity in the World 2001*. Food and Agriculture Organization, Rome.

FAO. (2009). *The State of Food Insecurity in the World 2008*. Food and Agriculture Organization, Rome.

Hassan, M. K., & Khan, J. M. (2007). Zakat, external debt and poverty reduction strategy in Bangladesh. *Journal of Economic Cooperations, 28*(4), 1–38.

Institute of Microfinance. (2011). Interest rates in Bangladesh microcredit market. Dhaka, Bangladesh. Available at: http://inm.org.bd/wp-content/uploads/2016/01/Interest-Rate.pdf.

Josling, T. (2011). *Global food stamps: An idea worth considering? ICTSD programme on agricultural trade and sustainable development*. Geneva: International Centre for Trade and Sustainable Development.

Kahf, M. (1995). Applied institutional models for Zakat collection and distribution in Islamic countries and communities. In el-Ashker & Sirajul Haq (Eds.), *Institutional framework of zakat: Dimensions and implications* (pp. 197–228). Jeddah: Islamic Research and Training Institute, Islamic Development Bank.

Kahf, M. (2013). *Zakah*. Available at http://monzer.kahf.com/papers/english/Zakah.pdf.

Kahf, M., & Khan, M. (1988). *Principles of Islamic finance: A survey*. Jeddah: Islamic Research and Training Institute, Islamic Development Bank.

Laila, T. (2009). *Zakat based solution to food security*. In 4th Garnet Annual Conference, Rome.

Mahmud, K. T. (2010). Does microcredit really matter to women borrowers of Bangladesh? A case of BRAC's agribusiness program. *The Global Journal of Finance and Economics, 7*(2), 111–121.

Mahmud, K. T., Hassan, M. K., Alam, M. F., Sohag, K., & Rafiq, F. (2014). Opinion of the Zakat recipients on their food security: A case study on Bangladesh. *International Journal of Islamic and Middle Eastern Finance and Management, 7*(3), 333–345.

Mallick, D. (2012). Microfinance and moneylender interest rate: Evidence from Bangladesh. *World Development, 40*(6), 1181–1189.

McKernan, S. M., Pitt, M. M., & Moskowitz, D. (2005). *Use of the formal and informal financial sectors: Does gender matter. Empirical evidence from rural Bangladesh* (World Bank Policy Research Working Paper 3491). Washington, DC: World Bank.

Mesbahuddin, T. (2010). Religion in development: An Islamic model emerging in Bangladesh. *Journal of South Asian Development, 5*(2), 221–241.

Nurzaman, M. S. (2011). *Zakat and human development: An emparical analysis on poverty alleviation in Jakarta, Indonesia.* In 8th International Conference on Islamic Economics and Finance, Doha.

Oran, A. F. (2009). Zakat funds and wealth creation. *Review of Islamic Economics, 13*(1), 143–154.

Patel, R. (2007). *Stuffed and starved: The hidden battle for the world food system* (2nd ed.). New York: Melville House Publishing.

Pinstrup-Andersen, P. (2009). Food security: Definition and measurement. *Food Security, 1*(1), 5–7.

Qardawi, Y. (1999). *Fiqh az-Zakat.* London: Dar Al Taqwa.

Raquib, A. (2011). Islamic banking and zakat-an alternative approach to poverty reduction in Bangladesh. *Journal of Islamic Economics, Banking and Finance, 7*(2), 11–26.

Savaş, A., & Haneef, M. A. (2015). *Integration of Waqf and Islamic Microfinance for Poverty Reduction: Case Studies of Malaysia, Indonesia and Bangladesh.* The Statistical, Economic and Social Research and Training Centre for Islamic Countries (SESRIC). Ankara and International Islamic University Malaysia (IIUM), Kuala Lumpur.

Sen, A. (2010). Hunger: Old torments and new blunders. *Hunger, The Little Magazine, 2*(6), New Delhi.

USDA. (2009). *Food security assessment, 2008–09.* Washington, DC: United States Department of Agriculture.

Wahid, H., Kader, R. A., & Ahmad, S. 2012. *Localization of Zakat distribution, religiosity, quality of life and attitude change* (Perceptions of Zakat Recipients in Malaysia). In 13th Malaysia Indonesia Conference on Economics, Management and Accounting (MIICEMA), Palembang.

World Bank. (2009). *Improving food security in Arab countries.* Washington, DC: World Bank. Available at: http://siteresources.worldbank.org/INTMENA/Resources/FoodSecfinal.pdf.

World Bank. (2011, February). Food price watch. World Bank: Washington, DC. Available at: http://www.worldbank.org/foodcrisis/food_price_watch_report_feb2011.html.

World Bank. (2012). *The grain chain: Food security and managing wheat imports in Arab countries* (World Bank Policy Research Paper No. 68075). Washington, DC: World Bank.

Zeller, M., Sharma, M., Ahmed, A. U., & Rashid, S. (2001). *Group-based financial institutions for the rural poor in Bangladesh: An institutional and household-level analysis* (Research Report No. 120). Washington, DC: IFPRI.

6

Behavioral Dimensions of Islamic Philanthropy: The Case of *Zakat*

Mohammed Obaidullah and Turkhan Ali Abdul Manap

Abstract This chapter studies the behavior of individual Islamic donors who make a specific type of religious contribution called *zakat*. It seeks to provide a fundamental understanding of what governs the behavior of these donors—the triggers and motivators, traits and attributes, and preferences. The study uses hierarchical cluster analysis to develop psychographic profiles of individual Islamic donors or groups among them. Interestingly, two of the three clusters closely resemble subsets of the overall sample, when disaggregated on the basis of donor's country of origin, indicating the possibility that Islamic donors from a given country may be displaying a distinct behavioral pattern. This raises a more profound possibility that the national identity of the donor associated with a unique social, economic, legal, and political environment

M. Obaidullah (✉) · T. A. A. Manap
Islamic Research and Training Institute,
Islamic Development Bank Group, Jeddah, Saudi Arabia
e-mail: mobaidullah@isdb.org

T. A. A. Manap
e-mail: turkhanali@isdb.org

© The Author(s) 2017

M. Zulkhibri and A. G. Ismail (eds.), *Financial Inclusion and Poverty Alleviation*,
Palgrave Studies in Islamic Banking, Finance, and Economics,
https://doi.org/10.1007/978-3-319-69799-4_6

may be a key influencer of the way she/he engages in matters pertaining to faith. The evidence highlights the need to give due importance to the observed diversity among *zakat* donors in any initiative to develop core principles, regulatory standards, institutional infrastructure, and models of governance for the development of this component of the global Islamic social finance sector.

JEL Classification G20 · G21 · G28

Keywords Islamic philanthropy · *Zakat* · Behavioral · Development

6.1 Introduction

Zakat is a unique form of charity in Islam. For a believing and practicing high net worth Muslim, it is a compulsory annual levy. In the classical framework, *zakat* is to be mobilized by the Islamic state and utilized for beneficiaries as ordained by the Shari'ah. In the absence of a state enforcement mechanism, however, *zakat* is clubbed with other forms of philanthropy that is undertaken by the individual. At the same time, given that the primary beneficiaries of *zakat* are the poor and the destitute, *zakat* is deemed to be a tool of poverty alleviation. The voluntary dimension of *zakat* payment naturally requires an understanding of donor behavior. Every donor has unique behavioral traits that motivate and trigger his/her action. It may be simple obedience and servitude to the commands of the Almighty as transmitted through religion. Or, it may be rooted in benevolence and a sense of obligation to help the poor and the needy. Or, it may be borne out of "affinity" for members of extended family and clan. Such action may also be a result of a strong desire to please the Creator by helping His creation. Donors may also be triggered by a sense of guilt and the need to expiate sins committed consciously or unconsciously. Donor behavior may also be shaped by the existing practices with respect to the management of the charity funds. Arguably, every donor has a unique set of preferences that may vary with respect to the role of a centralized or decentralized system, local and institutional actors, and the clergy. A donor may also prefer a "collectivist" scenario that is built on "trust" where measures to ensure transparency, accountability, and good governance are in place. If such measures are not or cannot be put in place, she/he may prefer an "individualist" scenario and self-management of *zakat*.

The purpose of this chapter is to provide a fundamental understanding of what governs the behavior of *zakat* donors—the triggers, motivators, preferences, and inclinations as well as aversions and discomforts—and then map the same with what the environment offers to them. A gap, if any, will naturally have policy implications and call for reforms. Since the regulatory infrastructure and policy environment usually differ across countries, the study also documents and compares donor behavior for country-specific subsets of the overall sample. The rest of the chapter is organized as follows. Section 6.2 undertakes a survey of related literature, primary in conventional and secular domain on what motivates the donors. Section 6.3 describes the objectives, data, and methodology. Section 6.4 presents the findings and discusses the same. Section 6.5 provides a summary of the paper.

6.2 Prior Studies

A number of studies have been undertaken to investigate a fundamental question: "what motivates an Islamic donor to donate?"

The intrinsic and extrinsic motivations for charitable giving can vary from donor to donor (Sargeant and Woodliffe 2007). A 2009 study by the Center for Philanthropy, Indiana university finds top three motivations for giving as follows: (i) providing for the poor's basic needs such as food and shelter; (ii) helping the poor help themselves; and (iii) making the community better. Bekkers and Bowman (2008) link charitable giving to trust. They find that a higher level of general trust is associated with more confidence in charitable organizations and charitable giving. People who are more trusting and believing in altruistic values are more likely to have confidence in charitable organizations and to start volunteering.

Several studies examined the linkage between income differences and factors, such as altruism, trust, and responsibility. Andreoni (1990) finds that the degree of altruism varies by income level. Wiepking (2007), however, does not find an effect of income on the probability of giving, but finds a consistent negative effect of income on both total and religious donations as a proportion of income. A synthesis of the current research into "major" donors and philanthropic giving undertaken by the Institute for Fundraising has some interesting findings regarding what motivates the major donors (Lincoln and Saxton 2012). The synthesis clearly highlights that major donors in developed countries emphasize the importance of strategic philanthropy; most give to causes where they have a personal connection. Interestingly, religious organizations figure in the group that receives the least support.

Breeze (2011) summarizes various theories of philanthropy that emphasize (i) the "purchase" of donor benefits, including intrinsic benefits, such as the satisfaction and pleasure gained by the act of donation; (ii) the creation and communication of a certain individual identity; (iii) an attempt to shape the world, while also transforming self-image; (iv) the relationship building between donors, charities, recipients and other donors; and (v) the pursuit of a moral and purposeful life or self-actualization. Schervish (2008) argues that all giving is motivated by an array of factors. An extensive study of major donor motivation in the UK (Lloyd 2004) groups the varied motivations that drive giving among the wealthy into five categories: (i) belief in the cause; (ii) being a catalyst for change; (iii) self-actualization; (iv) duty and responsibility; and (v) relationships. Although economists, psychologists, sociologists, and other researchers have identified many motivations for giving, including a variety of predictors, such as tax implications, altruism, and others, the models and theories of the motives for donating have proven insufficient (Vesterlund 2006; Van Slyke and Brooks 2005; Burnett and Wood 1988).

A number of studies explore the link between religiosity and charitable behavior. Religiosity has been proven to be a significant contributor to charitable giving in American society (Schervish 1997). Religion provides a cognitive framework that fosters caring and benevolent behavior. The impact of religiosity on religious donations is explicit. Brown and

Ferris (2007) show that people with religious beliefs tend to be generous and have greater concern for disadvantaged groups. Lili and Elizabeth (2008) explore the impact of social capital on individual charitable giving to religious and secular organizations and find evidence of important differences in the determinants of religious and secular giving, suggesting the need to distinguish these two types of charitable giving in future work.

In relation to Islamic charity, studies are extremely rare. Bakar and Rashid (2010) examine the motivations underlying *zakat* on income for Malaysia. In a survey of 31 academics of the International Islamic University Malaysia, this study investigated the relative importance attached by Islamic donors to several motivators, e.g., *zakat* as a social obligation toward the Muslim Ummah; a payment toward the rights of the poor and needy; a religious obligation; a way to improve the economic condition of the Ummah; an effective mechanism for wealth distribution; and a way to claim tax rebate. The study witnessed a near agreement (ranging between 75 and 90%) among most respondents on all the factors. The study concludes rather hastily that Muslims do not take into serious consideration the issue of *zakat* distribution since what matters more to them is that they would get tax rebate out of the *zakat* on income paid. They base their conclusion on the finding that the availability of tax rebate is ranked higher in its influence toward the fulfillment of *zakat* obligation (80%) as compared to the effectiveness of *zakat* for wealth redistribution (74%). This is notwithstanding the fact that 84% of respondents stressed on *zakat* as a tool to improve the economic condition of the Ummah. Needless to say, there is a need for a study that uses a more exhaustive and comprehensive list of motivators, and a much larger sample size to arrive at realistic results.

In an early study, the first of its kind, Diabi (1993) sought to explain the underlying reasons for non-payment of *zakat*. Treating *zakat* similar to income tax, he hypothesized that the probability of a Muslim individual declaring his/her true income (and the *zakat* payable thereon) depends on the individual faith, attitude toward risk of being detected, and the enforcement of a penalty for *zakat* evasion. This framework is understandable in the context of Saudi Arabia, where *zakat* is compulsorily mandated by the state and enforced vigorously in a manner similar to income tax. A study to examine reasons for "*zakat* evasion" therefore makes sense in this context. It does not go very far, given the contemporary realities in most Muslim countries where *zakat* payment is treated as a voluntary contribution from the standpoint of legal compliance, even while it is compulsory from a religious point of view. In these countries, tax benefit may at best be seen as a tool to incentivize *zakat* payment.

In another study, Saad and Haniffa (2014) examine factors influencing business *zakat* compliance behavior using the theory of reasoned action (TRA) to investigate whether "attitude," "subjective norm," and "intention" are the determinants of *zakat* compliance behavior and find intention to be a significant predictor of *zakat* compliance behavior. Intention is further found to be influenced by both attitude and subjective norm, and it mediates the relationship between both factors with business *zakat* compliance behavior. In yet another study, Mustafa et al. (2013) investigate and seek to explain the factors underlying the inclination of Islamic donors to trust a particular *zakat* institution and find board capital, disclosure practices, governmental model of *zakat* institution, and stakeholder management as being the antecedents of Islamic donors' trust.

6.3 Objective, Data, and Methodology

The purpose of this study is to gain a fundamental understanding of what governs the behavior of *zakat* donors—the triggers and motivators, traits and attributes, preferences, inclinations as well as aversions and discomforts—and then map the same with what the environment offers. Based on their responses to a set of statements that connote specific motivators, traits, and preferences, an attempt has been made to develop psychographic profiles of individual Islamic donor groups. Various statements used in the study capture the following factors.

"Servitude to God" is expected to be the dominant motivator for a believing and practicing Muslim for whom *zakat* is compulsorily mandated by the Creator. It is a religious obligation that opens the possibility of earning His pleasure through helping His creation. "Purification and expiation" is also expected to be key motivators. *zakat* is paid by the believers and faithful as a way to purify wealth, to expiate one's sins. The study also considers "feel good" as well as "getting rid of feeling of guilt" as possible motivators. Since *zakat* is primarily targeted at alleviating poverty and helping the needy including the near-and-dear ones, "altruism," "benevolence and concern for others," "affinity and relationship" are also expected to motivate *zakat* payment. Additional motivators considered in the study are "self-actualization" through "making a difference to the society" and/or "helping a cause that is dear to one's heart," such as "propagation of Islam."

It may be noted here that some of the factors above may be interrelated because every action for a believing and practicing Muslim is, in the ultimate analysis, undertaken with a view to seek the pleasure of the Almighty and is motivated by "servitude to the Creator." The factors, however, connote specific concerns and are, therefore, considered independently as influencers and motivators. Other factors may be in the nature of more mundane considerations, such as immediate returns in the form of "tax benefits" and "self-recognition." *Zakat* may be paid simply for "compliance with dictates of the state" or to bring "social change through local and voluntary organizations."

The study also aims to examine the relationship if any, between the various motivators, influencers, and preferences of Islamic donors and their own individual traits—piety, benevolence, vigilance, accountability, responsibility, ability to trust, penchant for details, apathy, indolence, and indifference—as well as the characteristics of *zakat* organizations, e.g., governance, transparency, accountability, information sharing, frugality, extravagance, etc.

In addition to measuring the relative importance of factors that motivate the individual *zakat* donor, the study also seeks to profile the donors in terms of specific behavioral traits and preferences. The study has the additional objective of examining whether the above-mentioned factors are influenced by the country of origin of the *zakat* payer.

Another important objective of the study is to examine if and to what extent specific motivators, behavioral traits, and preferences are interrelated and go together. For instance, it may seek answers to the following types of questions. Do the individuals who pay *zakat* to seek the pleasure of God are also motivated by altruism, affinity or kinship? Do they show responsibility and accountability? Do they appreciate frugality and caution? Do they demand a lot of information? Do they prefer the state or non-state actors to be entrusted with *zakat* management? The study seeks to find answers to such questions by subjecting the statements to pair-wise correlation analysis, and cluster analysis.

6.3.1 Clustering Approach

Clustering is the method of identifying the distribution of patterns and intrinsic correlations in large data sets by partitioning the data points into similar classes. The major goal of cluster analysis is to separate n individual observations, or items, into k groups, or clusters, on the basis of the values for the q variables measured on each individual. There are three major classes of clustering algorithms, namely (1) hierarchical, (2) partitioning, and (3) model-based methods. Given that the nature of our data set is binary and is relatively small, we employ hierarchical cluster analysis with binary squared Euclidian distance and Ward-linkage to identify the number of clusters and thus the number of groups of Islamic donors with similar motivators, traits and preferences. Hierarchical cluster is well suited for binary data because it allows selecting from a great many distance functions invented for binary data and is theoretically more sound for them than simply Euclidean distance. More specifically, we use the following approach in clustering:

Suppose for each individual ($i = 1, \cdots, n$), let the binary variable X_{ij} take the value 0 or 1, where $j = 1, \cdots, q$. Then two individuals have a "match" on a binary variable if both individuals have the same values for that variable either both 0 or 1. Otherwise, the two individuals are said to have a "mismatch" on the binary variable. To determine the closeness of the clusters, we calculate the squared Euclidean distance $\sum_{ij}^{q} \left(X_{ij} - X_{i'j}\right)^2$ between each pair of rows of 0s and 1s.

Data for the study was collected through a survey. It required respondents to tick if they agree with a given statement. Respondents were asked to respond to 52 statements relating to their motivation and

Table 6.1 Servitude to God

Statement(s)	Total Sample	India	Nigeria	Malaysia
It is compulsorily mandated by God	77	88	67	77
It is a religious obligation for every rich Muslim	89	88	78	93
God is pleased with those who help his creation	57	67	40	58

preferences and 4 questions relating to their nationality, education, profession, and income. The survey was announced widely on the social media, including Twitter, Facebook, and several large networks, e.g., Thomson Reuters Islamic Finance Gateway, Global Islamic Economy, IBF Net, Islamic Finance Info, NRIndians, Bihar Anjuman and Sadaqa. In. The survey elicited a total of 226 respondents.

6.4 Findings and Discussion

First, we consider the relative importance attached to various motivators, triggers, and preferences. A simple calculation of the relative frequency of responses to a given statement throws up some interesting findings as below. We also consider three specific subsets from Nigeria, India, and Malaysia and examine if "country of origin" is a significant influencer of their behavior.

The primary motivator for *zakat* payer is "Servitude to God" (Table 6.1) as the related statements elicit maximum responses. The significance seems to be relatively lower for *zakat* payers from Nigeria.

Related to the above is the purification and expiation aspect of *zakat*. Islamic donors are motivated by positive statements without the use of terms, such as "sin" or "guilt." As high as 64% pay *zakat* because it "purifies" their wealth. The percentage comes down to 36% when the statement is rephrased as "wipes off sins." Similarly, a high 51% say they pay *zakat* because "it feels good" while only 30% say, they pay *zakat* because "it helps get rid of his/her feeling of guilt" (Tables 6.2 and 6.3).

"Benevolence and concern for the poor and the needy" motivates 63% of respondents and 44% pay *zakat* to an organization because it

Table 6.2 Purification and expiation

Statement(s)	Total Sample	India	Nigeria	Malaysia
Zakat payment purifies his/her wealth	64	79	53	55
Zakat payment wipes off his/her sins	36	43	26	41
He/she feels good after paying *zakat*	51	48	38	51
Zakat payment helps get rid of his/her feeling of guilt	30	21	32	34

Table 6.3 Altruism

Statement(s)	Total Sample	India	Nigeria	Malaysia
He/she must help the poor and the needy	63	67	42	70
His/her relatives and near and dear ones seek financial help	33	50	24	28
The organization receiving his/her *zakat* helps the poor and makes a difference to the society	44	39	10	57

can help the poor and make a difference to the society. Further, their "affinity" with potential beneficiaries motivates 33% of the Islamic donors. Altruism and affinity seem to be of relatively lesser significance in Nigeria as compared to India and Malaysia

"Self-actualization" is not a major motivator as a meager 27% say they pay *zakat* to an organization because it helps a cause dear to his/her heart. This percentage is unusually low at 5% for Nigeria, 30% for India, and 40% for Malaysia.

A higher percentage, 36% of all respondents pay *zakat* because it may be utilized for "propagation of Islam." This percentage is 24%, 33%, and 58% for Nigeria, India, and Malaysia, respectively.

"Self-recognition" is a motivator for a little more than one-third of respondents. 37% of them feel that *zakat* organizations must acknowledge his/her contribution through a letter or a note or some other form of recognition. This ratio is 19%, 64%, and 31% for Nigeria, India, and Malaysia, respectively.

Zakat payers may not be motivated significantly by immediate returns in the form of "tax benefits." It is a motivator for a mere 17% of the respondents and elicits almost zero response in Nigeria and India. It is, however, a significant motivator in a country like Malaysia.

Table 6.4 Tax benefits

Statement(s)	Total Sample	India	Nigeria	Malaysia
Zakat results in savings in income tax	17	0	2	50
If an individual pays *zakat*, he/she should get full deduction in income tax payable	46	55	29	68
If an individual pays *zakat*, he/she should get partial deduction in income tax payable	20	10	27	25
If a business pays *zakat*, it should get full deduction in income tax payable	31	48	16	38
If a business pays *zakat*, it should get partial deduction in income tax payable	18	12	24	13
Zakat and taxes should not be mixed up	46	79	57	17

The overall picture may be biased due to the absence of substantial tax benefit on *zakat* in a given jurisdiction. While Malaysia provides for tax rebate or a reduction in tax payable by the full amount of *zakat* paid, other countries provide tax benefit similar to other donations equal to a reduction in tax base or taxable earnings by the *zakat* amount. This is supported by the fact that 46% of Islamic donors feel if an individual pays *zakat*, he/she should get full deduction in income tax payable. The ratio is quite high in India at 55% and in Nigeria at a more modest 29%. A relatively lower percentage advocate partial deduction in tax payable. A relatively lower percentage also advocate tax benefit to businesses. However, an equally high 46% feel that *zakat* and taxes should not be mixed up; neither individual nor business should get any tax reduction for paying *zakat*. It is as high as 79% in India and extremely low at 17% in Malaysia, arguably for reasons cited above (Table 6.4).

"Compliance with dictates of the state" does not appear to be a significant motivator as only 12% acknowledge they pay *zakat* because it is compulsorily required by the state, even when the sample includes countries like Malaysia, Saudi Arabia, and Pakistan that have mandated *zakat* to be compulsory. Predictably, the ratio is higher at 33% in Malaysia, but does not explain the low overall ratio. The ratio, predictably is zero for India, consistent with the fact that state plays no role in *zakat* management) and a meager 7% in Nigeria (*zakat* is compulsorily

Table 6.5 Role of state, non-state actors in *zakat* collection/distribution

Statement(s)	Total Sample	India	Nigeria	Malaysia
Zakat should be collected/distributed by central government	40/41	17/12	31/27	73/72
Zakat should be collected/distributed by provincial government	34/40	14/12	24/27	62/70
Zakat should be collected/distributed by local entities	33/38	24/36	24/24	42/45
Zakat should be collected/distributed by individuals	18/23	24/43	22/16	12/12
Zakat should be collected/distributed by NGOs	49/52	79/76	53/51	27/28
Zakat should be collected/distributed by Ulema	20/18	33/31	29/22	8/10

mandated in a few provinces). Does this imply that Islamic donors are not in favor of the state having a role in *zakat* management? Quite contrarily, 40–41% of respondents feel that the central government should collect and distribute *zakat*. Similarly, 34% feel that the provincial government should collect *zakat* and a higher percent (40%) feel that it should distribute *zakat* as well. A country-wise analysis, however, offers quite interesting contrasts. India and Malaysia seem to be placed at opposite extremes with Nigeria placed in between. Few Indian Islamic donors see any role for the state at the central or provincial levels, a large majority batting for non-government organizations and some opting for the ulema. An exactly opposite set of preferences is reported for Islamic donors from Malaysia. Preferences from Nigeria are similar to India, albeit less intense (Table 6.5).

Overall, a sizable percentage of Islamic donors perhaps look forward to "social change through local and voluntary initiatives" if we bracket local entities with NGOs and ulema together.

Islamic donors display a high sense of responsibility/accountability in the matter of *zakat* estimation and payment with 67% asserting that they have a fair knowledge of how to estimate their *zakat* liability. 27% need professional advice and assistance. A high 46% feel it is their responsibility and religious obligation to ensure that *zakat* is utilized properly for the benefit of the poor and the needy. 14%, however, display extreme apathy, indolence and indifference and say they are unconcerned about how *zakat* is utilized once the obligation

Table 6.6 Responsibility and accountability

Statement(s)	Total Sample	India	Nigeria	Malaysia
Have fair knowledge of how to estimate my *zakat* liability	67	81	67	55
Need the assistance of experts to estimate my *zakat* liability	27	21	20	47
Not concerned about how *zakat* is utilized once I pay my *zakat* to the collection	14	10	9	27
Own responsibility to ensure that *zakat* is spent for the benefit of the poor and asnaf	46	69	36	37
A religious obligation to ensure that *zakat* is utilized properly	46	64	27	38

to pay is over. Is there a pattern too in the country-specific responses (Table 6.6)?

Indian *zakat* donors demonstrate a high sense of responsibility and accountability. Feeling that they are adequately knowledgeable, they hold themselves personally responsible and accountable for the end-use of *zakat.* Nigerian respondents also demonstrate fair level of knowledgeable but a far lesser degree of personal accountability for the end-use of *zakat.* Malaysian *zakat* donors feel they need expert assistance and also demonstrate moderate levels of personal accountability. The felt need for expert advice may also demonstrate a "quest for accuracy and perfection." However, the straightforward response that "I am not concerned about how *zakat* is utilized" among 27% of Malaysian Islamic donors compared to 10% and 9% of Islamic donors from India and Nigeria, respectively does indicate "apathy" and "indifference" as being the reason for seeking expert assistance (Table 6.7).

Islamic donors clearly feel that the *zakat*-collecting organizations should heavily promote their campaigns to raise funds, similar to modern fund-raising organizations, through roadshows, conferences, etc. (42%) and use mainstream media—newspaper, TV, Internet, etc. for advertising and fund-raising campaigns (50%). An equally large number of respondents (48%) feel that they should avoid costly and expensive methods of creating awareness. Only a meager 16% believe that they should use masjids alone for creating awareness regarding *zakat.*

Table 6.7 Frugality

Statement(s)	Total Sample	India	Nigeria	Malaysia
Heavily promote through fund-raising campaigns, roadshows, conferences, etc.	42	21	31	77
Use mainstream media—newspaper, TV, Internet, etc.	50	31	47	70
Avoid costly and expensive methods of creating awareness	48	60	40	40
Use masjids only for creating awareness regarding *zakat*	16	24	7	10

Table 6.8 Conservatism/Caution

Statement(s)	Total Sample	India	Nigeria	Malaysia
Never use *zakat* to cover own administrative expenses	39	29	31	52
Never use more than one-eighth of *zakat* collected to cover their own administrative expenses	48	45	33	57
Never carry undistributed surplus *zakat* to next year	36	48	24	30
Never invest *zakat* surplus to generate good long-term returns	35	38	27	50
Never invest *zakat* surplus in safe and liquid avenues, even if for a short term	26	33	20	28

Indian *zakat* donors tend to be far more frugal than their Nigerian and Malaysian counterparts with 60% preferring a cautious approach and avoidance of promotional methods that cost money. Malaysian *zakat* donors (77%) seem to be quite comfortable with aggressive marketing and promotional campaigns to raise funds. Once again Indian *zakat* donors display distinct inclination for frugality, with only 21% in favor of promotion and some even opting for the traditional use of masjid for creating public awareness about *zakat* (Table 6.8).

Islamic donors, overall, display a high degree of conservatism in the matter of utilization of *zakat* by organizations to cover their own administrative expenses with 39% entirely ruling this out and 48% opting for the standard practice of permitting *zakat* organizations to use up to one-eighth of *zakat* collected to cover their own administrative

Table 6.9 Governance

Statement(s)	Total Sample	India	Nigeria	Malaysia
Audited every year by independent financial auditors	58	48	29	82
Audited every year by independent Shari'ah auditors	65	69	49	75
Report the figure for total *zakat* collections every month to the public	40	33	27	50
Report the figures for *zakat*, Sadaqa, and cash waqf separately to the public	48	52	31	45
Report the category-wise distribution of *zakat* every year to the public	49	57	29	53
Report the project-wise distribution of *zakat* every year to the public	48	52	24	52

expenses. Since *zakat* flows are meant for the poor and the destitute, scholars recommend that *zakat* collected during a year should be fully spent during that year. 35–36% of Islamic donors seem to take an extreme position in this matter and prefer a prohibition on organizations from carrying undistributed surplus *zakat* to the next lunar year and/or investing such surplus to generate good long-term returns. Even when such surplus is invested in safe and liquid avenues for a short term, 26% find the idea repugnant. While respondents from Malaysia bat for aggressive marketing and fund-raising campaigns, they also display at the same time a higher degree of concern. Fifty-two percent feel that the entire cost should be absorbed by non-*zakat* funds and 57% prefer to place a cap at one-eighth of *zakat* funds collected. In the matter of carry forward of undistributed surplus, they display more flexibility with only 30% rejecting this possibility. The corresponding percentage for India is 48% (Table 6.9).

Individual *zakat* donors place a lot of value on "audit" with 58% opting for mandatory and independent financial audit and 65% for Shari'ah audit. 40% seem to be avid seekers of information requiring that organizations must report the figure for total *zakat* collections every month to the public. They also seem to place high value on transparency in the form of separation of *zakat* from Sadaqa, cash waqf funds and their disclosure to the public (48–49%). An equally large percent of respondents require annual disclosure of category-wise as well as project-wise distribution of *zakat* to the public. The inter-country comparison clearly shows that there are major differences in the way Islamic donors demand good governance and seek transparency. Respondents from Nigeria are least concerned about audit and are least demanding in terms of relevant information. *Zakat* donors from Malaysia display maximum vigilance and concern for good governance.

While making inter-country comparison and interpreting the country-specific findings, it is useful to juxtapose the social, economic, legal, and political environment present in these countries. It may be noted that in Malaysia, *zakat* management is undertaken in a fairly organized manner with involvement of state and private corporate entities, with a legal regulatory framework in place and with a policy environment that coordinates between financial institutions, religious councils, inland revenue authorities, and other relevant institutions. In India, on the other hand, *zakat* management takes place in a regulatory and policy vacuum and is undertaken informally with minimal involvement of any institutional and organizational infrastructure, the ulema playing a key role in creating public awareness, collecting and utilizing *zakat* funds. In such an environment, "trust" reposed in the ulema essentially replaces the need for timely sharing of information; with the ulema accountable only to God. Nigeria interestingly, is characterized by a mix of formal and informal *zakat* management with involvement of the state entities, as well as non-state actors at local levels; a regulatory framework being in place in only a few provinces. The perceived significance of financial audit, Shari'ah audit, information sharing, and good governance practices may thus be explained in terms of the impact of these environmental differences on the Islamic donor's motivators, traits, and preferences.

As the next step in analysis, the study finds motivators, traits, attributes, and preferences that go together and based on this, clubs them together forming groups or clusters with similar psychographic profiles. We also use descriptors (as distinct from definitions) based on behavioral traits, attributes, and preferences as presented in Appendix 1. Based on the cluster dendrogram presented in Fig. 6.1, we identify three distinct clusters as follows.

The first cluster includes God's servants, who pay *zakat* simply because it is ordained by God. They take it on themselves to acquire the

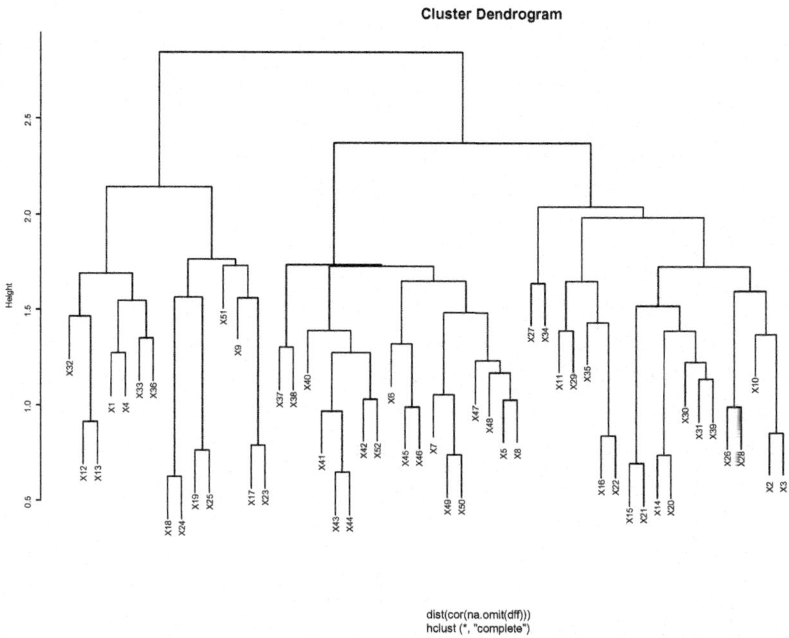

CLUSTER I	CLUSTER II	CLUSTER III
x32: conformist, frugal, x12:responsible, x13:accountable, x1: religious-dutiful, x4: God's servants, x33: traditionalist - parsimonious, x36: traditionalist — conservative, x18: institutionalist, x24: institutionalist, x19: ulema - loyalist, x25: ulema-loyalist, x51: purist, x9: knowledgeable, x17: individualist — anarchist, x23: individualist - anarchist	x37: greed-buster, x38:traditionalist, x40: Shari'ah-conformist, x41: control-freak, x43: information-seeker, x44: information-seeker, x42: Shari'ah-conformist, x52: recognition-seeker, x6: propagator-of-faith, x45: reformist, x46: change-agent, x7: affinity-seeker, x49: sin-expiator, x50: guilt-expiator, x47:feel-gooder, x48:purist, x5: do-gooder, x8: God's-pleasure-seeker	x27: tax-saver, x34: skeptical, x11: indolent-apathetic, x29: tax-saver, x35: cautious - compliance-freak, x16: localist, x22: localist, x15:federalist, x21: federalist, x14: statist — collectivist, x20: statist — collectivist, x30: prodigal-campaigner, x31:communicator, x39: reckoner, x26: return-seeker, x28: return-seeker, x10: ignoramus, x2: tax-saver, x3: statist -law-abiding

Fig. 6.1 Descriptors based on behavioral traits, attributes and preferences

necessary knowledge regarding *zakat* rules. They tend to favor *zakat* management by "non-government actors" including the NGOs, ulema and even by pious individuals. They display high degree of responsibility and accountability and consider it as their own responsibility and/or religious obligation to ensure that *zakat* is spent for the benefit of the poor and the needy. They prefer a frugal and traditional approach to creating public awareness, such as the masjids. They feel the *zakat*-collecting organizations should avoid costly and expensive methods of creating awareness. They tend to believe in the traditional view that the *zakat* organizations must never carry undistributed surplus *zakat* to next year. A juxtaposition and careful comparison of this cluster with the observations for the sub-sample from India throws up strikingly similarities.

The second cluster includes Islamic donors who display high degree of altruism, benevolence, and concern for the poor and the needy. They also pay *zakat* to be used for propagation of faith and also to help their near and dear ones. They believe this will purify their wealth, expiate their sins, and make them feel good. They pay *zakat* because they believe *zakat* is used for a cause dear to their heart and brings about a change in the society. They do it to seek God's pleasure as the ultimate objective. They do not display preference for any particular infrastructure of *zakat* management, but are more concerned about the governance aspects of *zakat* management. They are traditionalists, unconcerned about returns and feel that *zakat* surplus should not be invested, either to generate good long-term returns or even for short term in safe and liquid avenues. They are also conservative and place a high value on Shari'ah compliance, especially on the fulfillment of Shari'ah conditions like separation of *zakat* funds from other forms of donations. They demand transparency and expect to be informed routinely about category-wise and project-wise distribution of *zakat*.

The third cluster includes *zakat* players who primarily seek some form of immediate returns, in the form of tax savings. Tax savers show very high correlation with the statists and the law-abiding. They strongly believe that the state (central or provincial) should provide a complete infrastructure for *zakat* management. The state should provide tax rebate—full or partial—on *zakat* to all *zakat* payers, whether individuals or businesses. Tax savers tend to need expert assistance for estimation of their *zakat* liability and display apathy and indifference toward how their *zakat* is going to be utilized. They also seem to champion aggressive marketing and use of media and modern technology for *zakat* management. They display some distrust for *zakat* bodies and explicitly demand that the *zakat* organizations must never use more than one-eighth of *zakat* collected by them to cover their own administrative expenses. They also seek legal compliance in the form of periodic financial audit. A juxtaposition and careful comparison of this cluster with the observations for the sub-sample from Malaysia throws up strikingly similarities.

6.5 Conclusion

The study has attempted to gain a fundamental understanding of what governs the behavior of *zakat* donors—the triggers and motivators, traits and attributes, preferences, and inclinations as well as aversions and discomforts. Based on their responses to a set of statements that connote a specific motivator, attribute or trait, and preference, an attempt has been made to develop psychographic profiles of individual Islamic donors or groups among them. The study finds "servitude to God" as the dominant motivator. Other key motivators include "purification and expiation," "altruism, benevolence and concern for others." Additional motivators observed in the study are "self-actualization" through "making a difference to the society" and/or "helping a cause that is dear to one's heart," such as, "propagation of Islam." "Immediate returns" in the form of "tax-savings" or "self-recognition" appear to be insignificant motivators when results for the overall sample are considered. These, however, constitute major motivators for sub-sample comprising Islamic donors from Malaysia. This sub-sample also bats for a significant role for state in *zakat* management.

With increasing role of the state in religious matters, e.g., *zakat*, there is a clear and perceptible danger of the believers behaving more as citizens and perhaps seeking compliance with state laws and not as pious and benevolent Muslims seeking the pleasure of God. It is not difficult to see the complete turnaround in the objective function of the believer—from seeking to maximize pious and good deeds in the form of *zakat* payment to one of seeing *zakat* as a state-imposed tax and seeking to minimize "*zakat* burden." Indeed, this possibility manifests in the literature on *zakat* compliance cited in this study where researchers find the "probability of being detected and penalized by the state" as among the key factors bringing about "*zakat* compliance." Our study, however, correctly hypothesizes that the investigated factors should include motivators in an environment where *zakat* payment is similar to other forms of donations, for "there is no compulsion in religion" in the ultimate analysis. Our findings provide strong supporting evidence that Islamic donors pay *zakat* because it is required by the Creator, and not by the state.

The study presents interesting contrasts among Islamic donors in terms of their motivators, preferences, and behavioral patterns. It reduces the matrix of responses collected across 28 countries to a set of such factors to three distinct clusters. Interestingly, two of the three clusters closely resemble subsets of the overall sample, when disaggregated on the basis of country of origin, indicating the possibility that Islamic donors from a given country may be displaying a distinct set of motivators, preferences, and behavioral patterns. Given the significance of *zakat* as the third pillar of Islam, this raises a more profound possibility. The national identity of a Muslim is associated with unique social, economic, legal, and political environment and thus may be a key influencer of the way he/she develops an understanding of the Islamic tenets and displays unique behavioral traits and preferences in matters relating to faith, as important as *zakat*. The idea of unity of the Ummah in thought and action, though cherished by all faithful, does not quite dominate the impact of environmental differences rooted in nationality.

Appendix 1: List Statements and Descriptors

Code	Statement	Descriptor
X1	I pay *zakat* because it is a religious obligation for me	Religious–dutiful
X2	I pay *zakat* because I save on my income tax	Tax saver
X3	I pay *zakat* because it is compulsorily required by the state	Statist/law-abiding
X4	I pay *zakat* because it is compulsory mandated by God SWT	God's servant

Code	Statement	Descriptor
X5	I pay *zakat* because I must help the poor and the needy	Do-gooder
X6	I pay *zakat* because my *zakat* may be utilized for propagation of Islam	Propagator of faith
X7	I pay *zakat* because my relatives and near and dear ones seek my financial help	Affinity seeker
X8	I pay *zakat* because God SWT is pleased with those who help His creation	God's pleasure seeker
X45	I pay *zakat* because organization receiving my *zakat* helps the poor and makes a difference to the society	Reformist
X46	I pay *zakat* because organization receiving my *zakat* helps a cause that is dear to my heart	Change agent
X47	I pay *zakat* because I feel good after paying *zakat*	Feel gooder
X48	I pay *zakat* because *Zakat* payment purifies my wealth	Purist
X49	I pay *zakat* because *Zakat* payment wipes off my sins	Sin expiator
X50	I pay *zakat* because *Zakat* payment helps me get rid of my feeling of guilt	Guilt expiator
X9	As a *zakat* payer, I have a fair knowledge of how to estimate my *zakat* liability	Knowledgeable
X10	As a *zakat* payer, I need the assistance of experts to estimate my *zakat* liability	Ignoramus
X11	As a *zakat* payer, I am not concerned about how *zakat* is utilized once I pay my *zakat* to the collection	Indolent–apathetic
X12	As a *zakat* payer, it is my responsibility to ensure that *zakat* is spent for the benefit of the poor and asnaf	Responsible
X13	As a *zakat* payer, it is my religious obligation to ensure that *zakat* is utilized properly	Accountable
X14	Who should collect *zakat*: the Central government in a country or its agency	Statist/Collectivist
X15	Who should collect *zakat*: the local/provincial government in a country or its agency	Regionalist/federalist
X16	Who should collect *zakat*: village/town committees and sub-committees	Localist
X17	Who should collect *zakat*: individuals	Individualist/anarchist
X18	Who should collect *zakat*: Muslim NGOs	Institutionalist

Code	Statement	Descriptor
X19	Who should collect *zakat*: Ulema	Ulema-loyalist
X20	Who should distribute *zakat*: the Central government in a country or its agency	Statist/collectivist
X21	Who should distribute *zakat*: the local/ provincial government in a country or its agency	Regionalist/federalist
X22	Who should distribute *zakat*: village/ town committees and sub-committees	Localist
X23	Who should distribute *zakat*: individuals	Individualist/anarchist
X24	Who should distribute *zakat*: Muslim NGOs	Institutionalist
X25	Who should distribute *zakat*: Ulema	Ulema-loyalist
X26	If an individual pays *zakat*, he/she should get FULL deduction in income tax payable	Return seeker
X27	If an individual pays *zakat*, he/she should get PARTIAL deduction in income tax payable	Tax saver
X28	If a business pays *zakat*, it should get FULL deduction in income tax payable	Return seeker
X29	If a business pays *zakat*, it should get PARTIAL deduction in income tax payable	Tax saver
X51	*Zakat* and taxes should not be mixed up; neither individual nor business should get ANY tax reduction for paying *zakat*	Purist
X30	*Zakat*-collecting organizations should heavily promote their campaigns to raise funds, similar to modern fund-raising organizations, through roadshows, conferences, etc.	Prodigal campaigner
X31	*Zakat*-collecting organizations should use mainstream media—newspaper, TV, Internet, etc. for advertising and fund-raising campaigns	Communicator
X32	*Zakat*-collecting organizations should avoid costly and expensive methods of creating awareness	Conformist, frugal
X33	*Zakat*-collecting organizations should use masjids ONLY for creating awareness regarding *zakat*	Traditionalist, parsimonious
X34	*Zakat* organizations must NEVER use *zakat* to cover their own administrative expenses	Skeptical

Code	Statement	Descriptor
X35	*Zakat* organizations must NEVER use more than one-eighth of *zakat* collected to cover their own administrative expenses	Cautious—compliance freak
X36	*Zakat* organizations must NEVER carry undistributed surplus *zakat* to next lunar year	Traditionalist—conservative
X37	*Zakat* organizations must NEVER invest *zakat* surplus to generate good long-term returns	Greed buster
X38	*Zakat* organizations must NEVER invest *zakat* surplus in safe and liquid avenues for a short term	Traditionalist—conservative
X39	*Zakat* organizations must be audited every year by independent financial auditors	Reckoner
X40	*Zakat* organizations must be audited every year by independent Shari'ah auditors	Shari'ah conformist
X41	*Zakat* organizations must report the figure for total *zakat* collections every month to the public	Control freak
X42	*Zakat* organizations must report the figures for *zakat*, sadaqa, cash waqf separately to the public	Shari'ah conformist
X43	*Zakat* organizations must report the category-wise distribution of *zakat* every year to the public	Information seeker
X44	*Zakat* organizations must report the project-wise distribution of *zakat* every year to the public	Information seeker
X52	*Zakat* organizations must acknowledge my contribution through a letter or a note or some other form of recognition	Recognition-seeker

References

Andreoni, J. (1990). Impure altruism and donations to public goods: A theory of warm-glow giving. *Economic Journal, 100*(401), 464–477.

Bakar, N. B. A., & Rashid, H. M. A. (2010). Motivations of paying zakat on income: Evidence from Malaysia. *International Journal of Economics and Finance, 2*(3), 76–84.

Bekkers, R., & Bowman, W. (2008). The relationship between confidence in charitable organizations and volunteering revisited. *Nonprofit and Volunteer Sector Quarterly, 38*(5), 884–897.

Breeze, B. (2011). Philanthropy. In D. Southerton (Ed.), *Encyclopedia of Consumer Culture*. London: Routledge.

Brown, E., & Ferris, J. (2007). Social capital and philanthropy: An analysis of the impact of social capital on individual giving and volunteering. *Nonprofit and Voluntary Sector Quarterly, 36*(1), 85–99.

Burnett, J. J., & Wood, V. R. (1988). A proposed model of the donation decision process. *Research in Consumer Behavior, 3,* 1–47.

Diabi, A. (1993). The concept of Zakah evasion: An economic interpretation. *Review of Islamic Economics, 2*(2), 17–27.

Lili, W., & Elizabeth, G. (2008). Social capital, volunteering, and charitable giving. *VOLUNTAS: International Journal of Voluntary and Nonprofit Organizations, 19*(1), 23–42.

Lincoln, S., & Saxton, J. (2012). Major Donor Giving Research Report, Institute of Fundraising.

Lloyd, T. (2004). *Why rich people give*. London: Association of Charitable Foundations.

Mustafa, O. A. M., Mohamad, M. H. S., & Adnan, M. A. (2013). Antecedents of zakat payers' trust in an emerging zakat sector: An exploratory study, *Journal of Islamic Accounting and Business Research, 4*(1): 4–25.

Saad, R. A., & Haniffa, R. (2014). Determinants of Zakah (Islamic tax) compliance behavior. *Journal of Islamic Accounting and Business Research, 5*(2), 182–193.

Sargeant, A., & Woodliffe, L. (2007). Gift giving: An interdisciplinary review. *International Journal of Nonprofit and Voluntary Sector Marketing, 12*, November 2007, 275–307.

Schervish, P. G. (1997). Inclination, obligation, and association: What we know and what we need to learn about donor motivation. In D. F. Burlingame (Ed.), *Critical issues in fund raising*. New York: Wiley.

Schervish, P. G. (2008). Why the wealthy give: Factors which mobilize philanthropy among high net-worth individuals. In A. Sargeant & W. Wymer (Eds.), *The Routledge Companion to Nonprofit Marketing*. Routledge: Abingdon.

Van Slyke, D. M., & Brooks, A. C. (2005). Why do people give? New evidence and strategies for nonprofit managers. *American Review of Public Administration, 35*(3), 199–222.

Vesterlund, L. (2006). Why do people give? In W. W. Powell & R. Steinberg (Eds.), *The nonprofit sector: A research handbook* (2nd ed.).

Wiepking, P. (2007). The philanthropic poor: In search of explanations for the relative generosity of lower income households. *VOLUNTAS: International Journal of Voluntary and Nonprofit Organizations, 18*(4), 339–358.

7

The Impact of *Zakat* Programs from Human Development Perspectives: An Empirical Evaluation

Mohammad Soleh Nurzaman

Abstract This chapter analyzes the impact of *Zakat* on to the welfare of household of *Zakat* recipient (mustahiq). This study utilized human development index (HDI) as the indicator of welfare, which has been disaggregated at household level. The study performed two times repeated questionnaires to get the sample, and distributed to beneficiaries of productive-based *Zakat* who have received funding from *Zakat* institutions through two-stage cluster sampling. The study suggests that the level of human development index of household who receives productive-based *Zakat* is significantly higher than the first period. Moreover, through panel data regression, the results show that the variable of productive-based *Zakat* is positively correlated with the level of HDI. Therefore, it can be concluded that *Zakat*, particularly productive-based *Zakat*, can play important role to improve the welfare of poor household.

M. S. Nurzaman (✉)
University of Indonesia, Jakarta, Indonesia
e-mail: dedenmsn@gmail.com; ms.nurzaman@ui.ac.id

© The Author(s) 2017

M. Zulkhibri and A. G. Ismail (eds.), *Financial Inclusion and Poverty Alleviation*,
Palgrave Studies in Islamic Banking, Finance, and Economics,
https://doi.org/10.1007/978-3-319-69799-4_7

Keywords Productive-based *zakat* · Mustahiq · Disaggregated human development index

7.1 Introduction

The importance of *Zakat* in Islam can be gauged by the number of times it is mentioned in the Holy Qur'an. It is clear that without *Zakat*, prayer is not established. The Prophet Muhamad (pbuh) further emphasized its importance by referring to one of the five pillars of Islam. Although the eight recipient categories of *Zakat* include some non-poor, the practice of the Prophet Muhamad (pbuh) and the opinion of *fuqaha's* place a lot of emphasis on the poor and needy. It is overwhelmingly believed that giving *Zakat* to the poor and needy has first priority (Kahf 2006).

The increasing impact of *Zakat* on human welfare is theoretically significant and built-in in the Islamic system. Al-Qur'an mentions that the needy and the poor are the first two groups from eight groups within recipient of *Zakat* (*mustahiq*). These two groups of recipients are given priority by al-Qur'an to receive distribution of *Zakat*. This implies that the main aim of *Zakat* is to address the problem of poverty in the society. Moreover, it is well-established that *Zakat* is a mode of cash transfer to the poor for the purpose of wealth redistribution in the society (Qardawi 1997).

From empirical perspectives, as the growth of Islamic financial and economic institution and its contribution in the economy in Muslim countries rise, *Zakat* as one of the importance of Islamic economic institution also getting increased attention from the society. Consequently, both at micro and macro level, tremendous studies have been made to analyze the significant of *Zakat* to increase the economic welfare of the poor in recent years. Such studies are very important since the claim of *Zakat* effectiveness on welfare needs to be evaluated and the impact on poverty alleviation needs to be proved.

In case of Indonesia, some related studies have been undertaken by Khatimah (2004), Sina (2004), Arif (2006), Muhtada (2008), and Beik (2009). Several other related studies have been conducted in other

Muslim countries with broader scope and methodology. For example, Shirazi (1994), Hussain and Shirazi (1994), Shirazi (1996), Patmawati (2006) focus on the relationship of *Zakat* to poverty and income distribution at micro level. Some other researches try to simulate impact of *Zakat* at macro level using several economic indicators (Billah 1996; Hossain 2005; Hassan and Khan 2007; Ahmed 2008).

One can identify the following shortcomings in the existing literature to which this chapter contributes. Firstly, most studies on *Zakat* contribution have not measured the impact on human welfare. Human welfare indicators are very important because improvement in income alone may not indicate improvement in the quality of life. Furthermore, better education and improvement in health condition should be considered as an improvement in welfare. These objectives are also in accordance with the Millennium Development Goals (MDGs) that advocated changing the revenue outlook as the sole measure of success in alleviating poverty.[1]

Secondly, majority of studies specifically at micro level empirical analysis investigate welfare indicators on *mustahiq* in utilizing the *Zakat* fund at one point of time (i.e., in one year only). In other words they do not take and analyze the indicators in the subsequent periods. By providing the indicators for at least two periods, one could provide a more consistent result on assessing the effectiveness of *Zakat* in improving the welfare of the poor.

Based on these conditions, this chapter examines the impact of productive-based *Zakat* programs[2] conducted by *Zakat* institutions from the perspectives of human development approach. Human development can be simply defined as a process of enlarging choices. In principle, human choices and their outcomes can be infinite and change over time. However, three essential elements at all levels of development are for people to lead a long and healthy life, to acquire knowledge and to have access to resources needed for a decent standard of living. These three elements are reflected by the indicator of Human Development Index (HDI).[3]

Indicators of achievement in the components of human development index (HDI) and all its component are expected to provide a better success parameters of the *Zakat* productive scheme that organized by *Zakat* organizations. Furthermore, this chapter analyses the data in the initial year and following year to make comparable analysis of the results.

7.2 *Zakat* and Welfare: Some Empirical Findings

Literature on *Zakat* can be classified under three categories. The first two have been explained by Dogarawa (2008). The first category deals with the *fiqh* (Islamic rulings and other juristic issues) of *Zakat*, contributed by mostly classical *fuqaha* (Islamic scholars) and a few contemporary Islamic economists. Among this category discusses the principle, ruling, and philosophy. Qardawi (1997) has also summarized most of the issues related to *Zakat* principle and philosophy, in which limited coverage has recently been elaborated by Mahmud and Haneef (2008).

The second category pertains to the management of *Zakat*. Islahi (2005) describes the management of *Zakat* by citing number of studies conducted in specific countries. On the other hand, Kahf (1999) covers comprehensively issues on management of *Zakat* by using cross-country data from some countries, including Saudi Arabia, Malaysia, Sudan, Pakistan, and Libya. The third category relates to the economics of *Zakat*. This category includes studies on the effects of *Zakat* on economic measures such as income. This also includes the relationship between *Zakat* and macroeconomic models; socioeconomic role of *Zakat* as a social welfare package and a distributive agent; and correspondence and difference between *Zakat* and taxation or other conventional social security systems.

Zakat is identified as an Islamic social security system because it is obligatory for each qualified Muslim[4] to give his payments to specified groups, which have the right to the possessions.[5] *Zakat* teaches Muslims to be concerned about others, especially the poor and needy. It is a symbol of justice that ensures equality and distribution of wealth among people, who are particularly Muslims. Qardawi (2007) argues that money will circulate more freely within the Muslim community as *Zakat* provides money to the poor. Moreover, as *Zakat* contains the principle of social justice and wealth redistribution for the eight groups of righteous recipients, its existence will further stimulate the economy of Muslim society.

With the general phenomenon of contemporary poverty classified as structural poverty, the tendency of utilization of *Zakat* funds is now increasingly focused on development and empowerment programs. Utilization of traditional *Zakat* programs that are exclusively charitable and consumptive oriented is no longer sufficient to liberate humankind from the downturn. By joining the development and empowerment programs, the poor people will have both physical and financial capitals that enable them to grab opportunities to be wealthier. It is expected that these people will have the ability to help themselves, regardless of dependency on social structure, political economy that is not aligned to them.

As a means of poverty alleviation, limited studies have been conducted in Indonesia. Khatimah (2004) elaborates the impact of *Zakat* to increase *mustahiq* society's economic welfare as the object of *Zakat* distribution through productive financing and examines deeply the counseling program conducted by Community Development Circle (CDC) at Dompet Dhuafa Republika, the biggest Lembaga Amil Zakat (LAZ) in Indonesia. Based on statistical test, the result shows most program partners get significant increase of their income after being given *Zakat* through financing models. The study finds that gender, education level, the total *Zakat* received, and the type of business are influenced by the rate of income. This result confirmed the findings by Sina (2004), who uses similar statistical method to examine the impact of *Zakat* on income of *mustahiq*. Sina uses the length of business instead of the business category, but this variable is statistically insignificant.

In a related paper, Muhtada (2008) reports an exploratory and descriptive study on a *Zakat* organization in Indonesia that has an empowerment program for poor people, particularly the peasants through productive schemes. The study analyzes the nature of the *Zakat* institutions, its efforts in promoting peasant empowerment, and its contribution to the solution for the peasantry's problems. The study found that the organization has been managing its resources efficiently. The organization has been seeking to improve the incomes of peasants by financing additional non-farm activities, but has not addressed the root cause of economic exploitation. Its microfinance activities are also adversely impacted by the fact that a large part of financial assistance is used for consumption purposes.

By using Sen Poverty Index, which combines the headcount ratio, income gap ratio, and the Gini coefficient, Susanto (2002) tries to discuss about *Zakat* as an alternative to anti-discrepancy and anti-poverty policy. The results show that this kind of charity is effective in reducing inequality and poverty in Indonesian society. In a broader and deeper context, the identical results are presented by Beik (2009) who simulated the role and scope of *Zakat* for poverty reduction in Indonesia. In terms of micro and macro views, the study finds that charity could play an important role in asset redistribution policies, capacity building, and creation of wealth.

The study conducted by Beik (2009) is more comprehensive, which analyzes the impact of *Zakat* on *mustahiq*'s welfare in Indonesia. It has used various well-known poverty indexes such as headcount ratio, poverty gap ratio, income gap ratio, Sen Index, and Foster-Greer-Thorbecke (FGT) Index as measures for knowing whether or not poverty can be reduced by using enormous sample, around 1000 respondents in Jakarta. According to the result, prior to *Zakat* distribution, the ratio of the poor people is 0.525. After *Zakat* is allocated, this ratio can be reduced to 0.45. This figure shows that the program of allocating *Zakat* as financing source for small scale and micro entrepreneurs is able to reduce poverty incidence from 52 to 45%. It means that the distributed *Zakat* fund is able to lower the number of respondents living below poverty line by 7.5% from its initial position.

Meanwhile, Febianto and Arimbi (2012) evaluate *Zakat* by using the more comprehensive indicators. The study employs economic empowerment indicators, which comprises not only economic measures such as the business assets, revenue, profit, and household income, but also other basic needs such as food, clothing, shelter, medical, and education needs. The influence of productive-based *Zakat* has a magnitude of 43% with a positive direction to the empowerment indicator. It means that the higher the performance of the *Zakat* financing implemented by the *Zakat* institution, the higher the recipients' economic empowerment will be. This finding is in line with that of Cokro and Ismail (2008), who conclude that *Zakat* financing can increase the economic conditions, as well as the basic needs of the recipients.

Studies on the impact of *Zakat* on welfare indicators are performed at some other Muslim countries, particularly in the economy of Pakistan, Bangladesh, and Malaysia. Most of these empirical studies are mainly focused on poverty alleviation, income distribution, the resources requirements for elimination of poverty, and possibility of bridging the resource gap through *Zakat*. Faiz (1991) explores the possibilities to eradicate poverty in Pakistan through the utilization of existing *Zakat* system. The study estimates that *Zakat* is a potential tool to eradicate poverty. In the study, *mustahiq* of *Zakat* are defined as the poor people who have income below the minimum level. Based on the findings, the number of *mustahiq* varied from 18.4 to 42.6% in 1988. The lower number indicates the percentage of the poorest households, while a higher number includes households that are not poor, yet they consider themselves poor.

Shirazi (1994) discusses the effects of *Zakat* on poverty alleviation in Pakistan, in which the potential of *Zakat* was found to lower poverty rate at about 2% in 1987–1988. Hussain and Shirazi (1994), however, show that the existing *Zakat* system in Pakistan is not able to bridge the poverty gap. Nevertheless, the poverty gap could be reduced if *Zakat* collection can be reached to its potential amount. In addition, Shirazi (1996) built upon this study to analyze the impact of *Zakat* and *'ushr* on poverty alleviation in Pakistan.

Patmawati (2006) examines the role of *Zakat* in reducing income inequalities and poverty in Selangor, Malaysia in 2006. By employing purposive sampling methods, the Lorenz curve and Gini coefficient, the study finds that *Zakat* distribution has positive contribution in reducing income inequality, whereby the bottom 10% of population receiving almost 10% of the total income and the top 10% of the population income portion reduced to 32%. Before *Zakat* is distributed, the bottom 10% of the population enjoy only 0.4% while the top 10% of the population enjoy 35.97%. The Lorenz curve shows that, with *Zakat* distribution, it moves closer to the perfect equality line as compared to pre-*Zakat* Lorenz curve. Gini coefficient depicts that *Zakat* distribution has reduced income inequality in Selangor, which is indicated by the declining value of Gini coefficient from 0.52 to 0.47.

In Bangladesh economy, Hossain (2005) proposes a new methodology of *Zakat* payment and utilization, to achieve optimal success in poverty eradication in Bangladesh. This paper shows with simulation analysis using household income and expenditure data, and that following the proposed methodology of converting *Zakat* from a temporary consumption item to investable wealth poverty can be eradicated in Bangladesh in 10–12 years. This would exceed the Millennium Development Goals (MDGs) by a long shot. It could also pave the way for the existing interest-based micro-credit programs to make a transition to interest-free Islamic microfinance as well as macrofinance.

Hassan and Khan (2007) demonstrate model that simulates the effectiveness of *Zakat* on helping government of Bangladesh to reduce external debt and poverty. The result indicates that *Zakat* fund can replace government budgetary expenditures in amount ranging from 21% of annual development plan (ADP) in 1983/1984 to 43% of ADP in the following year, which can be utilized for paying the external debt or other social expenditures. Another result shows that *Zakat* fund can increase the taxation potential of the government though the improvement of productivity, employment, and output.

Most empirical findings show that there is a positive relation of *Zakat* and welfare of *mustahiq*. However, there is no specific research on the relationship of *Zakat* and integrated welfare indicator such as human development index. The majority of studies are only examined the improvement on the perspective of income through productive financing, without cohesively analyzing the impact of *Zakat* further to other social indicators such as education and health. A few studies elaborate this impact by using their own integrated indicator. Another limitation is that those studies, particularly at micro level, are only conducted at a point of time without evaluating at the next period, thereby making incomparable result.

7.3 Research Methodology

Two sources of data are used in this study. The first source is primary data, which are obtained through questionnaire survey. The questionnaire survey is distributed to the beneficiaries of productive-based *Zakat* and non-*Zakat* that have received funding from *Zakat* institutions. The field study is conducted in the region of capital city of Indonesia, Jakarta, for several months. Jakarta is chosen to be a research area mainly because the best prototype of *Zakat* program in Indonesia is currently in the capital city.

The second source is secondary data from the (WHO) and Badan Pusat Statistik (Indonesia Statistical Office). This includes survey on journals, books, and other relevant materials, and accessing available data in relevant institutions such as BAZNAS (official institution appointed to manage *Zakat* fund), as well as the data from FOZ(association of *Zakat* institutions in Indonesia).

7.3.1 The Type and Procedure of Sampling

This study uses cluster sampling method to generate samples. Cluster sampling has been used in various studies that measure the impact of the financial institutions, mainly to microfinance-based institutions, in improving the welfare of the poor, for instance by Chowdhury, Gosh and Wright (2005)[6] and Amin, Rai, and Topa (2003).[7] This study, specifically, uses a two-stage sampling methods in conducting the survey. First, choose the *Zakat* institutions that become the object of this research. Second, do a simple random sampling of clusters from the chosen *Zakat* institutions to produce the survey respondents.

There are three *Zakat* institutions out of 10 that are selected at the first stage, which comprises about 15 clusters productive-based *Zakat* recipients. These clusters are categorized based on group of recipients or locations that have been arranged by the *Zakat* institutions and each cluster consists of 15–25 *Zakat* recipients. Then eight clusters are chosen at the second stage, which totally consists of 133 recipients or 615 family members. These 133 recipients are then asked again with the same questionnaire to see the comparison between the first and the second period, and to perform panel data regression.

7.3.2 Methodology

There are two quantitative techniques to answer the objective of study: methodology to estimate the value of Human Development Index at household level and panel data regression to determine whether the amount of *Zakat* and some other factors might have impact to the estimated HDI.[8]

The methodology to estimate household HDI follows Nurzaman (2011) with two important improvements.[9] The first improvement is by including aggregated health indicator as the independent variable in the imputation method of life expectancy index. This health indicator comprises two main elements—the ability of people to have a proper house and to have access to health facilities. A proper house is indicated by the components of electricity, toilet, tiles, roof, wall, and water, while access to health facilities is represented by having access to doctor, having access to health providers, and having ability to get medicine. These indicators are chosen following the standard questions formulated by the Statistics Indonesia in the National Socio-Economic Survey (SUSENAS).

Another improvement is extending the education index. An additional indicator is used in forming this index and the other two indicators remain utilized through some modifications. Informal education or community-based education.[10] is used as additional indicators for those who do not have formal education, while the average length of school will be replaced by schooling attainment for household members who are above 6 years.[11] and literacy is directly asked to the all respondents.

In the process of computation, there are two different calculation methods. First, the three indicators are combined after each is given weight of one-third equally for the person who has not completed the education up until minimum level required by the government,[12] but he/she might join informal education. For the person at the school age or a university graduate, the weighting scheme follows the government standard estimation, i.e., two-third for literacy and one-third for schooling attainment.

The disaggregated HDI for household of *mustahiq* is obtained from the composite index, calculated as the simple average of three components, as follows:

(1) Life expectancy index as measured by life expectancy at age for every member of household.

(2) Education index as measured by literacy rate, length of school, and participation in informal school for every member of household.
(3) Standard of living index, or income index, as measured by the total expenditure for daily needs consumption of each family adjusted for purchasing power.

$$HDI = \frac{1}{3}(Lifeexpectancyindex) + \frac{1}{3}(Educationindex) + \frac{1}{3}(IncomeIndex) \quad (7.1)$$

Meanwhile, to determine factors affecting the HDI, regression analysis is employed. The combination between cross-sectional data and time-series data, or panel data, is employed to regression model in order to evaluate the impact of *Zakat* financing to HDI. Panel data regression is used to make the researcher observations amount to (N * T).[13]

The regression model conducted in this study is developed to evaluate whether *Zakat*, and the other selected determinants, affect HDI (and the component indices, i.e., life expectancy index, income index, and education index). The model is as follow.

$$HDI = \alpha + \beta_1 Zakat + \beta_2 Number + \beta_3 income + \beta_4 Prog + \beta_5 House + \varepsilon \quad (7.2)$$

where the definitions of the variables are as follows:

Dependent variable *(HDI):*

The dependent variable is the value of estimated HDI, which has a range of 0.00–1.00.

Independent Variables:

1. The amount of *Zakat (Zakat)*: Total *Zakat* fund obtained by *mustahiq* from *Zakat* institution in Rupiah.
2. Number of family members *(Number)*: Family members are all members of the family who live together in a single house.
3. Empowerment programs *(Prog)*: This reflects participation of *Zakat* recipients and their families in the trainings or programs provided by the *Zakat* institutions. The value of program in the model is 1 if the recipient joins the program, or otherwise.
4. Basic facilities of the house of *mustahiq (House)*: The component of basic facilities for a house comprises six main elements, which are

included in the national socioeconomic surveys. A proper house is indicated by the accessibility of electricity, toilet, tiles, roof, wall, and water. In the model, the basic facilities are treated as dummy variable, hence 1 of the household has ability or complete basic facilities, or otherwise.

5. Family income *(Income)*: Family income is the amount of aggregate income received by the entire family member in nominal rupiah. Consequently, this variable will capture not only income received by the recipient of *Zakat*, which is usually the head of family, but also income from the other members in that particular family.

7.4 Findings

7.4.1 HDI of Household of Mustahiq

Table 7.1 displays the distribution of HDI and its components for household of *mustahiq*, at the first and second periods that are generated from estimation. The distribution is employing quantile distribution. There are 25% of families that have the value of HDI equal or less than 0.57 at the first period, and only increase slightly to at most 0.62, and 0.67 for accumulated of 50 and 75% of them. At the first period, the household of mustahiq can only get the highest HDI at 0.65.

This low achievement at first period can be further analyzed by evaluating its components. It can be seen that, though the realization and distribution of education index are substantially good, the index of life and index of income are relatively low. For example, while 50% of household can get education index at equal or less than 0.83, the equal proportion of household can only achieve life index and income index at equal or at less than 0.59, and 0.43, consecutively.

However, the household of *mustahiq* achieves a significant improvement of level of HDI and its distribution at the second period. The first quarter of household of *mustahiq* that can increase their HDI to equal or less than 0.64, while a half and three quarters of them can achieve HDI to equal or less than 0.69, and 0.75, respectively. The highest HDI that can be achieved by the household of mustahiq at the second period also increases to 0.87.

Table 7.1 Quantile distribution of HDI estimation (For household of *Mustahiq*)

(%)	*HDI1*	HDI2	*EDU1*	EDU2	*LIFE1*	LIFE2	*INC1*	INC2
1	*0.26*	0.36	*0.15*	0.43	*0.34*	0.3	*0.28*	0.34
5	*0.42*	0.56	*0.49*	0.8	*0.47*	0.42	*0.31*	0.47
10	*0.50*	0.61	*0.66*	0.84	*0.50*	0.47	*0.35*	0.50
25	*0.57*	0.64	*0.76*	0.88	*0.55*	0.5	*0.38*	0.54
50	*0.62*	0.69	*0.83*	0.92	*0.59*	0.56	*0.43*	0.61
75	*0.67*	0.75	*0.90*	0.93	*0.62*	0.6	*0.49*	0.72
90	*0.72*	0.8	*0.98*	0.98	*0.65*	0.61	*0.54*	0.8
95	*0.74*	0.83	*1*	1	*0.66*	0.62	*0.56*	0.86
99	*0.78*	0.87	*1*	1	*0.66*	0.62	*0.69*	1

Note HDI1 and HDI2 is Human Development Index for the first and second Period, EDU is index of education, LIFE is index of life expectancy, and INC is index of income

If the analysis is extended to each component of HDI, the description can be explained as follow. First component is index of education. Index of education contributes very positively in the formation of the *Zakat*'s recipient and their families' HDI. It appears that the majority of recipients of *Zakat* and their families have considerable fair education index at both periods. In fact this is consistent with the result of raw data where 99% of household of *mustahiq* are literate and the majority of them have high school education or take an informal education such as training and community-based program that is not only given by the *Zakat* institution but is also provided by the government.

Second component is index of life expectancy. In contrast to the result in the education index, none of household *mustahiq* has above high-level life expectancy index category, i.e., above 0.80.[14] In other words, the entire recipient of productive-based *Zakat* and their families are categorized at/or below middle level. This shows the health condition of *Zakat* recipients and their families should receive a larger share of attention from the *Zakat* institution as well as the policy makers. Some components of composite health indicator, such as ability to access doctors, to access to health providers, and ability to get medicines, are in fact getting worse at the second period.

The high cost of having access to the health facilities becomes the main reason behind those situations. The Global Medical Trends Survey Report of Towers Watson in 2012 showed the increased healthcare and hospital costs were much greater than the increase in income of the people of Indonesia.[15] As the result, some households have to treat themselves by buying only the counter medicines when they are sick or even let the disease without treatment because they assume it does not interfere with their activities, with disastrous consequences later. Consequently, the complement programs including the provision of facilities and access to free health services should become a priority, in addition to direct health consultation and other empowerment programs for *Zakat* recipients and their families.

A similar situation is occurred to the third component, index of income. The majority of recipients of productive-based *Zakat* and their families have only a low-level or middle-level index of income. However, the distribution of income index has considerably changed at the second period. Since the index of income is fundamentally representing achievement of all the basic needs, the significant improvement of income index indicator shows that the household is able to fulfill the basic needs including food and non-food components. At the second period, indeed the majority of *mustahiq* have succeeded their entrepreneurship further through having more income. However, many of the other family members also get or create new jobs by joining the empowerment program provided by *Zakat* institution, thereby contributing in forming more income to their household.

For instance, a community of one of the locations specializes in cooking and producing daily foods. The *Zakat* institution then gives financing to the households to buy all the equipment and facilities for the cooking and provides an instructor to train the participants to become skillful in this field. Because the training program is open to the public, participants in practice are not only the recipients of *Zakat* but other family members who also join the program. Thus, separately, other family members also sell food from the acquired expertise.

7.4.2 Regression Analysis

Regression analysis is performed to see whether productive-based *Zakat* has an effect on HDI and its components. The panel regression method is selected to allow more informative observation among the respondents. The other advantage of working with panel data is that we will be able to control individual-specific, time-invariant, unobserved heterogeneity, the presence of which could lead to bias in standard estimators like OLS. We can also further estimate dynamic equations.

There do exist three approaches in the analysis of panel data (i.e., the least squares approach or OLS), fixed effects approach (FE), and random effects approach (RE). The summary of the three approaches is presented followed by statistical tests to choose the best approach between these three approaches. Then the classical assumptions of regression method, such as homoscedasticity, no multicollinearity problem, and endogeneity, are evaluated to ensure that the result is conforming to the assumptions.

Table 7.2 shows the summary of the three panel data approaches, which use unbalanced panel data.[16] The explanation of variables used in the regression table is as follows: *HDI* is the value of estimated HDI for household of *mustahiq*; *Zakat* is the amount of productive-based *Zakat* received by the *mustahiq* of *Zakat*; *Member* is the number of people in a family of *Zakat*'s recipient; *Famincome* is the amount of total income received by all the household members[17]; *Prog* is dummy variable of empowerment programs, or community development offered by the *Zakat* institution, which is joined by the *mustahiq*; *Houseinfra* is basic facilities/infrastructure for the house.

It can be seen that only variables *famincome* and *Zakat* that are statistically significant in the models. The variable total income significantly affects the HDI at $\alpha = 1\%$, while the amount of productive-based *Zakat* is significant at $\alpha = 5\%$. The other three variables, i.e., *member*, *prog*, and *houseinfra* are not statistically significant in the model. However, these findings will be verified later by applying the panel model into each HDI component.

It has also been conducted a Wald test to choose between OLS and FE, and Breusch and Pagan LM-test to compare between POLS and RE. The Wald test assumes that the null hypothesis is rejecting the OLS, and consequently chooses FE, if the F test is significant for FE. It can be found that OLS cannot be rejected since the value of Prob > F = 0.9986.

Table 7.2 The summary of all panel data approaches (HDI as dependent variable)

Variable	POLS	FE	RE
Member	0.0001638	0.0089882	0.0009476
Famincome	0.00001343***	0.00001674***	0.0000134***
Zakat	7.06e−06**	4.86E−06	6.291e−06*
Prog	0.012293	−0.002577	0.004666
Houseinfra	0.005197	0.023816	0.008469
_cons	0.570583***	0.462220**	0.568214***
N	223	223	223
Adj R^2	0.35109515	−0.3345722	
F test that all u_i = 0 (Wald Test)		Prob > F = 0.9986	
Breusch Pagan LM-Test			Prob > chi^2 = 1.0000

Note *p < 0.10; ** p < 0.05; *** p < 0.001

As OLS is considered better than FE, then it is should be compared further by the RE approach to determine which one is preferred. Breusch and Pagan LM-test assume the null hypothesis is rejecting the OLS, and consequently chooses FE, if the F test is significant for FE. Since Prob > chi2 = 1.0000. Hence OLS is preferred than RE. It can be concluded that the OLS is the best panel data approach for explaining the HDI regression result.

It can also be shown from Table 7.2, the adjusted R-squared is 0.36 for the OLS regression, which means that 36% variation in the level of human development (HDI) can be explained simultaneously by variations in the level of all the independent variables in the model. Prob of F-statistic reaches 0.000, which gives the sense that this model is significant and the overall explanatory power is also significant. Therefore, the model can be used to explain the influence of the amount of *Zakat*, the household income, the empowerment program, the basis facilities of a house, and the household size the level of human development index.

The coefficient of each significant variable of OLS regression can be explained as follows. The variable constant is significant with the coefficient 0.57. This means the household has HDI about 0.57 at initial level, by assuming other variables are constant. There are correspondingly two significant independent variables: variable level of household

Table 7.3 The result of POLS regression (HDI components)

Variable	Inc_index		Life_index		Edu_Index	
HDI	coef	se	coef	se	Coef	se
Member	−0.025127***	0.004	0.0083436	0.003	0.0174126*	0.005
Famincome	0.0000329***	0.000	−4.17E−06*	0.000	0.0000104*	0.000
Zakat	0.00001*	0.000	2.18E−06	0.000	9.22E−06	0.000
Prog	0.04590**	0.015	−0.03523*	0.011	0.0240482	0.023
Houseinfra	−0.00238	0.009	0.02248**	0.007	−0.0129248	0.014
_cons	0.48715***	0.042	0.40315	0.030	0.7886389	0.064
Prob > F	0.00		0.00		0.01	
Adj R^2	0.59		0.10		0.06	

Note *p < 0.05; ** p < 0.01; *** p < 0.001

income, variable of *Zakat*, which have the coefficient 0.0000134, 0.00000706. These mean that the household needs to get more income of Rp1000 thousand (US$91) to increase 0.0134 point of their HDI, while they also need about Rp1000 thousand (US$91) of productive-based *Zakat* fund if they want to increase 0.007 point of HDI.

If the analysis is extended into the HDI components (for OLS), as shown in Table 7.3, it is revealed that the sources of positive impact of household income variable to the HDI are coming from income index and education index. Although the household income has statistically negative relation to life expectancy index, in overall the impact to HDI is positive.[18] Similarly, the component of income index is positively affected by the variable of *Zakat*, thus this is the reason of why this variable has a positive impact to the level of HDI in general.

The variable of empowerment program has also a relation to life expectancy index and income index, while the variable of house facilities has a positive effect to life expectancy index.[19] Yet because the significant values of empowerment program variable oppose each other, the result is mutually exclusive to HDI.[20] The analogous finding is also achieved for the variable household size, which has significant relationship to income index and education index. But again the overall impact of household size variable is neutral to HDI since its significant value is opposite to each other of income index and education index.[21]

Although that by using UNDP categorization the achievement values of HDI are still at middle level, in overall it is established that the *mustahiq* and their families are certainly having better welfare that is reflected by improved HDI. In addition, the panel data regression has verified further the positive impact of productive-based *Zakat* to the HDI of *mustahiq*'s household. Previous studies such as those of Khatimah (2004), Sina (2004), Susanto (2002), Beik (2009), Faiz (1991), Shirazi (1994, 1996), Sadeq (1996), Patmawati (2006) have also come out with similar findings that *Zakat* institution brings positive impact to the *mustahiq*. For instance, Beik (2009) shows that the program of allocating *Zakat* as financing source for small scale and micro entrepreneurs is able to reduce poverty incidence from 52.5 to 45%. It means that the distributed *Zakat* fund is able to lower the number of respondents living below poverty line by 7.5% from its initial position.

As this study finds that size of *Zakat* financing to have significant association with the level of HDI, we can conclude that Islamic microfinance, especially the institution of *Zakat*, may contribute to the improvement of recipients' lives in terms of income, health, and education. This is in line with the previous studies. For example, Febianto and Arimbi (2012) employ the economic empowerment indicator, which comprises not only economic measures such as the business asset, revenue, profit, and household income, but also other basic needs such as food, clothing, shelter, medical, and education needs. The influence of productive-based *Zakat* has a magnitude of 43% with a positive direction to the empowerment indicator. It means that the higher the performance of the *Zakat* financing implemented by the *Zakat* institution is, the higher the recipients' economic empowerment will be.

There are some possible reasons why receiving productive-based *Zakat* financing is able to improve clients' welfare status, which is indicated by better HDI. As the clients receive financing from *Zakat* institution, the improvement towards welfare status might occur due to investment in productive capital. Besides, while having micro financing may induce growth in income as well as basic need fulfillment, proper training and empowerment program could also become significant factor to strengthen households' awareness in having well education.

Furthermore, there are also some other plausible explanations behind these findings. At the initial period, financing received by the *mustahiq* provides opportunity for them to expand their business, undertake new activities and products, as well as improve the ownership of productive assets. At the second period, it may enhance the household's income and savings as well as strengthen households' ability to fulfill the basic consumption needs, while health expenditure remains the second priority. Thus, this indicates that, other than *Zakat*, income plays significant role to the development of household welfare.

Apparently, the households who succeed in gaining higher HDI after they receive the financial aid from the *Zakat* institutions are those who already have higher income. The above results of panel data regression verify that household income is statistically significant to the HDI. Monetary benefit seems to become the most important factor affecting the welfare level of household as having more income means having more opportunity to satisfy the basic consumption and all other household needs.

If a simulation is developed, it can be demonstrated that a household needs Rp10 million (US$909) more monthly income to increase their HDI to about 0.13, which mean they can achieve the level of HDI to be at 0.70. With same amount of money, productive-based *Zakat* fund can increase a household HDI from 0.57 to 0.64. As the variable of *Zakat* financing and household income might be highly related, i.e., having *Zakat* financing is expected might increase the income,[22] providing more *Zakat* financing can be put as the priority, while expecting the income will increase as well later. Consequently, the HDI in overall can increase significantly if the *Zakat* institutions can provide more amount of productive-based *Zakat*.

The evidence of this study has shown that the average of *Zakat* financing that can be provided is only at Rp2,362,031 (US$215). Thus, it needs about Rp7.7 million more of *Zakat* financing if the HDI of *mustahiq*'s households are expected to increase significantly by 0.07 point, which is essentially very difficult for *Zakat* institutions to give financing at this much amount. A study by Rulindo (2012) shows that BMTs, as the microfinance institutions that have profit orientation, can only give financing to their clients at Rp5,000,000 (US$454) in average.

Let there are 20 million Muslims who are categorized as *mustahiq* and need to be supported by productive-based *Zakat*, around

Rp14.4 trillion (US$1400 Million) more amount of financing would be needed. This is roughly only 6% of potential *Zakat* of Rp217 trillion (US$19.7 million) that could be collected from all the Muslims in Indonesia who are obliged to pay *Zakat*.

7.5 Conclusion

By using the empirical observations, this chapter has shown the method and result of estimated HDI at household level, which are rarely employed. Such a method shows that HDI can be disaggregated into household level, which then can further be utilized to evaluate welfare across household level of *mustahiq*. This method, absolutely, can be expanded so that it is not restricted to only *mustahiqs* as the object of measurement.

By using two periods of observation, it is found that the level of human development index of household who receives productive-based *Zakat* is significantly higher than the first period. The underlying distribution of household HDI also improves at the second period. Moreover, by evaluating the detail results of the HDI components, the education index, and income index are found statistically higher at the second period, while it is not significant for index of life expectancy. The life expectancy index of household of *mustahiq* is also considerably worse than the household who receives non-*Zakat* financing.

The household of poor people prefers securing first their basic consumption needs, particularly food and education to improving their health due to high cost of health facilities. Insecurity of basic needs, particularly food, does not only threaten the quality of life of individuals but also has negative social and economic impacts. However, since in general the overall index of HDI shows improved value, it can still be inferred that indeed there is an improvement of HDI of *mustahiq*'s household at the second period.

Meanwhile, the result of panel data regression shows that the variable of productive-based *Zakat* is positively correlated with the level of HDI. This implies that the more productive-based *Zakat* can be given, the wealthier the recipient is. The magnitude of the relation is 0.00000706, which economically can be interpreted that the household of *mustahiq* needs about Rp10,000 thousand (US$909) of productive-based *Zakat* fund if they want to increase 0.07 point of HDI. Monetary benefit seems to become the most important factor affecting the welfare level of household as having more *Zakat* and consequently income means having more opportunity to satisfy the basic consumption and all other household needs.

Therefore, it can be concluded that *Zakat*, particularly productive-based *Zakat*, can play important role to improve the welfare of poor household. However, it is required significant amount of *Zakat* to achieve this positive result. Since there is still a huge gap between the realization and the potential of *Zakat* revenues by the *Zakat* institutions in Indonesia, the source of the amount could be taken by keeping increasing the received *Zakat* from the *muzakki*. It needs effort not only from the *Zakat* institutions but also from the government to provide the favorable regulations and environment. The public awareness is also needed to pay their *Zakat* through *Zakat* institutions to make the financing well managed to be distributed to the *mustahiq*.

Notes

1. The Human Development Index is then chosen to represent welfare in this study for two reasons: first, the HDI purports to broaden the dimension of human development measured by income and basic need approaches. Second, the Human Development Index is accepted as a standard measurement of well-being by all three Bretton Woods Institutions (World Trade Organization 2002; The World Bank 2006; International Monetary Fund 2000).
2. Productive-based *Zakat* is an important concept regarding the mechanism of how to increase the welfare of *mustahiq* through working capital of *Zakat*. out of the financial capital alone, the additional programs could be designed to empower the recipients and build their capability to increase their wealth
3. In HDI, component indices for life expectancy, literacy and school enrollment, and income are combined together into a single index that can be used to compare the level of human welfare among countries or to monitor one country's progress over time

4. *Zakat* is applied for Muslim who has property which is potentially to grow, debt-free, owned a full year (*haul*), and well above the minimum value (*nishab*).
5. Eight groups of people (*asnaf*) are entitled to receive *Zakat* according to the Qur'an, Surah At-Taubah verse 60: the poor; the destitute; the agents employed therein; those whose hearts are to be won over; the freedom of slaves; the (relief of) debtors; expenditure in the way of Allah; the follower of the way—an ordinance from Allah
6. Chowdhury MJA, Ghosh D & Wright RE (2005) The impact of micro-credit on poverty: Evidence from Bangladesh, Progress in Development Studies, 5 (4), p. 298-309.
7. Amin, S., Rai, S. and Topa, G. (2003) 'Does Micro-credit Reach the Poor and Vulnerable? Evidence from Northern Bangladesh', Journal of Development Economics 70(1): 59–82.
8. HDI value ranges from "0.00" up to "1.00". The lower the HDI value of a community/household, the weaker/the more lagging development of the household.
9. The method of estimating household HDI is explained in my previous paper, which has been presented at eighth ICIEF. It can be accessed at http://conference.qfis.edu.qa/app/media/237.
10. In the Acton National Education System, No. 20/2003 Article 1, paragraph 16. It is stated that the sense of community-based education is to provide education based on the distinctiveness of religious, social, culture, aspirations, and educational potential of the community as a manifestation of, by, and for the community. Thus, it appears that community-based education is basically an education that gives independence and freedom in the community to determine the field of education in accordance with the wishes of the community itself.
11. In Indonesia, a person starts going to formal study at age 7.
12. Pursuant to Indonesian Government Regulation No. 47/2008, the compulsory education is 12 years or the school age is from 7 to 18 years old
13. T refers to time, while N refers to observations or generated samples.
14. UNDP categorizes HDI into four levels: Low (0.00–0.49), Middle (0.50–0.79), High (0.80–0.89), and Very High (0.90–1.00).
15. Based on Global Medical Trends Survey Reports of Towers Watson in 2012, the rate of healthcare and hospital cost in Indonesia increased by 13.55% in 2011, and 13.95% in 2012. The cost is the second highest in the Region of Asia Pacific

16. For the unbalanced one-way error component model, it can still be performed as a least squares regression (for discussion, see Baltagi and Chang 1994).
17. The variable household income as independent variable is different from index of income, which is part of HDI as dependent variable. While index of income is estimated through expenditure on basic needs, the household income is simply the income received from all the job of members.
18. The variable of *famincome* is also supposed to be excluded from the life index regression as it has been employed to the formulation of life expectancy index through imputation method.
19. The variable of *houseinfra* is also employed to formulate life index, thus supposed to be excluded.
20. The reason why the empowerment program has negative relation to the life index is because the household seems to put more priority to increase their income first other than more healthy condition.
21. Theoretically, the household member has negative relation to the index. Its positive relation to education index is due to the data characteristic where the majority of household members are well educated. Hence, the more members a family has, the higher HDI it will achieve.
22. In the regression result, however, the variable household income and *Zakat* are not related

References

Ahmed, H. (2008). Zakah, macroeconomic policies, and poverty alleviation: Lessons from simulation on Bangladesh. *Journal of Islamic Economics, Banking and Finance, 4*(2).

Amin, S., Rai, S., & Topa, G. (2003). Does micro-credit reach the poor and vulnerable? Evidence from northern Bangladesh. *Journal of Development Economics, 70*(1), 59–82.

Arif, M. N. R. (2006). *Efek multiplier zakat terhadap pendapatan di provinsi dki Jakarta: Studi kasus bazis DKI Jakarta* (Zakat multiplier effect on income in the province of Jakarta). Unpublished Master thesis, University of Indonesia.

Baltagi, B. H., & Chang, Y. J. (1994). Incomplete panels: A comparative study of alternative estimators for the unbalanced one-way error component regression model. *Journal of Econometrics, 62*(2), 67–89.

Beik, I. (2009). *The use of Zakah as financing source for micro and small scale enterprises and its role in reducing poverty: A case study in Jakarta, Indonesia.* Unpublished PhD Dissertation, IIUM Malaysia.

Billah, M. M. (1996). The modern social security system–the institution of Zakah: An appraisal. *Business Law Journal, 1996*(1), 18–29.

Chowdhury, M. J. A., Ghosh, D., & Wright, R. E. (2005). The impact of micro-credit on poverty: Evidence from Bangladesh. *Progress in Development Studies, 5*(4), 298–309.

Cokro, W. M., & Ismail, A. G. (2008). *Sustainability of BMT financing for developing micro-enterprises* (MPRA Paper 7434). University Library of Munich, Germany.

Dogarawa, A. B. (2008). *Islamic social welfare and the role of Zakah in the family system* (MPRA Paper 23192). University Library of Munich, Germany.

Faiz, M. (1991). Prospects of poverty eradication through the existing Zakat system in Pakistan. *The Pakistan Development Review, 30*(4).

Febianto, I., & Arimbi, M. A. (2012). The impact of Qardhul Hasan financing using Zakah funds on economic empowerment (case study of Dompet Dhuafa, West Java, Indonesia). *Asian Business Review, 1*(1), 15–20.

Global Medical Trends Survey Report. (2012). http://www.towerswatson.com/DownloadMedia.aspx?media=%7B80CE6971-6A5C-4E65-ACE3-EEE730624AF6%7D. Accesed in 15 January 2014.

Hassan, M. K., & Khan, M. J. (2007). Zakat, external debt and poverty reduction strategy in Bangladesh. *Journal of Economic Cooperation, 28*(4), 1–38.

Hossain, M. (2005). *Zakat based poverty eradication in Bangladesh: The millennium development goal is exceed able.* Institute of Hazrat Mohammad (SAW). Dhaka, Bangladesh.

Indonesia Act of Zakat No. 38/1999.

Indonesia Act of Zakat No. 23/2011.

Islahi, A. A. (2005). *Zakah: A bibliography.* Jeddah, Saudi Arabia: Scientific Publishing Centre, King Abdul-Aziz University.

Kahf, M. (1999). *The performance of the institution of Zakah in theory and practice.* Paper Presented at the International Conference on Islamic Economics towards the 21st Century, Kuala Lumpur.

Kahf, M. (2006). *Role of Zakat and Awqaf in reducing poverty: A case for Zakat-Awqaf-based institutional setting of micro-finance.* Paper for the Conference on Poverty Reduction in the Muslim Countries, Nov. 24–26, 2006.

Khatimah, K. (2004). *Pengaruh Zakat Produktif Terhadap Peningkatan Kesejahteraan Ekonomi Para Mustahik (Studi Kasus di Community*

Development Circle (CDC) Dompet Dhuafa Republika Tahun 2001–Maret 2004). Unpublished Master Thesis, University of Indonesia.

Mahmud, M. W, & Haneef, S. S. (2008). Debatables issues in Fiqh AL-Zakat: A jurisprudential appraisal. *Jurnal Fiqh, 5*.

Muhtada, D. (2008). The role of Zakat organization in empowering the peasantry: A case study of the rumah Zakat Yogyakarta Indonesia. In M. Obaidullah and S. A Latiff (Eds.), *Islamic finance for micro and medium enterprises*. Jeddah, Saudi Arabia: IRTI-IDB.

Nasional, B. A. Z. (2013). *Laporan Zakat edisi milad BAZNAS ke-12*. Jakarta: BAZNAS.

Nurzaman, M. S. (2011). *Zakat and human development: An empirical analysis of poverty alleviation*. 8th International Conference on Islamic Economics and Finance. http://conference.qfis.edu.qa/app/media/237.

Patmawati, I. (2006). *The economic role of Zakat in reducing income inequality and poverty in Selangor*. PhD Thesis, Faculty of Economics & Management, University Putra Malaysia.

Qardawi, Y. (1997). *Fiqh az-Zakah* (24th ed.). Beirut: Mu`assasat al-Risalah, 37–38.

Qardawi, Y. (2007). *Hukum Zakat: study komparatif mengenai status dan filsafat zakat berdasarkan Qur'an dan Hadits*. Jakarta: Litera AntarNusa.

Rulindo, R. (2012). *Spirituality, religiosity and economic performances of muslim micro-entrepreneurs*. PhD Dissertation. International Islamic University Malaysia.

Sadeq, A. H. M. (1996). Ethico-economic institution of Zakah: An instrument of self-reliance and sustainable grassroots development. *Humanomics,12*(2), 47–69.

Shirazi, N. S. (1994). *An analysis of Pakistan's poverty problem and its alleviation through Infaq*. PhD Dissertation. International Islamic University, Islamabad.

Shirazi, N. S. (1996). *System of zakat in Pakistan: An appraisal*. Islamabad: International Institute of Islamic Economics, International Islamic University.

Sina, I. (2004). *Analisis Pengaruh Dana Zakat, Infak, Sedekah (Zis), Tingkat Pendidikan & Lama Usaha Mustahiq Terhadap Peningkatan Pendapatan Usaha*. Unpublished Master Thesis, University of Indonesia.

Susanto, A. A. (2002). Zakah sebagai kebijakan alternatif antikesenjangan dan anti kemiskinan. *Jurnal Ekonomi Syariah Muamalah, 1*(1), 5–15.

8

The Nature of *Waqf* Land and Properties Development in Muslim Countries

Muhamed Zulkhibri

Abstract This chapter examines the nature of *waqf* land and properties development and reviews the role of institutions in *waqf* land and properties development in Muslim countries. The study shows that the development of *waqf* land faces many problems and challenges among others such as lack of financial resources, undeveloped and unproductive *waqf* land, loopholes in the legal framework, unregistered *waqf* land, *waqf* on leasehold land, and land classified as heritage. Accordingly, the potential contribution of these institutions hinges on improving its efficiency. Thus, this study proposes a new framework that *Awqaf* institutions in Muslim countries should consider undertaking *waqf* land development through the issuance of *sukuk* and developing cash *waqf* fund.

Keywords *Waqf* · Properties · Muslim · Development · *Sukuk*

M. Zulkhibri (✉)
Islamic Research and Training Institute,
Islamic Development Bank, Jeddah, Saudi Arabia
e-mail: khibri1974@yahoo.com; mzulkhibri@isdb.org

© The Author(s) 2017

M. Zulkhibri and A. G. Ismail (eds.), *Financial Inclusion and Poverty Alleviation*,
Palgrave Studies in Islamic Banking, Finance, and Economics,
https://doi.org/10.1007/978-3-319-69799-4_8

8.1 Introduction

There is no doubt that the existence of *waqf* since the time of the Prophet (pbuh) is meant for human beings to do good deeds for the society and in particular to benefit the Muslims. *Waqf* or endowment has been embodied in Islam as one of the good deeds in which the spiritual deed is rewarded by Allah with 70 times returns. In another verse, the act of philanthropy by disposing out property as an act of charity is encouraged in Islam. *Waqf* assets fall into two main categories: assets that produce goods and services for the needy; and investment *waqf*, which produces goods and services to be sold or usufruct that can be rented for a profit distributed to the beneficiaries of the *waqf*. The uniqueness and benefit of *waqf* in the poverty alleviation programs provide a powerful mechanism for developing the Ummah in form of charitable instruments.

In Islamic tradition, as an integral part of the Islamic socioeconomic system, *waqf* is very important for the Muslim society. A *waqf* can be described from an economic perspective as a way of diverting funds and other resources from consumption to investing into productive assets thereby providing revenue or usufruct, which can provide revenue. It has a dual role of saving and investment. The future potential of *waqf* development should not be underestimated. The average rate of return on investments made in developing *waqf* properties is in the range of 20–25% (Rashid 2012). *Waqf* land has also been used for other purposes rather than solely for religious such as health care, education sector, infrastructure development, and public amenities.

Hasan (2007) identifies that there are two types of *waqf*: (1) *waqf Ahli* (the family endowment). Until the distinction of his or her descendants, the *waqf* is held for the family or specific group; thereafter, it is diverted to a charitable purpose and (2) *waqf khairi* (the charitable or public endowment). It involves the permanent commitment of property to charitable purposes. In addition, *waqf* can also be identified as *waqf musytarak*, a combination between these two forms of *waqf*. Part of the *waqf* property is dedicated to family members and another part for the use of the public. *Waqf* assets can include not just immovable properties, but also sukuk and equities. To realize the huge advantages and benefits of *waqf*, every property entrusted as *waqf* should be governed and administered with the utmost excellence to bear the intended result of the founder.

Among the prominent education institutions that were founded and maintained using *waqf* land and properties are the University of Cordova in Spain, Universitas Islam Indonesia in Jogjakarta, Indonesia, Al-Azhar University in Egypt (Ahmad Zaki et al. 2008), and AlBukhary International University in Malaysia. In the healthcare sector, the hospital (Al Noori Hospital) in Damascus and clinics (Klinik Nur) in Malaysia were founded and maintained using *waqf* funds. The King Abdul Aziz Endowment (*Waqf*) complex (Abraj Albeit) in Makkah was constructed for the purpose of raising revenue to finance maintenance and development of the Grand Mosque in Makkah as well as the Prophets Mosque (Nabawi Mosque) in Madinah.

This chapter examines the nature of *waqf* land and properties development and reviews recent literature and the role of institutions in *waqf* land and properties development. The study also proposes a framework to undertake *waqf* land or property development for *Awqaf* institutions in Muslim countries using various Islamic modes of *waqf* for waqf institutions. This chapter is set out as follows: Sect. 8.2 provides a brief review of *waqf* developments. Section 8.3 outlines the binding constraints to *waqf* land and properties developments. Section 8.4 presents the proposed framework for *waqf* land and properties development, and Sect. 8.5 provides the conclusion.

8.2 Review of *Waqf* Development

Development of *waqf* land and properties requires an institutional framework that allows transactions to take place in an orderly manner and in which agents know that the decisions they take and the contracts they make will be protected by law and enforced. Reviving the *waqf* institutions is becoming increasingly important among scholars and religious authorities. In recent years, many international conferences and seminars on *waqf* have been organized (i.e., Harvard 2006, 2008; South Africa 2007; Singapore 2008; Kuwait 2008; Iran 2008; Malaysia 2010) to discuss the role of *waqf* in the modern societies. These conferences and seminars have discussed, among others, on how to revive *waqf* institutions, how to streamline the rules and regulations, and how to manage *waqf* land and properties in many parts of the Muslim world for the benefit of the Ummah. Box 1 provides some examples of development of *waqf* land and properties in Malaysia and Singapore. There are still a lot of undeveloped *waqf* land and properties, which have potential to be invested using various instruments. However, various efforts by the governments to optimize the utilization and to enhance the benefits of *waqf* land and properties do not generate the best outcome.

In recent years, several institutions at the international and national levels related to *waqf* were set up with the aims to develop and revive *waqf* sector. The World *Waqf* Foundation (WWF) was established by the Islamic Development Bank (IDB) in 2001 to promote and use *waqf* in the development, to support the development of *waqf* institutions, and to alleviate poverty. A state body in Kuwait, under the Ministry of *Awqaf* and Islamic Affairs, was founded in 1993 called Kuwait *Awqaf* Public Foundation (KAPF) to develop an innovative approach to *waqf* development. Furthermore, the *waqf* administration system in Kuwait is under the *Awqaf* and Religious Matters Ministry. The Ministry launched a community program, and activities are done in and out of the country to increase *waqf* events. Other than that, investment and increment in *waqf* are also done, and the proceeds are spent for the development of its society.

In Southeast Asia region, Singapore *waqf* administration was carried out by Majlis Ugama Islam Singapura (MUIS), under the Administration of Muslim Law Act (AMLA) 1966, to administer all *waqf* in the country. In order to oversee the management of *waqf* resources in the country, the Malaysian Government, in 2004, has established the Jabatan *Wakaf*, Zakat dan Haji (JAWHAR). In Brunei, Majlis Ugama Islam Brunei (MUIB) became the sole trustee for all *waqf* and was tasked to manage and administer the *waqf* property using e-government technology. MUIB also gives information and understanding to the public about the *waqf* procedure. MUIB has successfully generated a high income and gives full benefits to all the Muslims from *waqf* property's income. In Indonesia, most *waqf* is used for physical development such as mosque and cemetery. In semiprofessional stage of *waqf* management, the usage of mosques is being widened for place of discussion, wedding, and seminar. *Waqf* land and properties are also being utilized for other benefits such as farming activities, shop lots, and rice factories (Ramli and Sulaiman 2006).

From the perspective of research, the literature has discussed the different usage of Islamic modes of investment for *waqf* institutions (Kahf 1998; Hasan and Abdullah 2008). For instance, cash *waqf* has become increasingly well known due to its flexibility, which allows distribution of the *waqf*'s potential benefit to the poor (Mannan 1998). There are also some studies which have focused on the topics of *waqf* land and properties development. Most of the literature has discussed the historic development of these lands and their legal aspects (Hasan and Abdullah 2008). Moreover, there are researches that have classified *waqf* land and properties according to specific purposes, for example agriculture, mosques, school and cemeteries. However, according to Nor and Mohammed (2009), limited literature that has categorized *waqf* land and properties and how to match them with Islamic investment modes are based on its strategic location and usage.

There is no recent news of any worth-mentioning *waqf* development projects except in Malaysia during the last two years with 20 major and 70 minor *waqf* projects have been completed, worth over US$100 million (Rashid 2012). On the other hand, the number of properties sponsored by the *Awqaf* Properties Investment Fund of Islamic Development Bank (APIF) has not been up to the mark. During 2002–2003, only eight projects were developed, while seven projects in 2009, and 5 projects in 2010. The distribution of dividend from the funds was relatively low at only 2.5%. In comparison, Harta Tanah PNB Trust in Malaysia generated 6–7% of income distribution annually. In addition, the WWF has been inactive as there is no any publication from the foundation since 2004 (Rashid 2012).

8.3 Binding Constraints to Development of *Waqf* Land and Properties

In practice, many new applications of the *waqf* concept have emerged over time and space, including serving the needs of associations and cooperatives, markets and private enterprises, and other civic endowments. *Waqf* usually places under the administration of a *mutawali* (trustee) for any economic transaction (i.e., housing for the poor, construction of schools and mosques, cemeteries, and others general welfare for the poor). In this respect, the underlying principle of *waqf* occupies the central activities of many charities and philanthropists as well as other institutions. However, the donor or his heirs cannot re-appropriate *waqf* donation, or otherwise withdrawn from its original purpose, or used as collateral for mortgages or loans (Nagata 2002).

The inability of appointed *mutawali* to development the *waqf* land and properties, in which most of the time the right to administer the *waqf* property was kept within the founder's or *mutawalli*'s family or was assigned to any government-run institution as a *mutawali*, has resulted in inefficient management, lack of qualified expertise, and underdevelopment of the *waqf* land and properties. These common issues facing *waqf* institutions need to be overcome when it comes to the process of developing the *waqf* land and properties. For instance, complaints of bribery against the *waqf* officials are not uncommon as well as impartial and unjust decisions on the *waqf* administration are common (Karim 2010). There are also many examples of disputed *waqf* land and properties that are now in the process of court hearing around the Muslim world.

Mohammad and Iman (2006) argue that three main characteristics of classical *waqf* that impose development constraints on *waqf* land or property: irrevocability, perpetuity, and inalienability. These characteristics have resulted in underdevelopment of *waqf* land or property and ineffective *waqf* property management. As implied by the definitions of early and modern jurists, the two characteristics of *waqf*, that is perpetuity and inalienability, negatively affect the development of *waqf* property, which in turn causes stagnation of the Islamic charities. This negative effect may be seen in the lack of liquid assets and conflict with some laws on the other while the latter being a further cause to other legal and financial constraints. Among the three characteristics of *waqf*, irrevocability may not be harmful as manifested in the freezing of any dealing relating to the transfer of title.

The specific binding constraints faced by the development of *waqf* land and properties among others are: (i) unregistered *waqf* lands—without land titles registered in the name of the *waqf* authority, the land cannot be developed and they remain undeveloped; (ii) unexplored option of *Istibdal* on non-prime land or sale—*Istibdal* or substitution would be a suitable alternative to non-prime land being exchanged for prime or more suitable lands for identified development initiatives or refurbishment; (iii) *waqf* on leasehold land and properties classified as national heritage—*waqf* authority may encounter obstacles developing *waqf* land that is leasehold (till lease expires) or classify under the category of national heritage under the auspices of respective local authority; (iv) legal framework—to understand different legal frameworks of *waqf* administration and *waqf* matters; and (v) security for financing route—for project financing, the concept of *waqf* may not allow for *waqf* land becoming collateral as a basis for financing.

In terms of *waqf* institutions, there has been overwhelming unsatisfactory evidence of *Awqaf* in many areas. As a result, vast majority of *Awqaf* properties are ill-managed, while no proper attention is given by *Awqaf* institutions. The expected consequence is much shabbiness and disrepair of *Awqaf* properties. Basic repairs and maintenance are ignored despite the fact that the *waqf* buildings have tremendous commercial potential (Ahmad and Khan 1998). *Waqf* properties of the highest quality in the commercial markets are now becoming a cheap commodity. The dreadful state of *Awqaf* institutions has resulted in a vacuum, which in turn failed to fill the gap in socioeconomic development in most Muslim countries. Generally, the reasons for this problem include: (i) poor legislative framework; (ii) administrative lapses; (iii) lack of political will; (iv) indifferent attitude of the management committee of the Awqaf; (v) lack of funding; and (vi) lack of honesty and integrity.

8.4 Framework for *Waqf* Land and Property Development

The social wealth of Muslim around the world consists of vast un-managed assets of *Awqaf*. In the development process, these assets can be combined to produce necessary facility of social services especially for the poor people (Bellhachmi 2004). In the process of social and economic development, the institution of *Awqaf* could play a pivotal role.

Achieving this requires that the vast underused *Awqaf* land and properties are given special attention to reactivate their functions and ability to provide those important services. The inability to offer market-determined return, the shortage of funds for regenerating the productivity of the *waqf* land, and other obstacles faced by movable and immovable *waqf* assets have hampered the revival of *waqf* institutions.

The intended development of *waqf* land and properties may be either for the purpose of revivification or advanced in the sense of investment. There are several modes of financing that can be employed for the development of *Awqaf* land such as issuing output share, partnership share, and leasing. The development of *waqf* assets can be divided into three modes of financing: (i) credit-based finance; (ii) income sharing through joint venture or equity; and (iii) self-financing. These three methods of financing or two of them can be combined depending on the requirements to develop the *waqf* assets.

Based on the recent studies and practices, this study proposes the establishment of *waqf* assets as an offer of alternative investment through the issuance of *sukuk* and complemented by 'cash *waqf* fund.' The issuance of *Sukuk* is to provide long-term support with a focus on building capabilities and to achieve the desired outcomes. On the other hand, cash *waqf* alone is not suitable for the *waqf* construction due to several fundamental issues: (i) cash *waqf* is a type of *waqf al-manqul* (endowment of movable properties); (ii) cash *waqf* has no benefit unless it is consumed (exchanged) with other goods or services; (iii) the value of cash *waqf* is subject to time value of money (volatility); and (iv) the application of *Istibdal* is inevitable in cash *waqf*.

In order to develop *Awqaf* projects and enhance the financial benefit, issuing *sukuk* mode of finance (i.e., such as in Singapore) and creating cash *waqf* fund (i.e., such as in Malaysia and Singapore) will build up trust between investors, depositors, and the *Awqaf* institutions. This mechanism provides more transparency and clarity among all parties involved in developing *waqf* land and properties in terms of their rights and obligations. These two sources of Islamic investment funds are expected to fulfill the objectives of the *Awqaf* and to attract the *Ummah* or *waqf* contributors to finance *Awqaf* projects. The details of these two sources of funding for the development of *Awqaf* institutions are discussed below:

- Before undertaking the development of *waqf* land and properties, *Awqaf* institutions need to fulfill three basic requirements: (i) develop a coordination mechanism between *Awqaf* institutions, *waqf* authority, and land authority for the purpose of compiling *waqf* land and properties information; (ii) identify and profile strategic *waqf* land and properties for the purpose of commercial activities (i.e., hospitals, educational and training institutions, and real estate); and (iii) form a potential partnership in the form of SPV—*Awqaf* institutions as a partner (*sharik*)—with the potential *waqf* authority to undertake specific *waqf* projects/investments.
- *Waqf* assets through the issuance of *sukuk* against the assets on the balance sheet of various investors offer an alternative investment since many *Awqaf* institutions simply do not have the funds to develop new capacity. Moreover, *sukuk* as a product is linked to the returns and cash flows of financing the assets purchased, in other words, the returns generated from an asset purchased, while keeping their existing work going on. The main objective is to provide long-term support with a focus on building capabilities and ensuring the completion of the projects. Therefore, *sukuk* can be used as a tool to finance for the development of the *waqf* properties.
- Figure 8.1 summarizes the cycle for *waqf* land development via sukuk. The *waqf* management board creates a *musharakah* venture. *Waqf* management board also will appoint a *Waqf* asset manager as an agent to develop the land. In order to mobilize the fund through *musharakah sukuk*, the following mechanics can be employed (Hassan and Shahid 2010): (i) the *waqf* asset manager and special purpose vehicle (SPV) enter into a *musharakah* venture to develop *waqf* land for a period with predetermined profit sharing; (ii) the *waqf* asset manager enters into a two-year forward lease agreement with construction company[1]; (iii) on behalf of the *waqf* management board, *waqf* asset manager contributes land to the *musharakah*

[1]Some of the development of the *Waqf* properties after assessing its risk and return analysis has resort to the method of joint development. In the leasing contract (*hukr*) which includes the terms for the refurbishment against the lease terms and condition, an amount will be computed for the total amount of refurbishment to be undertaken.

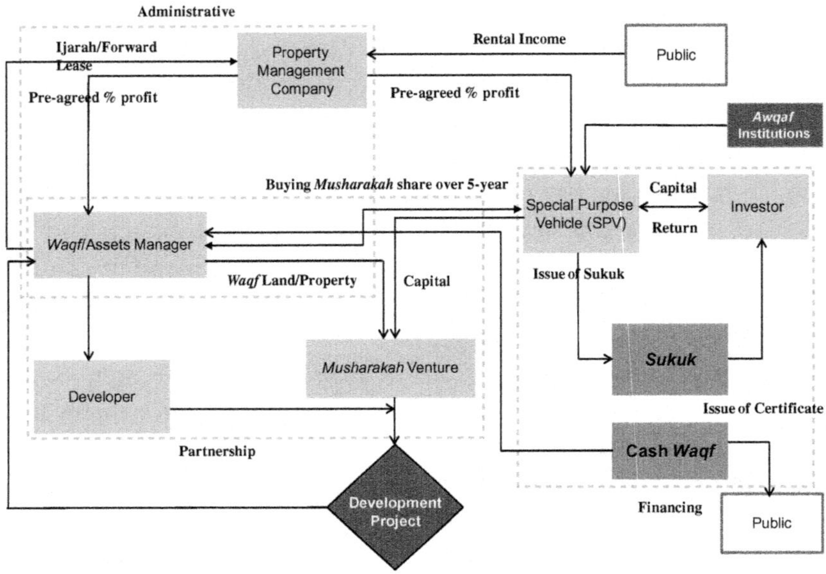

Fig. 8.1 Illustration for *Waqf* land development. *Source* Author's own illustration

venture; and (iv) the SPV contributes cash as capital to build commercial building on the *waqf* land.

- There are several types of *sukuk*, but in the real estate financing and for creating funds for construction of new complexes, *Ijara sukuk* and *musharakah sukuk* are the most popular. *Musharakah* financing principle for the development of *waqf* assets through the issuance of *sukuk* may be most suitable due to three elements: (i) profit and loss-sharing is the basis of new source of funds; (ii) mid- to long-term finance is vital to developing *Awqaf* land and properties; and (iii) Islamic financial institutions have great surplus of cash to be tapped.
- The *musharakah sukuk* can be complemented by cash *waqf* fund. Cash *waqf* has become increasingly popular among Muslim, which allows distribution of the *waqf's* potential benefit to the poor as well as more distribution flexibility compared to *Zakah*. *Waqf* fund may be opened for public with the intention to support services to mankind and cash contribution for charity purposes. The donors (*waqifs*) of this fund will give their cash money for the purpose of financing

the development of *Awqaf* land/building/properties. The *waqf mutawalli* will manage this fund, and the fund will be utilized for providing revolving loans for development of *Awqaf* properties. For financing other *Awqaf* properties, loans that are payable to the fund will be utilized again.

The new framework should also provide clarity on the management of *waqf* land. Some forms of regulations are required between the *waqf* management, the *waqf* authority, and investors. Baskan (2002) argues that the solutions for *Awqaf* need to be privatized by returning their assets to private management by creating *waqf* boards of trustees independent of the Government Ministry. Therefore, it is advisable to make development compulsory for the person who may be managing a *waqf* land. The *waqf* authority should ensure that if nothing has been done to develop the *waqf* land or lack of financial resources to initiate any forms of development on the *waqf* land, the *waqf* authority may take responsibility or it may delegate this work to a party which is capable (i.e., Islamic bank, business venture, and investor). The developed *waqf* land should be returned to the *mutawalli* after the fund invested in the development has been recouped.

8.5 Conclusion

This study examines briefly the nature of *waqf* land development, reviews recent literature and practices on *waqf* land development and proposes a solution to undertake *waqf* land development for *Awqaf* institutions in Muslim countries. The development of *waqf* land and properties is an important milestone for many Islamic institutions around the world given the fact that there are a large amount of undeveloped and ill-managed *waqf* land and properties in the Muslim world. Inevitably, the development of *waqf* land also involved problems and challenges such as lack of financial resources, undeveloped and unproductive *waqf* land, loopholes in the legal framework, unregistered *waqf* land, *waqf* on leasehold land, and land classified as heritage. Furthermore, there are impediments such as bureaucracy, lack of expertise, and the need to revisit religious rulings on *waqf*, in order to realize the true intent and spirit of *Awqaf*. If the size of the *Zakah* and *Awqaf* institutions can be enhanced, it can play a greater role in the society. The potential contribution of these institutions hinges on improving its efficiency. Thus, creative and innovative solutions are urgently needed in order to expedite *waqf* development and its *Zakah* and *Awqaf* institutions.

By providing the expertise on enhancing the *Awqaf* institutions and developing *waqf*, it is expected from this undertaking that the institution of *Awqaf* could not only play a better role in the process of social and economic development but also generate an additional source of income for *Awqaf* institutions in the Muslim countries to combat poverty. Financing and development is possible for *waqf* assets and should not be a deterrent for the further development of *waqf*. The existing frameworks and various instruments of investment approaches taken by the *waqf* institution contributed positively to the development of *waqf* land. However, this study proposes a new framework that *Awqaf* institutions in Muslim countries should consider undertaking *waqf* land development through the issuance of *sukuk* and developing cash *waqf* fund together with Muslim countries.

References

Ahmad, H. & Khan, A. (1998). *Strategies to Develop Waqf Administration in India*. Research Paper No. 50, Jeddah: Islamic Research and Training Institute.

Ahmad Zaki, A. L., Norzaidi, M. D., & Che Zuina, I. (2008). Pengurusan harta wakaf dan potensinya ke arah kemajuan pendidikan umat Islam di Malaysia. *Jurnal Pengurusan JAWHAR*, *2*(2), 13.

Baskan, B. (2002). *Waqf system as a redistribution mechanism in Ottoman empire*. Paper presented at 17th Middle East History and Theory Conference, 10–11 May 2002, Center for Middle Eastern Studies, University of Chicago.

Belhachmi, Z. (2004). Revealing al-Waqf as a systemic cultural policy of governance. *WAQF*, *7*(4), 5–35.

Hasan, Z. (2007). *The effectiveness of the administration of waqf land in Malaysia*. Shariah Law Reports: LexisNexis.

Hasan, Z., & Abdullah, M. N. (2008). *The investment of waqf land as an instrument of muslims' economic development in Malaysia*. Paper presented at the Dubai International Conference on Endowments' Investment, 4–6 February 2008, Waqf and Minors Affairs Foundation, Dubai, UAE.

Hassan, A., & Shahid, M. A. (2010). *Management and development of the awqaf assets*. In 7th International Conference—The Tawhidi Epistemology: Zakat and Waqf Economy, Bangi, Malaysia.

Kahf, M. (1998). *Financing the development of awqaf property*. Paper presented at International Conference on Awqaf and Economic Development, 2–4 March 1998, Islamic Research and Training Institute (IRTI), Kuala Lumpur.

Karim, M. F. (2010). *Waqf estates in Bangladesh—Analyzing socio-economic profile and exploring potential but unexplored expenditure options*. In 7th International Conference—The Tawhidi Epistemology: Zakat and Waqf Economy, Bangi, Malaysia.

Mannan, M. A. (1998). *Cash waqf: Enrichment of family heritage generation to generation* (1st ed.). Social Investment Bank Press, Dhaka, Bangladesh.

Mohammad, M. S., & Iman, A. H. (2006). Obstacles of the current concept of waqf to the development of waqf properties and the recommended alternative. *Malaysian Journal of Real Estate, 1*(1), 1–95.

Nagata, J. (2002). *The changing perceptions of waqf, as social, cultural and symbolic capital in Penang*. The Penang Story—International Conference, 18–21 April 2002, organized by The Penang Heritage Trust and STAR Publications, Penang.

Nor, N. B. M., & Mohammed, M. O. (2009). Categorization of *Waqf* Lands and their Management Using Islamic Investment Models: The Case of the State of Selangor, Malaysia. International Conference on *Waqf* Laws & Management: Reality and Prospects, IIUM, Kuala Lumpur, 20–22 October 2009.

Ramli, A. H., & Sulaiman, K. (2006). Pembangunan tanah *wakaf*: pengalaman negara-negara Islam, Konvensyen *Wakaf* Kebangsaan, 12–14 September 2006, organized by Department of Awqaf, Zakat and Hajj, Kuala Lumpur.

Rashid, S. K. (2012). *Certain legal and administrative measures for revival and better management of awqf* (Unpublished).

9

Relationship Between Intention and Actual Support Toward the Construction of Modern *Waqf-Based* Hospital in Uganda

Mustafa Omar Mohammed and Umar Ahmed

The paper was presented at the *10th International Conference on Islamic Economics and Finance (ICIEF)*, March 23–24, 2015, Doha, Qatar.

Abstract This chapter makes use of the theory of planned behavior to identify factors that motivate intention toward *Waqf* giving. The chapter examines the relationship between intention and actual support toward the construction of modern *Waqf*-based hospital in Uganda. The study adopted factor analysis, principal component analysis, and Structural Equation Modeling (SEM) to analyze data from 300 valid questionnaires. The findings reveal that three motivating factors, namely attitude, moral duties, and religious duties significantly and positively influence Muslim community's intentions to provide actual financial

M. O. Mohammed (✉)
International Islamic University Malaysia, Kuala Lumpur, Malaysia
e-mail: mustafa@iium.edu.my

U. Ahmed
Modern College of Business & Science, Bausher Street, Muscat
Oman
e-mail: umar.ahmed@mcbs.edu.om

© The Author(s) 2017

M. Zulkhibri and A. G. Ismail (eds.), *Financial Inclusion and Poverty Alleviation*, Palgrave Studies in Islamic Banking, Finance, and Economics,
https://doi.org/10.1007/978-3-319-69799-4_9

and non-financial support for the construction of modern *Waqf*-based hospital in Uganda. Accordingly, Muslim religious authorities and relevant parties should use these three motivating factors to influence Muslim community decision to support *Waqf*-based projects for their socioeconomic development.

Keywords Waqf · Hospital · TRA · SEM

9.1 Introduction

Good health is one of the main determinants of economic growth and a component of well-being of the population (ILO 2008; Scheil-Adlung et al. 2006). Accessibility to healthcare services makes society healthier and raises their earning capacities. In addition, good health has positive impacts on school attendance, employment, and human capital development (Lamiraud et al. 2005). Better health means much higher survival rates for infants and children, which raise GDP per capita by increasing the ratio of workers to dependents. Better health among adults increases labor force participation and improves the productivity of those who are at work (ILO 2008). These together have significant positive impact on sustainable economic growth and social development, which in turn improves social welfare (Victor 2004).

However, not all countries enjoy good health care services and its benefits. For instance, Uganda's health care performance is still ranked among the worst in the world by the World Health Organization (WHO 2009). Uganda is a landlocked country in East Africa with estimated population of 34 million, and its population growth rate is 3.4% (WHO 2013). Uganda is still a low-income developing country ranking 161 on the Global Human Development Index in 2012 (HDI 2013). In Uganda, total health expenditure is US$52 per capita while household expenditure on health as a percentage of total health expenditure is 42%. The resources available for health are less than required to deliver the Uganda National Minimum Health Care Package. Indeed, household continues to carry a heavy burden with a high out-of-pocket expenditure on health care services (WHO 2014). This is because government investment on health is still low, and according to health ministry report (2013), financial investment in health by government shows a further decline over the years from 9.6% in 2009/2010 to 7.4% in 2012/2013.

With low government investments on health coupled with unaffordable private health care services, societies resort to other viable alternatives to meet their needs. For example, according to Sen (2000), nations adopt two pathways to increase the provision and accessibility of health care services to their citizens. The first route is through rapid economic development, where high-income nations can afford to provide high-quality health care services for all their citizens likewise citizens can afford to pay for high-quality health care services. The second pathway is a "support-led," where individuals, corporations, charitable organizations, and religious and non-religious affiliated NGOs provide health care services to the poor and the needy section of society through donations. Today, the second pathway is increasingly contributing significantly toward providing health care services to the poor and the needy in both developed and developing countries.

For instance, in the USA, social services are regarded as the responsibilities of active citizen. In 1989, contribution of nonprofit institutions to the health care services was 56% of the total health care services in the country. They financed 3427 hospitals compared to public sector, which financed 1142 hospitals during the same period (Salamon 1999). In 1996, the sector spent US$262.5 billion on health care services, and the largest part of these incomes came from donations. By 2000, the nonprofit sector accounts for half of the USA's health care services (Salamon et al. 2000). Weisbrod (1998) reported that 212 of the UK's top 500 charities are health care service providers. In Pakistan, Imran Khan (former national cricket team captain) built Shaukat Khanum Memorial Cancer Hospital and Research Centre (SKMCH&RC) as Trust. The hospital opened to patients on December 29, 1994, upon completion of the first of its three phases at the cost of US$22 million. Sixty-seven percent of this fund was raised in the form of donation (SKMCH&RC annual report 2010). In Malaysia, *Waqaf* An-Nur Corporation Berhad (WANCorp) was established as part of Johor corporation social responsibilities. JCorp via WANCorp in cooperation with State Islamic Councils and support from KPJ Healthcare Berhad built and managed 20 *Waqaf* An-Nur Clinics (KWAN). This is in addition to one *Waqaf* An-Nur Hospital (HWAN) and two mobile clinics, both also being financed through *Waqf*. Today, WANCorp provides good health care services at affordable price of RM5 Malaysian Ringgit (inclusive of medication) to more than 1 million patients across states in Malaysia (Jcorp Annual Report 2013).

In Uganda, while the role of NGOs toward health care services is increasingly becoming prominent, the role of trusts, foundations, and endowments, particularly *Waqf*, is very appalling. Apart from few *Waqf* assets such as mosques, schools, and the Islamic Universities in Uganda built by the Organization of Islamic Cooperation (OIC) as *Awqaf* (Basar 1987), unfortunately, most of *Waqf* assets in the country are scattered, mismanaged, expropriated, underdeveloped, and in some instances sold privately by the trustees. The revival of *Waqf* to meet the socioeconomic needs of Muslim communities in Uganda, particularly a health care project such as hospital, is imperative. Reviving *Waqf* in Uganda will primarily depend on the extent to which the donors are motivated, and how these motivations influence their intention to support a *Waqf*-based health care project in the country. To the best knowledge of the authors, hardly any empirical study has examined the relationship between intention to donate and actual support of Muslim communities toward *Waqf-based* health care projects.

This chapter attempts to fill the gaps by examining the relationship between four antecedents (attitude, moral duties, perceived behavioral control, and religious duties), intentions, and actual financial and non-financial support by Muslim community for the construction of modern *Waqf-based* hospital in Uganda. Against this backdrop, this chapter attempts to answer the following research questions:

1. What is the relationship between Muslim community attitude, intention, and the actual support for the construction of modern *Waqf-based* hospital in Uganda?
2. What is the relationship between moral duties, intention, and the actual support for the construction of modern *Waqf-based* hospital in Uganda?

3. What is the relationship between perceived behavioral control, intention, and the actual support for the construction of modern *Waqf-based* hospital in Uganda?
4. What is the relationship between religious duties, intention, and the actual support for the construction of modern *Waqf-based* hospital in Uganda?

9.2 Theory of Planned Behavior (TPB)

This study is based on the theory of planned behavior (TPB) coined by Azjen (1991). TPB is one of the most influential and well-supported social psychological theories for predicting human behavior. The theory is an extension introduced to overcome the limitations of TRA—Theory of Reasoned Action.

The Theory of Reasoned Action (TRA) studies attitude–behavior relationship by connecting attitudes, subjective norms, behavioral intentions, and actual behavior (Ajzen and Fishbein 1975; Fishbein and Ajzen 1980). According to the theory, behavior is a consequence of behavioral intention, which is in turn a consequence of combination of people's attitude toward performing the behavior in question and their perceptions of the pressure put upon them by referents to perform or not to perform that behavior (Ajzen and Fishbein 1980). The TRA is based on two main antecedents (attitude and subjective norm), which predict intention. Attitude refers to the evaluative effect of individuals' positive or negative feelings in order to perform a particular behavior (Fishbein and Ajzen 1975). A subjective norm, on the other hand, refers to an individual's perception of other people's opinions on whether he or she should perform or not a particular behavior (Ajzen 1991). In other words, subjective norm is an individual perception of the likelihood that potential referent groups or individuals would approve or disapprove performing a given behavior (Ryan and Bonfield 1980).

Despite the fact that a high correlation of attitudes and subjective norms to behavioral intention and subsequently to behavior has been confirmed in many studies, the theory was found to be limited in explaining behaviors over which an individual has no volitional control.

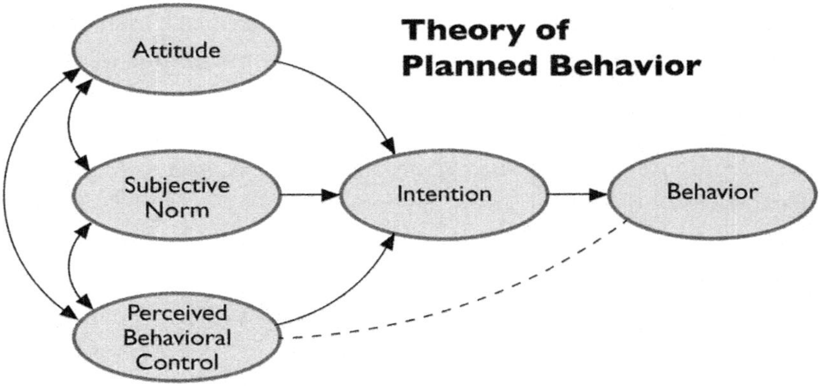

Fig. 9.1 TPB Theoretical framework. *Source* http://www.healthcommcapacity.org/ retrieved on December 30, 2014

In order to overcome these limitations, Ajzen (1991) extended TRA by introducing Theory of Planned Behavior (TPB) where he added a new component, i.e., "perceived behavioral control." The extension of the theory was necessitated to accommodate the correlates of behavior that are covered by the TRA and the correlates behavior that are not totally under a person's control (Ajzen 1991). He asserts that behavioral decisions are not made all of a sudden, but are the consequences of attitudes, subject norms, and perceived behavioral control over the behavior. Ajzen further supported the integration of additional variables into the model. Figure 9.1 below shows Ajzen's TPB theoretical framework.

TRA and TPB are widely applied in psycho-social studies including, Islamic banking and finance (Echchabi and Olaniyi 2012; Yousafzai et al. 2010; Syed et al. 2011), study of health behaviors such as healthy eating (Astrom and Rise 2001; Corner et al. 2002), alcohol, and tobacco use (Mcmillan and Corner 2003), and exercise behavior (Bozionelos and Bennett 1999), blood donation (Giles and Cairns 1995), and volunteering behavior (Warburton and Terry 2000). There are a number of studies that have focused on altruistic and helping behavior (Konkoly and Perloff 1990; Becker 1974; Arrow 1975; Andreoni 1989, 1990; Rose-Ackerman 1997). Similarly, several studies have been conducted on charitable giving behavior (Linden 2011; Smith and Mcsweeney 2007; Osman et al. 2014). For instance, Linden (2011) used the theory of planned behavior as the underpinning theory in determining charitable giving behavior.

This study has modified TPB model to examine the extent to which the intention of Muslim community in Uganda to support the construction of *Waqf-based* hospital can be translated into actual financial and non-financial support. In addition to attitude, moral duties, and perceived behavioral control, the study adds religious duties as the fourth variable.

9.3 The Variables

The present study aspires to examine the relationship between four antecedents (attitude, moral duties, perceived behavioral control, and religious duties), intentions, and actual financial and non-financial support by Muslim community for the construction of modern *Waqf-based* hospital in Uganda.

9.3.1 Attitude

Attitude is said to arise from a combination of people's belief about behavioral outcomes and their evaluation of those outcomes (Ajzen and Fishbein 1977; Sparks and Shepherd 1992). Hence, attitude toward behavior is determined by a person's evaluation of the outcomes associated with the behavior and by the strength of these associations. Generally, a person who believes that performing a given behavior will lead to mostly positive outcomes will hold a favorable attitude toward performing the behavior, whereas a person who believes that performing the behavior will lead to mostly negative outcomes will hold an unfavorable attitude.

In the context of support for the construction of modern *Waqf-based* hospital in Uganda, the donor's response might be used to understand attitude toward the support behavior. For example, belief that

Waqf contributes to the socioeconomic development of the Muslim community in Uganda, belief that *Waqf* support could reduce government and individual expenditure, and belief that *Waqf* is a source of fund that can support health care projects might be taken as evidence of positive attitude toward the actual support. By way of contrast, an unfavorable attitude would be implied by expression of beliefs suggesting that *Waqf* support is difficult to perform. Numerous studies have documented the significant relationship between attitude and intention (Shih and Fang 2004; Lada et al. 2009; Amin and Chong 2011). Therefore, it is expected that there would be a positive relationship between Muslims attitude, intention, and the actual support for the construction of modern *Waqf-based* hospital in Uganda.

9.3.2 Moral Duties

Linden (2011) hypothesized that moral norms rather than social norms are likely to play a significant role in the formation of charitable intentions. In addition to moral norms, "attitude," "perceived behavioral control," and "past behavior" were also identified as significant predictors. Similarly, Smith and McSweeney (2007) findings from study on charitable giving behavior using a theory of planned behavior (TPB) reveal that attitudes, perceived behavioral control, injunctive norms, moral norms, and past behavioral control influence charitable giving intention. Hence, moral duties are expected to have positive relationship with attitude, intention, and the actual support for the construction of modern *Waqf-based* hospital in Uganda.

9.3.3 Perceived Behavioral Control

Perceived behavioral control is defined as people's perceptions of their ability to carry out a given behavior (Ajzen 1991; 2011). It measures the degree to which a person has mental and physical control over his behavior and how confident he feels about being able to perform the behavior. This includes access to money, time, and other resources needed to perform a given behavior (Ajzen 2011).

In the support for the construction of *Waqf-based* hospital, such information like campaign or promotion about the project could enhance the awareness and knowledge of donor and eventually increase his or her support. Besides, financial commitment and income level will also determine his or her ability for contributing.

Smith and McSweeney (2007) conducted a study on charitable giving behavior using a theory of planned behavior (TPB) as a baseline theory to determine the influence of attitudes, norms, perceived behavior control, and past behavior on intention to donate money to charitable organizations. Their findings reveal that attitudes, perceived behavioral control, injunctive norms, moral norms, and past behavioral control influence charitable giving intention. Perceived behavioral control is expected to have positive relationship with attitude, intention, and the actual support for the construction of modern *Waqf-based* hospital in Uganda.

9.3.4 Religious Duties

Kamri (2010) mentioned that the practice of *Waqf* giving behavior is a form of *ibadah* that brings oneself closer to God (Allah) by entrusting the *Waqf* for the benefit of the public. Several verses of the Quran and Prophetic tradition or *hadith* stipulate that the *Waqf* founder (*Waqif*) is promised a continuous reward from the *Waqf* he/she made. For example, Allah says in the Quran (al-Hadid, 57:11):

> Who is he that will loan on God a beautiful loan for (God) will increase it manifold to his credit, and he will have (beside) a noble reward.

Kotler and Keller (2012) argued that religion is part of culture, and culture influences and shapes one's intention and behavior. Religion is one of the most important cultural institutions which has significant influence on people's attitudes, values, and behaviors at both micro—and macro-societal levels (Echchabi and Aziz 2012).

Several researches (Amin 2012; Amin et al. 2011; Sun et al. 2012) have focused directly on examining the relationship of religious obligation with behavioral intention. For example, the study by Alam et al. (2012)

found that religiosity is a significant factor on the intention to undertake Islamic home financing among Muslims in Klang Valley. Similarly, Sun et al. (2012) examine religious and commitment and perceived attributes of Islamic mobile banking service adoption among 135 Southeast Asian young adults, and findings from the multiple regression analysis reveal that Islamic mobile phone banking is moderated by religious affiliations and commitment. Ong and Moschis (2006) and Mokhlis (2006) have documented the importance of religiosity in determining one's consumption behavior.

In the context of this study, religious duties refer to the degree to which a person believes that participating in *Waqf* giving would be of religious influence, as it is strongly encouraged in Islam in order to earn *mardhatillah* (Allah's blessings). It is therefore expected that religious duties would have positive relationship with attitude, intention, and the actual support for the construction of modern *Waqf-based* hospital in Uganda.

9.3.5 Intention

Intentions are assumed to capture the motivational factors that influence behavior; they are indications of how hard people are willing to try, of how much of an effort they are planning to exert, in order to perform the behavior. The stronger the intention to engage in a behavior, the more likely is the performance. These intentions remain behavioral characters until, at the appropriate time and opportunity, an attempt is made to translate them into action.

Empirical studies on *Waqf* giving behavior intention have yet to be documented although such acts have been strongly emphasized in Islamic heritage. For example, the beloved Prophet Muhamad (pbuh) mentioned in his *hadith* pertaining to intention and action:

> Verily actions are by intentions, and for every person is what he intended, so the one whose hijrah was to Allah and His messenger, then his hijrah was to Allah and His messenger, and the one whose hijrah was for the world to gain from, or for a woman to marry, then his hijrah was to what he made hijrah for (Al-Bukhari).

The *hadith* mentions that every action or behavior is determined by the individual's intention, which is the basic criteria for every act in all spheres of the individual's life such as religious, social, economic, and political. Ajzen (1985) theories about intention support what had been said by the Prophet Muhamad (pbuh) several centuries ago. Fishbein and Ajzen (1975) define intention as a person's readiness to do or perform a particular behavior as a result of two influential factors, namely attitude and subjective norm. Therefore, intention is expected to have positive relationship with the actual support for the construction of modern *Waqf*-based hospital in Uganda.

9.3.6 Financial and Non-Financial Support (Charity)

As discussed earlier, this chapter examines the extent to which attitude, moral duties, religious duties, and perceived behavioral control can translate the intention of donors into actual financial and non-financial support (in this case charity) toward the establishment of *Waqf*-based hospital in Uganda. Charity is a universal value although the motive toward giving behavior can ideologically vary.

Islam views charity not only as a means of wealth transfer to the poor but also as a mechanism for self-development and an avenue for seeking Allah's pleasure and His reward in the Hereafter. Thus, the motive for giving alms is solely to seek Allah's pleasure. Allah says in the Quran: "It is neither their meat nor their blood that reaches Allah, but it is piety from you that reaches Him" (22:37).

In the Western worldview, the motives for giving charity include social desirability, career advancement, religious, expectations of respect and recognition, positive attitudes toward community as well as altruism or humanitarian (Olson 1965; Becker 1974; Arrow 1975; Andreoni 1989, 1990; Rose-Ackerman 1997). According to Laffont (1975), individuals choose action they would mostly prefer everyone would choose when donating to charities or supplying public goods. He analyzes the case where individuals believe that others will act as they do, then maximize their utility given this belief. Under these beliefs, he shows that individuals voluntarily contribute certain amount toward public goods and social welfare, with the hope that others will do the same.

While Andreoni (1989) argues that individuals may be motivated by altruism, this depends on the extent to which they care about the level of public goods produced, warm glow, and their own responsibility for the production of these public goods.

Andreoni (1990) added that when people donate to privately provided public goods, they may not only gain utility from increasing its total supply, but they may also gain pleasure from the act of giving (warm glow). Rose-Ackerman (1997) argues that some people give to charity because of the result of feelings of commitment; some results from sympathy; some arises from belief in the moral value of reciprocity; and some is motivated by private benefits of the donor such as prestige, pride, and attendance at elite parties. Motivations for giving are inextricably linked. One can obtain prestige from making a gift only if others view one's action as worthy. If the narrow private benefits of giving gifts are too obvious and large, gift givers will not be praised for their self-sacrifice (Rose-Ackerman 1997). Johnson (1968) opines that an individual will donate to charity only to avoid "societal costs" in the form of social pressure and religious belief. The height of societal costs depends on the folkways and custom of the society, the type, and the quantity of the public good as well as the social position and wealth of the individuals in question.

9.4 Conceptual Framework

Based on the literature survey, we develop a conceptual framework to investigate the extent to which attitude, moral duties, perceived behavioral control, and religious duties translate the intention of Muslim community in Uganda into actual financial and non-financial support for the construction of *Waqf*-based hospital. Figure 9.2 shows the conceptual framework of the study adapted from the TPB.

9.4.1 Hypotheses

Based on the literature review and the adapted TPB, the following hypotheses were developed to test the relationships between the dependent and independent variables:

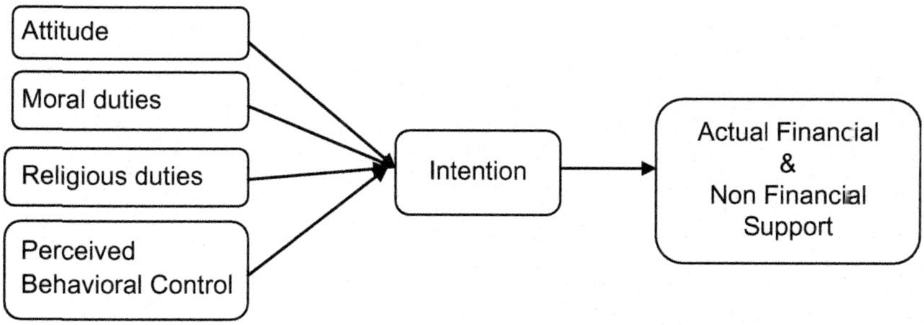

Fig. 9.2 Conceptual framework. *Source* author's own illustration based on TPB

H1 There is a significant and positive relationship between Muslims attitude, intention, and the actual support for the construction of modern *Waqf-based* hospital in Uganda.

H2 There is a significant and positive relationship between Muslims commitment to fulfill their moral duties, intention, and the actual support for the construction of modern *Waqf-based* hospital in Uganda.

H3 There is a significant and positive relationship between perceived behavioral control (such as abilities and willingness to donate), intention, and the actual support for the construction of modern *Waqf-based* hospital in Uganda.

H4 There is a significant and positive relationship between Muslims commitment to fulfill their religious duties, intention, and the actual support for the construction of modern *Waqf-based* hospital in Uganda.

9.4.2 Research Methodology

This study has used quantitative research method for data collection (self-administered survey) and analysis. According to Burns and Bush (2000), a survey is a suitable method for collecting data about attitudes and opinions. It also allows quantitative analysis to be conducted in the testing of inferences and permits generalization of findings. The process of developing the questionnaire began with an extensive survey of the related literature. The literature survey provided bases for identifying the relevant variables and related instruments that were used in past studies. The questionnaire was designed based on the Likert scale that consisted of statements that express agreement and disagreement of the respondents toward the object of interest (Cooper and Schindler 2006). The Likert scale is easy to develop, easy for the respondents to answer questions, and is reliable (Emory 1985). Therefore, this study used four-point Likert scale, and the responses ranges from "agree to strongly agree" to "disagree and strongly disagree" for all the questions in the questionnaire. Cronbach's Alpha test was conducted to measure reliability of the instrument. A total of 330 questionnaires were distributed to the Muslim population across the central, southern, and northern Uganda. Respondents were classified by gender, age, marital status, and education level. The study used SPSS for descriptive analysis and reliability test and later adopted AMOS software for Confirmatory Factor Analysis (CFA), Measurement Model, and Structural Equation Modeling (SEM), which is considered a superior method of analysis for multivariate behavioral research that involves a complex structural relationship among variables (Buhi et al. 2007).

9.5 Results and Discussion

This section presents the findings from the quantitative survey. The section comprises the profiles of the respondents, analysis of the SEM results, and results of the hypotheses testing.

9.5.1 Profile of the Respondents

The majority of the respondents are: male (68%), young—aged between 20–30 years (42%) and 31–40 age group (33%), educated class comprising degree holders (47%), middle-income earners (31%) and work as professionals (24%), academicians (11%), and business community (22%). Twenty-four percent (24%) had more than 10 years work experience, and 37% worked between 5–10 years. Hence, the respondents represent young male Muslims who are professionals, educated, well-informed, and of middle-income section of the society. This reflects positively on the quality of the data collected.

9.5.2 Reliability Statistics, Fitness of SEM, and Results of Hypotheses Testing

The Cronbach's alpha obtained a value of 0.791, which indicates a satisfactory level of internal consistency, and the scale can be considered reliable with our sample (Tabachnick and Fidell 2001). A total of 300 questionnaires, representing 83% of the responses were collected as valid and complete. The SEM results show that the model is acceptable as it obtained the required values for each of the indices such as CFI = 0.990 and RMSEA = 0.046. Figure 9.3 shows Structural Model of the overall model fit. The figure shows the intention–behavior relationships, which connect religious obligations, moral norms, behavioral intention, and actual behavior.

Accordingly, the model supports the four hypotheses, i.e., there are significant and positive relationships between the four antecedents (attitudes, moral duties, perceived behavioral control, and religious duties), intentions, and the actual support for the construction of modern *Waqf-based* hospital in Uganda. In other words, the model predicts that positive attitude, positive perceived behavioral control, and commitments to fulfill both the religious and moral duties will positively influence the decision of Muslim community to provide actual financial and non-financial support for the construction of modern *Waqf-based* hospital in Uganda.

Meanwhile, the regression's weights that substantiate the findings given by AMOS 5.0 are reported in Table 9.1. Overall, regression model reveals significant and positive relationship among the variables at p-value greater than 0.05, and the path coefficients of the causal structure are statistically significant at C.R above 5.00.

The results in Table 9.1 reveal that there are positive and significant relationships between three antecedents (attitude, moral duties, and

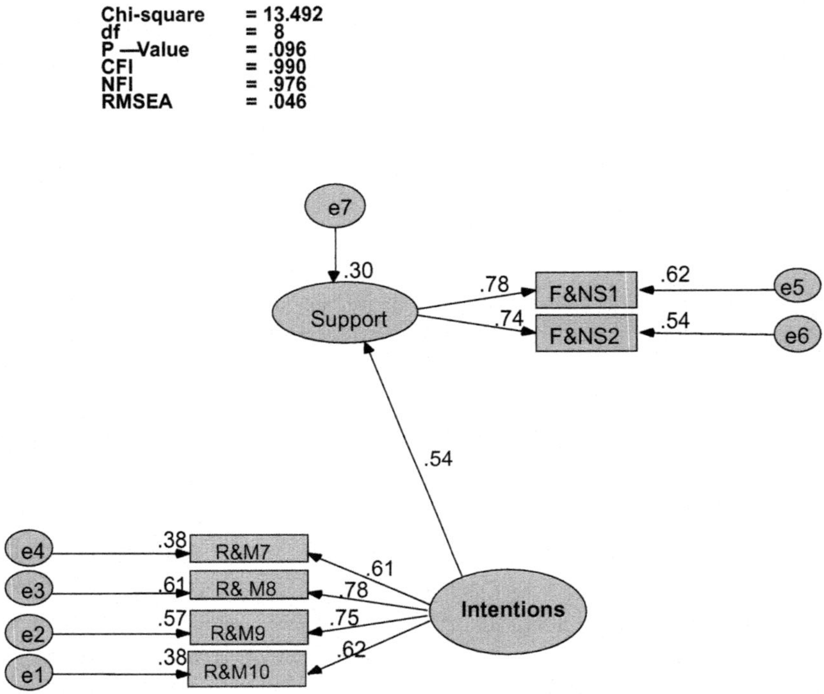

Fig. 9.3 Relationship between intention to support the construction of Waqf-based hospital and actual behavior. *Source* authors' own computation

Table 9.1 Maximum likelihood estimate of path coefficient of the model

			Estimate	S.E.	C.R.	P
Support	<---	Intentions	0.544	0.088	6.416	***
R &M10	<---	Intentions	0.620			
R&M9	<---	Intentions	0.754	0.118	9.852	***
R&M8	<---	Intentions	0.780	0.120	9.988	***
R&M7	<---	Intentions	0.613	0.111	8.623	***
F&NS1	<---	Support	0.784			
F&NS2	<---	Support	0.736	0.164	7.188	***

Note *** Significant at 0.05 level

religious duties), intentions, and actual financial and non-financial support for the construction of modern *Waqf-based* hospital in Uganda, $\beta = 0.54$, $C.R = 6.42$. In addition, desire to assist others for a noble cause ($\beta = 0.62$), for humanity ($\beta = 0.78$), for seeking the pleasure of Allah ($\beta = 0.61$), and His rewards in the Hereafter ($\beta = 0.75$) positively and significantly influence the decision of Muslim community to support the construction of modern *Waqf-based* hospital in Uganda financially ($\beta = 0.784$) and non-financially ($\beta = 0.736$). In other words, Muslim community in Uganda in reality will support (financially and non-financially) the constructions of modern *Waqf-based* hospital because of humanity, a belief that it is a social responsibility to help the poor and the needy to get decent and affordable health care services (moral duties), it is an avenue to seek Allah's pleasure and His rewards in the Hereafter (religious duties), and also due to the belief that it is a virtue or noble cause to assist in the construction of *Waqf-based* hospital so that every individual will have equal access to affordable good health care services irrespective of their income status (attitude). These findings are consistent with many studies on altruism and donors giving behavior.

9.6 Conclusion

In nutshell, this study has predicted that intentions to endow for the construction of modern *Waqf-based* hospital can be materialized in the form of financial and non-financial support. Commitment to fulfill both moral and religious obligations and believe in noble cause will positively and significantly influence Muslim community's intentions to actually provide financial and non-financial support for the construction of modern *Waqf-based* hospital in Uganda. It is, therefore, imperative for Islamic religious institutions in Uganda including Uganda Muslim Supreme Council (UMSC), which is the highest body managing the affairs of Muslim community in the country, to emphasize on these three motivating factors when they want to raise fund for the construction of *Waqf-based* hospital and other projects. These factors will influence Muslims decision to donate for socioeconomic development. This in turn will improve on the social welfare of Muslim community in Uganda.

References

Ajzen, I. (1985). From intentions to actions: A theory of planned behavior. Germany: Springer-Verlag.

Ajzen, I. (1991). The theory of planned behavior. *Organizational Behavior and Human Decision Processes, 50*(2), 179–211.

Ajzen, I. (2011). The theory of planned behaviour: Reactions and reflections. *Psychology & Health, 26*, 1113–1127.

Ajzen, I., & Fishbein, M. (1975). *Belief, attitude, intention, and behavior: An introduction to theory and research* (1st ed.). Reading, Mass: Addison-Wesley Pub. Co.

Ajzen, I., & Fishbein, M. (1977). Attitude-behavior relations: A theoretical analysis and review of empirical research. *Psychological Bulletin, 84*(5), 888–918.

Ajzen, I., & Fishbein, M. (1980). *Understanding attitudes and predicting social behavior*. Upper Saddle River, NJ: Prentice-Hall Inc.

Alam, S. S., Janor, H., Zanariah, Che-Wel, C. A., & Ahsan, M. N. (2012). Is religiosity an important factor in influencing the intention to undertake Islamic home financing in Klang Valley? *World Applied Sciences Journal, 19*(7): 1030–1041.

Amin, H. (2012). Patronage factors of Malaysian local customers toward Islamic credit cards. *Management Research Review, 35*(6), 512–530. https://doi.org/10.1108/01409171211238271.

Amin, H., & Chong, R. (2011). Is the theory of reasoned action valid for Ar-Rahnu? An empirical investigation. *Australian Journal of Basic and Applied Sciences, 5*(10), 716–726.

Amin, H., Abdul-Rahman, A. R., Chooi Hwa, A. M., & Sondoh, S. L., Jr. (2011). Determinants of customers' intention to use Islamic personal financing: The case of Malaysian Islamic banks. *Journal of Islamic Accounting and Business Research, 2*(1), 22–42.

Andreoni, J. (1989). Giving with impure altruism: Applications to charity and Ricardian equivalence. *Journal of Political Econom, 97*(6), 1447–1458.

Andreoni, J. (1990). Impure altruism and donations to public goods: A theory of warm—glow giving. *Economic Journal, 100*(401), 464–477.

Arrow, K. J. (1975). Gifts and exchanges. In E. S. Phelps (Ed.), *Altruism, morality and economic theory*. New York: Russell Sage Foundation.

Astrom, A. N., & Rise, J. (2001). Young adult's intentions to eat healthy food: Extending the theory of planned behavior. *Psychology and Health, 16*(2), 223–237.

Basar, H. (1987). *Management and development of Awqaf properties*. Jeddah: Islamic Research and Training Institute, Islamic Development Bank.

Becker, G. S. (1974). A theory of social interactions. *Joumal of Political Economy, 82*(2), 1063–1093.

Bozionelos, G., & Bennet, P. (1999). The theory of planned behavior as predictor of exercise: The moderating influence of beliefs and personality variables. *Journal of Health Psychology, 15*, 383–405.

Buhi, E., Goodson, P., & Neilands, T. (2007). Structural equation modeling: A primer for health behavior researchers. *American Journal of Health Behaviors, 31*(1), 74–85.

Burns, A. C., & Bush, R. F. (2000). *Marketing research*. London: Prentice Hall.

Conner, M., Norman, P., & Bell, R. (2002). The theory of planned behaviour and healthy eating. *Health Psychology, 21*(2), 195–201.

Cooper, D. R., & Schindler, P. S. (2006). *Business research methods* (9th ed.). USA: McGraw-Hill.

Echchabi, A., & Aziz, H. A. (2012). The relationship between religiosity and customers' adoption of Islamic banking services in Morocco. *Arabian Journal of Business and Management review* (OMAN Chapter), *1*(10), 89–94.

Echchabi, A., & Olaniyi, O. N. (2012). Using theory of reasoned action to model the patronisation behaviour of islamic banks' customers in malaysia. *Research Journal of Business Management, 6*, 70–82.

Emory, W. C. (1985). *Business research methods* (3rd ed.). Homewood, Ill: Irwin. ISBN: 9780256030099.

Giles, M., & Cairns, E. (1995). Blood donation and Ajzen's theory of planned behavior: An examination of perceived behavioural control. *British Journal of Social Psychology, 34*(2), 173–188.

Human Development Report. (2013). Key to HDI countries and ranks, 2012. New York: United Nations development Programme. Online Source at: http://hdr.undp.org/en/2013-report.

ILO. (2008). Social health protection: An ILO strategy towards universal access to health care, *Social Security Policy Briefings, Paper No 1*, Social Security Department, Geneva: International Labour Organisation.

Johnson, D. (1968). *The fundamental economics of the charity market*. PhD Dissertation, University of Virginia.

Johor Corporation. (2013). *Annual report*. Online source, available at: http://www.jcorp.com.my/waqaf-an-nur-hospital-clinics-35.aspx.

Kamri, N. (2010). The roles of ethics in waqf management: Case of jawhar. *Shariah Journal, 18*(3), 659–680.

Konkoloy, T. H., & Perloff, R. M. (1990). Applying the theory reason action to charitable intent. *Psychological Report, 67*(1), 91–94.

Kotler, P., & Keller, K. L. (2012). *Marketing management* (Vol. 14). New Jersey: Pearson-Prentice Hall.

Lada, S., Harvey Tanakinjal, G., & Amin, H. (2009). Predicting intention to choose halal products using theory of reasoned action. *International Journal of Islamic and Middle Eastern Finance and Management, 2*(1), 66–76.

Laffont, J. J. (1975). Macroeconomic constraints, economic efficiency and ethics: An introduction to kantian economics. *Economica, 42*, 430–437.

Lamiraud, K., Boysen, F., & Scheil-Adlung, X. (2005). The impact of social health protection on access to health care, health expenditure and impoverishment: A case study of South Africa, *Extension of Social Security Paper Series 23*, Geneva: International Labour Organisation.

Linden, S. (2011). Charitable intent: a moral or social construct? A revised theory of planned behavior model. *Current Psychology, 30*(4), 355–374.

McMillan, B., & Conner, M. (2003). Using the theory of planned behavior to understand alcohol and tobacco use in students. *Psychology, Health and Medicine, 8*, 317–328.

Mokhlis, S. (2006). The effect of Religiosity on shopping orientation: An exploratory study in Malaysia. *Journal of American Academy of Business, 9*(1), 64–74.

Olson, M. (1965). *The logic of collective action*. Harvard University Press.

Ong, F. S., & Moschis, G. P. (2006). Religiosity and consumer behaviour: A cross cultural study. *Paper presented at the BAI Conference Proceedings*. Singapore, July 12–14.

Osman, A. F., Muhammed, M. O., & Amin, H. (2014). An analysis of cash waqf participation among young intellectual. Paper published in Book Article. Waqf Iqlimi. Universiti Sains Islam Malaysia.

Rose-Ackerman, S. (1997). Altruism, nonprofits, and economic theory. *Journal of Economic Literature, 34*(2), 701–728.

Ryan, M. J., & Bonfield, E. H. (1980). Fishbein's intentions model: A test of external and pragmatic validity. *Journal of Marketing, 44*(2) (Spring, 1980), 82–95.

Salamon, L. M. (1999). *America's nonprofit sector: A primer* (2nd ed.). New York: Foundation Center.

Salamon, L. M., Sokolowski, S. W., & Anheier, H. K. (2000). *Social origins of civil society: An overview*. Baltimore, MD: The Johns Hopkins University Center for Civil Society Studies.

Scheil-Adlung, X, Guy, C., Johannes, J., & Ke, X. (2006). What is the impact of social health protection on access to health care, health expenditure and impoverishment? A comparative analysis of three African countries, *Extension of Social Security Paper Series 24*, Geneva: International Labour Organisation.

Sen, A. K. (2000). *Development as freedom*. New York: Anchor Books.

Shih, Y. Y., & Fang, K. (2004). The use of a decomposed theory of planned behaviour to study internet banking in Taiwan. *Internet Research, 14*(3), 213–223.

Smith, R., & Mcsweeney, J. (2007). Charitable giving : The effectiveness of a revised theory of planned behaviour model in predicting donating intentions and behaviour. *Journal of Community and Applied Social Psychology, 17*(5), 363–386.

Sparks, P., & Shepherd, R. (1992). Self-identity and the theory of planned behavior: Assessing the role of identification with green consumerism. *Social Psychology Quarterly, 55*, 388–399.

Sun, S., Goh, T., Fam, K. S., & Xue, Y. (2012). The influence of religion on Islamic mobile phone banking services adoption. *Journal of Islamic Marketing, 3*(1), 81–98.

Tabachnick, B. G., & Fidell, L. S. (2001). *Using multivariate statistics* (4th ed.). Allyn and Bacon. [2007].

Victor, R. F. (2004). Reflections on the socio-economic correlates of health. *Journal of Health Economics, 23*(6), 1083–1099.

Warburton, J., & Terry, D. J. (2000). Volunteer decision making by older people: A test of a revised theory of planned behavior. *Basic and Applied Social Psychology, 22*(3), 245–257.

Weisbrod, B. (1998). *To profit or not to profit: The commercial transformation of the nonprofit sector*. New York: Cambridge University Press.

WHO. (2008 & 2009). Uganda cooperation strategy 2009–2014. Geneva: World Health Organisation. Online Source at http://www.who.int/nha/en.

WHO. (2013 & 2014). Health expenditure. Geneva: World Health Organisation. Online Source at http://apps.who.int/gho/data/view.main.HEALTHEXPRATIOUGA?lang=en.

Yousafzai, S. Y., Foxall, G. R., & Pallister, J. G. (2010). Explaining internet banking behaviour: Theory of reasoned action, theory of planned behavior, or technology acceptance model. *Journal of Applied Social Psychology, 40*, 1172–1202.

Glossary

Bay al-dayn: Sale of debt. The provision of financial resources is required for production commerce and services by way of sale/purchase of trade documents and papers. Bai al-Dayn is a short-term facility with a maturity of not more than a year. Only documents evidencing debts arising from bona fide commercial transactions can be traded.

Bay inah: Sale contract followed by repurchase by the seller at a different price.

Bay muajjal: Sale contract based on deferred payment at a certain price. It is a contract involving the sale of goods on a deferred payment basis.

Fatwa: A religious decree.

Faraid: The knowledge or rules on estate distribution according to Islamic principles.

Fiqh: Islamic jurisprudence, the science of the Shari'ah. It is an important source of Islamic economics.

Hibah: Gift or an act of giving away one's property with the immediate effect of the transfer of ownership without any return.

Ijarah: Lease or service contract that involves benefit/usufruct of certain asset or work for an agreed payment or commission within an agreed period.

Khalifah: The civil and religious leader of a Muslim state considered to be a representative of Allah on earth.

Maqasid-al-Shari'ah: The goals and objectives of Islamic law an evidently important and yet somewhat neglected theme of the Shariah.

© The Editor(s) (if applicable) and The Author(s) 2017

M. Zulkhibri and A. G. Ismail (eds.), *Financial Inclusion and Poverty Alleviation*,
Palgrave Studies in Islamic Banking, Finance, and Economics,
https://doi.org/10.1007/978-3-319-69799-4

Maslahah: Public interest.

Mutawalli: One entrusted with something (the trustee of a waqf).

Mudarabah: Profit sharing contract. As a financing technique adopted by Islamic banks it is a contract in which all the capital is provided by the Islamic bank while the business is managed by the other party. The profit is shared in pre-agreed ratios, and loss, if any, is borne by the investor.

Murabahah: Sale contract with a disclosure of the asset cost price and profit margin to the buyer.

Musharakah: An investment partnership in which profit sharing terms are agreed in advance and losses are pegged to the amount invested—basically Private Equity.

Musaqah: A type of partnership in which the owner of an orchard agrees to share a stipulated portion of the produce of the orchard's trees with a worker in exchange for the latter's irrigation of the garden.

Muzara'ah: Share-cropping; an agreement between two parties in which one agrees to allow a portion of his land to be used by the other in return for a part of the produce of the land.

Qard Hassan: Benevolent loan.

Qawaid Fiqhiyyah: Principles of Islamic law.

Riba: One of the three fundamentals prohibitions in Islamic finance (the other two being Gharar and Maysir). This term literally means an increase or addition. Technically it denotes any increase or advantage obtained by the lender as a condition of the loan. Any risk-free or "guaranteed" rate of return on a loan or investment is riba. Riba, in all forms, is prohibited in Islam.

Sadaqa: Usually refers to voluntary donations.

Salam: Sale contract based on order of certain asset with certain specifications. Full payment is made in cash at the time of conclusion of the contract whereas the delivery of the asset is deferred to a specified time.

Shari'ah *Supervisory Board:* Committee of Islamic scholars available to an Islamic financial institution for guidance and supervision in the development of Shari'ah compliant products.

Sukuk: Islamic securities/bonds.

Takaful: A scheme which is based on the spirit of cooperation and helping each other by providing financial assistance to participants when needed and all participants mutually agree to give contribution for the said purpose.

Tawarruq (*Commodity Murabahah*): Purchasing an asset with deferred price either on the basis of Musawamah or Murabahah, then selling it to a third party to obtain cash.

Wa'ad: Promise.

Wadiah: Safe keeping contract in which a party entrusted his property to another party for safe keeping and to be returned upon request.

Wakalah: Agency contract.

Waqf (*Awqaf plural*): A form of the endowment by an owner of a property for public benefit and well-being which is allowed by Shari'ah.

Zakat/Zakah: Alms-giving is the practice of charitable giving by Muslims based on accumulated wealth and is obligatory for all who are able to do so. It is considered to be a personal responsibility for Muslims to ease economic hardship for other Muslims and eliminate inequality for followers of Islam.

Index

© The Editor(s) (if applicable) and The Author(s) 2017
M. Zulkhibri and A. G. Ismail (eds.), *Financial Inclusion and Poverty Alleviation*, Palgrave Studies in Islamic Banking, Finance, and Economics, https://doi.org/10.1007/978-3-319-69799-4